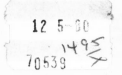

W9-AQO-265

VALIANT FRIEND

Lucretia Mott's statue stands in the crypt at the United States capitol, along with those of Susan B. Anthony and Elizabeth Stanton. Her life is a personification of the historic and spiritual forces that gave birth to the equal rights movement. In *Valiant Friend*, Margaret Hope Bacon vividly recreates every side of this notable, multi-faceted woman.

THE AUTHOR

Margaret Hope Bacon has written numerous articles and short stories for national magazines, and columns, reviews, and features for the Philadelphia *Evening Bulletin* and Philadelphia *Inquirer*. She is the author of four previous books related to Quaker history and the history of reform: *The Quiet Rebels* (Basic Books); *Lamb's Warrior, The Life of Isaac T. Hopper* (Thomas Y. Crowell); *I Speak for My Slave Sister, The Life of Abby Kelley Foster* (Thomas Y. Crowell); and *Rebellion at Christiana* (Crown Publishers), which was nominated for the Newbery Award for excellence in children's literature. She lives in Philadelphia, where she is Assistant Secretary for Information and Interpretation of the American Friends Service Committee.

Lucretia Mott (Quaker Collection, Haverford College Library)

VALIANT FRIEND

THE

LIFE

OF

LUCRETIA MOTT

By
Margaret Hope
Bacon

WALKER AND COMPANY ☀ NEW YORK, NEW YORK
720 5th ave.   10019

First published in the United States of America in 1980 by the Walker Publishing Company, Inc.

Published simultaneously in Canada by Beaverbooks, Limited, Pickering, Ontario.

ISBN: *0-8027-0645-2*

Library of Congress Catalog Card Number: 79-91253

Printed in the United States of America

Book design by Robert Barto

10 9 8 7 6 5 4 3 2 1

CONTENTS

ACKNOWLEDGMENTS

THE LARGEST single collection of Lucretia Mott's letters, diaries, obituaries, and other documents is located at the Friends Historical Library, Swarthmore College, Swarthmore, Pennsylvania. Members of the staff of this library helped and encouraged me every step of the way in the writing of this book, and I owe them all a debt of gratitude: Jane Rittenhouse Smiley, Patricia Neiley, Nancy Speers, Jane Thorson, Albert Fowler, Claire Shetter, and Bernice Nichols. Dr. J. William Frost, the director, was helpful in many ways, including reading the manuscript in galley.

Among other librarians who made the book possible are Barbara Curtis of the Quaker Collection at Haverford College; Dr. Edwin Bronner, director of the Haverford College Library; Eleanor Perry of the Philadelphia Yearly Meeting Library, who, with Charles Perry of the Development office of Haverford, kept me supplied with books; and Dr. Mary-Elizabeth Murdock of the Sophia Smith Collection at Smith College.

Other libraries and historical societies that I consulted and whose staff I would like to thank include the Nantucket Historical Society; the Worcester Historical Society; the Library Company of Philadelphia; the Record Room, Westtown School, Westtown, Pa.; the Haviland Room, New York Yearly Meeting; the Schlesinger Library of Radcliffe; the Department of Rare Books and Manuscripts at Cornell University Library and at Harvard University Library; and the Special Collection at the New York Public Library.

Letters in the body of the text are quoted by courtesy of the Trustees of the Boston Public Library; the American Antiquarian Society; the Historical Society of Pennsylvania; the James Fraser Gluck Collections of Manuscripts and Autographs in the Rare Book Room of the Buffalo and Erie County Public Library; the Autograph Collections, Library of Vassar College; the Department of Rare Books, Manuscripts and Archives of the University of Rochester Library; and the George Arents Research Library at Syracuse University. Six letters from the Manuscript Division of the Library of Congress are also briefly quoted.

I am grateful to Dr. Judi Breault, Dr. Dana Greene, and Dr. Ira Brown for reading all or part of the manuscript and giving me criticism from their perspectives as historians of the period; to Ruth and Robert Seeley for patiently and cheerfully typing many drafts; to Ruth Cavin for her sensitive and sympathetic help as an editor; and to Allen Bacon for his unfailing support.

VALIANT FRIEND

CHAPTER

I

"THE TRUTH
AND JUSTICE
OF OUR CAUSE"

THROUGHOUT the summer of 1853 New York City had been crowded with visitors to the city's first world's fair. The Crystal Palace, a block-long structure of glass and steel patterned after its original in London, was situated between Forty-first and Forty-second streets east of Sixth Avenue, in Bryant Park. Inside there were industrial exhibitions from all over the world, including such curiosities as the new foot-pedal sewing machine. Next to the Palace a cylindrical glass tower served as an observatory in which visitors were carried skyward in a steam-driven elevator. From the tower you could see the whole gigantic city, stretching northward as far as Fiftieth Street and southward to the green of Castle Gardens at the Battery. Out-of-towners stood in patient lines for admission to these glories. Native New Yorkers, having already seen the show and being tired of jammed eating places and crowded streets, began to long for the end of the exhibition.

And now in the first week of September, just as the city was locked in a heat wave and tempers were getting thin, a new onslaught of visitors had arrived, more troublesome than all the others. The radical reformers had come to town, to hold conventions one after the other. There were two rival temperance gatherings, one for those who would admit women as delegates and one for those who would not. An antislavery convention was scheduled, sure to make trouble in a town dominated by Tammany Hall and the proslavery Democrats. And to top it all off, there was a gathering of radicals dedicated to woman's rights. GRAND RALLY OF THE BLOOMERS, James Gordon Bennett's *New York Herald* proclaimed derisively. SPEECHES BY

MALE AND FEMALE BLOOMERS. STRONG-MINDED WOMEN ARE
GETTING THEIR PLUCK UP.

On the night of September 6 a Tammany mob had broken up
the woman's rights convention, held at Broadway Tabernacle
near Worth Street. On the morning of the seventh the women
began to gather in twos and threes. A few wore the new bloomer
costume, a sort of tunic over Turkish trousers, but most were
sedately dressed in the high-necked, wide-skirted dresses of the
period. Many had an anxious look. On their way up Broadway
they had seen several of the Tammany toughs, easily recogniz-
able by their white Panama hats, heavy gold chains, pantaloons,
and polished boots. Most were members of a sporting club
managed by Capt. Isaiah Rynders, an ex–riverboat tramp now
enjoying a patronage job as a weigher at the New York Customs
House by virtue of his usefulness to Tammany. Would the
Rynders gang strike again tonight? Inside the dim vastness of
the Tabernacle the women glanced anxiously about them.

Promptly at ten A.M. a small woman in Quaker gray stepped
to the podium and called the second day of the New York
Woman's Rights Convention to order. Her voice was sweet and
firm, her carriage erect, her cameolike face beautiful in repose.
She was not only president of the convention, she was widely regarded as the wise elder stateswoman of the newly formed
woman's rights movement. A gentle sigh of relief and satisfaction ran through the audience as Lucretia Mott began to speak.

"The uproar and confusion which attended the close of our
proceedings of last night, although much to be regretted, as in-
dicating an unreasonable and unreasoning disposition on the
part of some to close their ears against truth, or rather, to
drown its voice by vulgar clamor, yet, when viewed aright, and
in some phases, presents us with matter of congratulation," she
began.

Despite the disruption of the night before, which was the
worst she had ever experienced, none of the women had screamed
or shown signs of fright, she noted. Was not their courage an
argument for the very claims they advocated?

"I think it was really a beautiful sight to see how calm the
women remained during last evening's excitement; their self-
possession I consider something truly admirable.... Had there

been here a company of women who were taught to rely upon others, they would doubtless have felt bound to scream for their 'protectors,' but the self-reliance displayed, which must have its basis in a consciousness of the truth and justice of our cause, gives us matter for real congratulation.''

In the audience were many who regarded Lucretia Mott's own self-possession as a beautiful sight. For if the mob had been asked to pick a single target for their rage, it might indeed have been the small figure in gray. Called the Black Man's Goddess for her pioneering role in the antislavery movement, a religious liberal often attacked as a heretic anti-sabbatarian, sometimes even called a socialist, Lucretia Mott was the very symbol of those meddling reformers and "rampant, unsexed women" the *Herald* thundered against and whom the Rynders mob was determined to silence.

She had not wanted to preside at this convention. There were younger women who should be in her place. But the arguments the women gave her were familiar. No one else had the poise and authority to keep order nor the leadership to carry the frightened women through such ordeals. Moreover, there was the inner compulsion to obey manifest duty. She had come all this weary distance walking in the Light, in the faith that obedience would sustain her through any trial.

Lucretia Mott introduced the speakers: Charles Burleigh, an abolitionist journalist, famous for his long red curls and his flamboyant speech; dark-haired Ernestine Rose, born a Polish Jew, now a famous agnostic, reformer, and feminist; round-faced Lucy Stone and sharp-featured Susan B. Anthony, co-workers with Lucretia in the woman's rights movement; wispy, balding, mild-looking William Lloyd Garrison, the editor of the *Liberator*, hanged in effigy throughout the South.

As the day progressed, the hall slowly filled with rowdies, and each speaker was interrupted by catcalls and jibes. Lucretia kept order with apparent self-possession, although within her her stomach knotted and spat.

She was not surprised by the heckling. Yesterday she had warned her sister delegates to expect nothing but increase hostility now that it was at last perceived that woman was demanding nothing less than full equality. "Any great change must expect opposition, because it shakes the very foundation of privilege,'' she reminded them.

It was a lesson she had learned through twenty years of bitter experience. While the good people of New York deplored the excesses of the Rynders gang, they did little to halt the violence. The Rynders mob must be deplored, of course, but what else, polite New Yorkers asked each other, could you expect? Heavily dependent on the South for trade, entertaining a thriving liquor industry, its wheels kept turning by Irish immigrant workers who had been taught to fear the competition of free blacks, New York stood to lose much in addition to its serenity if the radicals had their way. Not content with threatening the economic underpinnings of society, the abolitionists proclaimed themselves openly opposed to a church and a state that upheld slavery. And now they were invading man's last stronghold, the sanctity of his home, with this talk of woman's rights.

The New York attitude mirrored that of the urban North at large. Most moderates had breathed a sigh of relief when the Compromise of 1850, engineered by Calhoun and Webster, had settled forever the troublesome question of slavery in the new territories and saved the Union from the disaster of civil war. But now the radical abolitionists daily threatened the entire delicate balance with their denunciations of the Compromise and their refusal to obey it. When Rynders struck, he was simply acting out the anger many good citizens felt in their hearts.

By evening the galleries were packed. Weary now, Lucretia introduced Sojourner Truth, a tall black woman, an ex-slave, who had electrified a woman's rights convention in Akron, Ohio, the year before with a speech that began, ''That man over there says that women need to be helped into carriages and lifted over ditches, and to have the best place everywhere. Nobody ever helps me into carriages or over mud puddles or gives me the best place, and ain't I a woman?'' She responded to the growing disorder of the New York audience by mirroring back its feelings: ''I know it feels kind of hissin' and ticklin' like to see a colored woman get up and tell you about things, and woman's rights. We have all been thrown down so low that nobody thought we'd ever get up again, but we have been down long enough now; we will come up again, and here I am.''

But neither Sojourner's eloquence nor Lucretia's commanding presence was enough to stem the mood of the mob, now increased still further with recruits from local bars. "Shut up!","Take a drink!", "Go home!" they shouted derisively at the speakers.

Some of the women began to panic. One clutched at Lucretia's arm as she banged for order. Would she call the police? But that was against her principles of nonresistance. Then, would she yield the floor to Ernestine Rose, an officer of the convention, who had no such scruples against force? Lucretia quickly agreed to the compromise. Ernestine took the gavel to announce the meeting adjourned. Her pounding was swallowed up by the din. The hall exploded in confusion.

The rowdies went after the men—Garrison, Burleigh, the black minister Henry Highland Garnet—but the women were jostled and shoved rudely aside. Outside the door additional rowdies seemed intent on beating up the speakers as they emerged. Some of the women, whose bravery Lucretia had praised that morning, hesitated to leave. Seeing their trouble, Lucretia asked her own escort to see several of them safely out.

"But who will take care of you?" he asked.

"This man will see me through," Lucretia said, tucking her hand under the arm of the nearest bully.

It was, some say, Captain Rynders himself. He had stayed away from the meetings until now, but since some of his boys were in danger of being arrested, he had come to see into the matter personally. Lucretia's friends were alarmed; Rynders's pals watched to see how he would react. Clearly he was taken aback, but after a moment's pause and a glance into that cameo face an impulse of courtesy took over. Gravely he conducted the little woman through the hall, which had been thrown into an uproar by his own doing. There was too much noise for them to exchange a word until they stepped outside. Then Lucretia thanked him hastily and joined some friends.

That might have been the end of the astonishing encounter had Lucretia not seen him the next day in a New York restaurant. Excusing herself from her friends, she went and sat at his table. In the daylight he must have seen that the beautiful woman of the night before was a well-preserved sixty. They chatted for a few minutes, she thanked him again for his courtesy of the evening before, and they said good-bye.

As soon as she left, Rynders asked someone what her name was. That's Lucretia Mott, he was told.

"Lucretia Mott?" He was surprised. This kindly grandmother the infamous Lucretia Mott? "Well, she seemed like a good, sensible woman."

Sensible grandmother, radical reformer, gentle nonresistant, militant advocate of woman's rights, Lucretia Mott was a leading figure in nineteenth-century America. Her long life, which all but spanned the century, both reflected and influenced the currents of American thought as the country moved from a nation of small shopkeepers and farmers into the Industrial Age. Her passionate identification with the underdog, along with her Yankee talent for finding practical solutions to complex problems, made her a creative force in social reform. Many of her ideas were at least a century ahead of her time.

The Victorians made a living legend of Lucretia Mott, emphasizing her sweetness and calm and deemphasizing her assertive qualities. Subsequent biographers have maintained the same image. It is true that she was a warm and loving woman of great poise, but she was also a very human person with a quick temper, a sharp tongue, and a stubborn streak. She had more than a little vanity, and she basked in the good opinion of others. At times she took herself too seriously, but a wry sense of the ludicrous kept her from becoming pompous. She had a healthy love of life, which made her seem too earthy to her more refined daughters.

In a day when women were not supposed to show anger, Lucretia struggled for years to suppress hers and suffered from dyspepsia as a result. In her middle years, however, she learned to channel that anger into righteous indignation and to use that energy in her crusades. It was too late to save her stomach, but as she learned to accept and express her angry feelings, she became more open to love and to spiritual impulses. By releasing the restraints, she also gained new reserves of energy, which made it possible for her to respond to the increasing demands upon her from all quarters. And decade after decade she opened herself to new growth, so that she became in her old age a fully evolved human being.

CHAPTER
II

NANTUCKET GENESIS

WHEN Lucretia Mott announced, as she often did, that she was born on the island of Nantucket, it was more than a statement of fact, it was an affirmation of identity. The history, geography, and customs of the island of her birth shaped her and gave her a sense of herself that she carried with her all her life. Although she moved away from the island at the age of eleven, she remained a Nantucketer at heart. She was still revisiting, bringing children, grandchildren, and great-grandchildren with her, until she was eighty-three, and she quoted Nantucket sayings and Nantucket ways until her last breath.

Thirty miles south off the coast of Cape Cod, Nantucket is a crescent-shaped sandbar eleven miles long and surrounded by treacherous shoals. The trees were cut long ago for fuel, and much of the island is bare except for moors covered with heather, beach plum, and wild cranberry. When the fog lifts, the island is bathed in a certain stark, brilliant light that leaves sharp shadows. Its shingled cottages are low, seeming to huddle against the land, weathered silver by wind and salt. In the summer rambling roses climb over the houses and the fences, and the moors are patchwork quilts of greens and mauves. In the winter it is all blacks and grays and whites, a desolate landscape to some, beautiful to those who have learned to love it. And always there is the pounding surf and the crying of the gulls.

Settled in 1659 by ten "proprietors," Nantucket grew slowly until whaling was discovered. From 1700 to 1850 it was the center of the whaling industry in the United States, its men sailing as far as China in quest of whale oil and blubber while its women operated the farms and shops and ran the affairs of the island. The result was the development of a hardy, self-reliant breed of both sexes, famous for their sharp wit, shrewd trading, and fierce independence.

Lucretia Mott was a true daughter of the island, a descendant of two of its original settlers, Tristram Coffin and Peter Folger. Since Benjamin Franklin was a grandson of Peter Folger, he and Lucretia were distant cousins. Both were fighters and innovators, but because Lucretia was a woman, her role was circumscribed and her talents forced to find different outlets. Had she been raised anywhere but on Nantucket, she might have remained obscure. But the life of the island, giving women a great deal of responsibility, plus the belief of Quakerism, the dominant religion, that men and women are equal, created a climate in which a woman could find her way. Mary Starbuck, a collateral ancestor of Lucretia's, was known as the Great Woman for her role in the early governance of the island. Maria Mitchell, a cousin, was the nation's first woman astronomer.

Lucretia's father was Thomas Coffin, Jr., a sea captain, who was away from home for long stretches of time as he chased sperm whales over the deep. Her mother, Anna Folger Coffin, was a warm, strong, humorous woman who supported herself and her children by keeping a shop while her husband was away at sea. The two were married in January 1790 and set up housekeeping in a little house on Fair Street, overlooking the great harbor. Here their first daughter, Sarah, was born on October 13, 1790, and their second, Lucretia, on January 3, 1793.

It was an exciting time to be born. The Constitution of the United States, embodying a compromise on slavery, had been ratified in 1788. The French Revolution, with a burst of new ideas about human equality, had broken out in 1789. The venerable Benjamin Franklin had led a major lobbying effort against the slave trade in the U.S. Congress in 1790. Mary Wollstonecraft, an Englishwoman living in France, had published a new work, *The Vindication of the Rights of Woman*, in 1792. The Age of Reason was passing; the Age of Romanticism had begun.

Nantucket itself was just recovering from a long period of severe deprivation during the Revolutionary War. Neutralist due to its Quakerism, Nantucket had seen its ships captured by

British and American patriots alike until its fleet of 150 was reduced to 12. Desperately needed supplies from "the continent"
were cut off, and bands of escaping loyalists landed in force and
pillaged what little was available. A few sailors running small
boats late at night managed to bring in a few necessities; otherwise the islanders starved and shivered.

At the end of the war Nantucketers had to begin the slow and
arduous task of rebuilding the whaling industry.

In the early days of Lucretia's childhood, her father's sailing
trips were successful. In 1797, when she was almost five, he
bought land on the corner of Fair and School streets, down the
way from his early, little house, and here erected a large, handsome dwelling that still stands today, a four-square house with a
pine-paneled fireplace in each room, wide stairs with a curving
railing, and a huge kitchen in which the whole family could
gather. Facing along School Street was a narrow parlor where
Anna Coffin kept her shop when Thomas was away at sea.
Coming home from school, Lucretia could always tell when her
mother was home, for then the shutters of the shop were open.
There would be a warm greeting, a dish of tea, perhaps a piece
of cornbread waiting for her.

In the big house on Fair Street Lucretia grew up, sweeping the
hearth, washing the dishes, rocking the cradle as four additional
sisters and one brother were born to the Coffins on Nantucket
island. Anna taught each of her daughters to knit and sew, but
especially to cook the Nantucket dishes that were passed down
from generation to generation. There was a special Folger codfish and onion dish, a particular way of cooking veal, of making
blackberry pudding, of preparing pork with pig sauce. Though
small and slight, Lucretia had a lusty appetite. All her life she
preserved her special love for food cooked Nantucket style.

Right down the hill lay the wide harbor and the big Straight
Wharf, where the largest ships lay at anchor. There a motley
crew of sailors—some Yankees, some Indians, some blacks
from Cape Verde, some Portugese—lifted bales and bundles.
Standing about were crates of tea and silk from far-off China.
Near the wharf other sailors tended try-pots, in which the whale
blubber was reduced to oil. Here were the craft shops that supported the whaling industry; the cordage shops, where ropes

were twisted; the coopers, where barrel staves were made; the forge, where harpoons and spikes were hammered into shape. As a vessel prepared to sail, the seamen were in and out of these shops, running and cursing. By the dockside, pigs squealed and chickens squawked, waiting to be loaded. And then at last the lines would be loosened and a few sails bent on as the vessel prepared to creep its way out of the narrow mouth of the harbor.

Along the tree-shaded cobblestone streets at the very edge of town the wealthier sea merchants had built mansions of brick trimmed with white, each with a graceful fanlight over the door. Some of the wealthy Nantucketers were not Quakers but ''people of the world.'' If one loitered near their houses, one might see a woman dressed in bright colors or even a man with a wig.

On one of these excursions into the center of town Lucretia Coffin saw a sight that was to remain with her for years afterward. On the town square a crowd had gathered to watch a woman being whipped at the public whipping post. The little girl did not learn her crime, or promptly forgot it, but indignation over the whipping flared within her. Seventy-five years later she led grandchildren and great-grandchildren to the spot where the whipping post had been and told them in a trembling voice how angry it had made her.

Beyond the town lay the farmlands, where sheep and cattle grazed and corn ripened in the summer sun. Lucretia's Folger grandparents were farmers, and she liked to visit them, to watch the sheep being sheared or to ride on the jouncing, sweet-scented hay wagon with her grandfather. Every spring there was a veal feast. Fresh meat was a luxury on the island, and the killing of a calf had become a traditional time of celebration and of family reunion. According to Nantucket custom, all the husband's relatives were invited on the first day of the veal feast, and the wife's on the second. Since practically everyone was related to everyone else on the island, the family gatherings were huge, and the excitement great for the children.

But Lucretia's Folger grandmother was strict, and when the child visited, she was kept busy with chores. Sometimes, when corrected, her sharp tongue would get the better of her, and she would answer back. One day at the end of a visit her grandmother told her that she had intended to let Lucretia ride up to the field with her grandfather on a load of hay, but because Lucretia had been so naughty, the treat was canceled. Then why, Lucretia wondered, did she have to tell me about it at all? "What I had done left no impression, but her unkindness I couldn't forget," she afterward recalled.

A mystery surrounds the oldest Coffin daughter, Sarah. She seems to have been handicapped in some fashion. She was never given any responsibility as a child and never sent away to school. At the age of thirty-four she died of a fall in her mother's house. Above all she was never spoken of in the family correspondence. Many years after her death a niece let it slip that she was "queer." The exact nature of her handicap is lost to us in the mists of time.

As a result of Sarah's problems, Lucretia actually functioned as the oldest child. She was Anna Coffin's chief helper in running errands and minding the younger children. During her father's long absences at sea she served as her mother's chief companion and even took charge of the household, under the watchful eye of her aunts, while her mother went to "the continent" to purchase goods for her store. This closeness developed within Lucretia a deep love of her mother and an identification that lasted a lifetime. Until Lucretia was fifty-one, she lived with or near her mother, turning to her for advice and support. After Anna Coffin's death Lucretia carried her memory as an inward monitor and frame of reference. "Mother's sayings" and mother's ways were part of her life until she was a very old woman. Although she grew beyond the older woman's sphere, the warmth of this relationship was a source of her strength.

Her relationship with her father is less clear. Since he was away much of her childhood, he seems to have been a shadowy figure, loved and respected but never really close. When his adventures, seafaring and mercantile, did not succeed and brought hardship on Anna, Lucretia was always at her mother's side. But it was from Thomas Coffin that she got the tremendous physical energy and the sense of adventure that were parts of her developing personality.

Functioning as the oldest child, Lucretia developed an assertiveness and a strong sense of self. Her sister Eliza, born in

December 1794, became Lucretia's lifelong companion and always played the role of a good-natured but submissive second child. In 1797 the Coffins lost a baby girl, and in 1798 Thomas Mayhew, the only son, was born. Later three additional sisters were born: Mary, in 1800, Lydia, 1804 (died in infancy), and Martha, 1806. Toward all these siblings Lucretia Coffin manifested a proprietary, slightly bossy attitude. She never hesitated to tell them how to behave. She had a sharp tongue, a quick temper, and a strong sense of injustice as a child, but also a special warmth, gaiety, and aliveness that drew other children to her.

From the time she was four, Lucretia spent five hours of the day, every day, at school. At home, hard-pressed Anna Coffin had managed to teach Lucretia her letters and her figures, but at school she learned to read, to write a clear, legible hand, to do sums, to memorize. The school she attended was built by the Nantucket Quakers in 1797, adjacent to the meetinghouse. Here boys sat with the schoolmaster, and girls with the schoolmistress, poring over their lessons until it was their time to recite.

In a book called *Mental Improvement*, by Priscilla Wakefield, an English Friend, Lucretia read about the slave trade. The capture of the blacks on the Guinea coast, the separation of families, and the packing of the slaves into the holds of the slave ships were all vividly described. Horrified, Lucretia read how, on the Middle Passage from Africa to the Caribbean, many of the slaves died from lack of air, water, adequate food, and exercise, while others starved themselves to death or threw themselves into the sea or were mutilated by cruel shipmasters. Shocked, she read the section over and over again. The thought of infants torn from their mother's arms was more than she could bear. It wasn't fair that human beings could so mistreat one another. Someone must put a stop to it. She memorized a long passage and recited it many times, almost in tears as she came to the last line, "Humanity shudders at your account."

There were no slaves on Nantucket. Slavery was never a part of the economy of the island. The Nantucket Quakers had gone on record against it as early as 1716. But slaves had been held in Massachusetts until 1780, and the sea captains of Newport and New Bedford had played a prominent role in the Triangular

Trade: rum from New England to Africa, slaves from Africa to the Caribbean, molasses from the Caribbean to New England. Some of these captains, Lucretia learned to her horror, had been Quakers. Where there was money to be made, even Quaker consciences could be strangely silent.

During the debate over the U.S. Constitution many had believed that slavery would die a natural death. But the invention of the cotton gin and the expansion of the cotton industry in the North served to ensure the life of the "peculiar institution." The Louisiana Purchase of 1803, which added to the United States a vast territory ripe for Southern agrarian expansion, further guaranteed the need for a continuous supply of slaves. As a result, slave breeding became important in the Southern states. These developments were in process during Lucretia's early childhood, but she heard little talk about them. The Nantucketers were now too busy with their own survival problems to keep in close touch with trends on "the continent."

The classroom provided no opportunity to discuss slavery; the children were expected simply to read and recite, no matter what the topic. The school session was long and boring, but there were brief intervals of recess, when the children could play together in the school yard. Lucretia's ready wit and talent for mimicry drew others to her, but some of her classmates feared her a little for her sharp tongue and quick temper. They called her spitfire, and said she was a tease. Lucretia tried to bridle her sharp tongue, but she was too quick herself to have much patience with what she considered slowness or stupidity, and time and again a snappy retort would come to her lips. At Quaker Meeting she earnestly sought ways to curb this fault.

Like other Quaker children, Lucretia Coffin had been taught to believe that God spoke directly to men and women, boys and girls, through an Inward Light that illuminated their consciences. By minding the Light within, one could learn where one's duty lay. Then it was just a matter of obedience. All the troubles of the world, all the evils including slavery, could be traced not to human depravity but to disobedience to manifest duty.

To stress the importance of this emphasis on the Light within, the Quaker meetinghouse was bare of all adornment and all ceremony. Quaker worship consisted simply of sitting in silence, waiting until one or another member of the Meeting felt moved by the Holy Spirit to speak. The person would then rise and deliver a message, sometimes in a peculiar singsong fashion, often quoting a verse from the Bible. Several men and women in the meeting spoke so regularly that they came to be recognized as ministers. They were given a special status and sat on the facing bench, or gallery. Some of the ministry were very dull, but once in a while someone spoke as though his or her words did indeed come from a spirit beyond human limitations.

Every Fifth-day, as the Quakers called Thursday, the entire school would line up and proceed to the nearby Friends Meetinghouse, for mid-week worship.

On First-days, Sundays, Lucretia came to Meeting with her mother, brother, and sisters. Now the meetinghouse was packed. The women, looking like so many rosy-cheeked chickadees in their black bonnets, white shawls, and gray dresses, filled one side of the room with the girls between them; the men, with their broadbrimmed hats and somber coats, filled the other, along with the older boys. The silence on First-days was deeper, more awesome. Lucretia prayed earnestly that she might be good and overcome her hasty temper.

Sitting on the facing bench on First-days were all the elders of the Meeting in their majesty. These men and women were entrusted with the supervision of the membership. If a young woman behaved in an unseemly fashion, if a man drank too much rum or beat his wife or defaulted on his debts, if there was dancing or too much wine bibbing at a Quaker wedding, the elders would pounce. The erring member would be reprimanded and, if he or she did not repent, disowned. The power of the elders was absolute, and their prying was often petty. Young Quakers learned to fear them and hold back the expression of feelings, either of joy or of anger. In its early days Quakerism had been a joyous religion, and its meetings democratic, but in recent years the power of the elders had grown. Sometimes their decisions seemed entirely arbitrary and unfair.

There were, Lucretia saw, many injustices in the world. But how was one to fight against them when one was weak and small?

One day in Meeting a woman minister talked about Joseph's exile in Egypt and how he was able to endure persecution because he was made strong by the mighty God of Jacob. Suddenly Lucretia felt as though the message was meant especially for her. If she would follow duty, strength would come. The early Quakers, she knew, had endured persecution not only in England but in the New World. One woman, Mary Dyer, had been hanged on Boston Common. These valiant early Quakers were the ones to copy, not their conservative descendants. Lucretia would become a true Quaker from this day on. As an outward sign of her conviction, she would change the way she dressed. Most of her clothes were already quite simple, but she had a new pair of shoes with bright blue bows she rather fancied. As soon as she got home from Meeting, she took a pair of scissors and cut off the worldly adornment.

A few years later a minister, Elizabeth Coggeshall, came from Rhode Island to Nantucket on a religious visit. She was a married woman of thirty-three with such a gift in the ministry that her own Meeting released her to travel and preach at other Meetings. Such men and women were known as Public Friends. If the Public Friend was a woman, members of the family took care of her household and children so that she could follow her leading. Four years earlier Elizabeth Coggeshall had made an extensive trip to England. Lucretia stood in awe of her. To be a Public Friend, to travel and be listened to, to what higher calling could a Quaker girl aspire?

Elizabeth Coggeshall not only preached at Nantucket Meeting but visited each household and had a sitting with each family. Thomas Coffin was again away at sea when she came. Anna gathered her little brood around her and sat with Elizabeth in the larger front parlor. Elizabeth spoke to the children simply about the importance of obeying the Inward Monitor, and of praying for strength to follow its commandments. Lucretia took the message to heart, aware that she would need much strength to control her wayward spirit. It seemed easy for her gentle little sister Eliza to be good, and even her sturdy little brother Thomas was not as mischievous as she. Despite her best efforts, her mother still called her Long Tongue and accused her of "liking to give as good as she got." She must pray for strength and try harder.

By now there was another baby sister to take care of, Mary, born in March 1800. A few months before her birth Thomas Coffin had thrown all his resources together to purchase a ship of his own, the *Trial*, in order to sail to China. The expense of outfitting the *Trial* strained the Coffins to the limit. When Thomas departed, he gave Anna power of attorney, but his estate was reduced to little more than the house on Fair Street. She immediately reopened her shop and settled down for a long time of managing without him.

For many children a fatherless household might seem forlorn. The children of Nantucket, however, were used to it. The seafaring fathers came and went; it was the mothers who kept the family going. For support in their loneliness the women turned to each other. There was a constant visiting back and forth on the island. When the men were home, they fitted themselves in and went along to family teas and suppers. This seemed to Nantucket children the natural way of doing things. Years later, when Lucretia lived on "the continent" and discovered that men and women had separate social circles, she was shocked and disapproving. "How odd it would seem to the natives [of Nantucket] for husbands not to be as ready as wives to visit," she commented.

But whenever father was away, there was always the lurking fear that he might never return. Whaling was dangerous; sometimes the harpoon line tangled around the leg of a sailor and carried him away down to Davy Jones's locker; sometimes the wounded whale would smash the whole longboat with one flip of its powerful flukes; and sometimes whole vessels would be lost at sea. There would be no mail, frequently no messages for months at a time. Whenever a vessel was sighted at the mouth of the harbor, mothers and children would climb up to the walks on top of the houses for a first glimpse of it. Was it the ship they longed to see? But often the vessel was at anchor along the Long Wharf before they learned whether the particular sailor they sought was alive or dead.

In 1802, when it was surely time for Thomas's ship to return, there came dreadful news. Uncle Uriah Hussey, Aunt Phebe Folger Hussey's husband, had gone down with his ship. The Folger sisters gathered to give what comfort they could to the stricken family. Lucretia even tried to cheer up little cousin Mary Hussey, with whom she could never get along. But at the memorial service in the Quaker meetinghouse it was hard to keep one's thought on Uncle Uriah without wondering, what if this were to happen to us?

Another year passed. Lucretia was now ten and in complete charge of the baby. Anna was often away getting supplies for her store. Lucretia managed the little ones, with the help of grandmother and the aunts. She was much admired for this early maturity, and she basked in the approval. But as day followed day, and week week, it seemed likely that word from Thomas Coffin would never come.

Then one day the regular sailing cutter from Woods Hole brought a deeply suntanned man to Nantucket Harbor. He had climbed the hill and was at the door of the house on Fair Street before Anna Coffin knew anything about it. Thomas Coffin had lost his ship and been forced to part company with its crew, but he himself was hale and hearty. The rejoicing in the big back kitchen that morning was something none of the Coffin children ever forgot.

After the first rush of hugs and tears he told them of his adventures. While the *Trial* was cruising for whales along the coast of South America, it was seized by a Spanish man-of-war, on the charge that it had violated neutrality. Against Thomas's protests they were hauled into the port of Valparaiso, Chile, and the ship impounded. In a few days it became clear that there was no way to get the ship back, except through a lengthy court suit. Reluctantly Thomas Coffin freed his crew to make what other arrangements they could, and prepared to stay and fight his case. A hospitable Spanish family took him in and taught him the language so quickly and so well that he was able to serve as his own attorney. He won some decisions, but it seemed as though the case would drag on forever. He finally decided to give up and, setting out on foot, crossed the Andes by himself. For a man in his late forties it was a trial of strength. Reaching Brazil, he found a ship in a port city ready to offer him passage back to the United States. He had tried time and again to send messages; none had reached Nantucket. But here he was at last.

It was a story of endurance under pressure, and it inspired all the Coffin children. They were proud of their adventurous father and never tired of the stories he told of his experiences in South America. He taught them to say "good morning" and "good evening" in Spanish and impressed upon them that they must have respect for the Catholic religion, since a Catholic family had been kind and generous to him. For the insular children, it was a broadening touch with the world beyond their little island.

Wonderful though his adventures had been, Thomas Coffin had decided that he was through with seafaring; he would now stay at home and try to make a living as a merchant. Before his ship had been seized in Valparaiso, he had sent a load of seal skins off to China. With the money from this trade he was able to enter into partnership with Jesse Sumner, a successful Boston merchant. In less than a year's time it was apparent, though, that this meant moving his family to Boston. Anna's widowed sister, Phebe Hussey, bought the house on Fair Street, and in July 1804 the Coffins set forth, Anna holding a new baby, Lydia, in her arms.

For Lucretia, now eleven and a half, it was a wrenching break. She loved every inch of her native island—its food, its customs, its people, its weather-beaten houses, and its long, barren vistas. She loved the sea and ships and the smell of salt. She loved its stark, revealing light, so like the Light within that she earnestly sought. Whenever she had been angry or unhappy, the sweeping moors and the whisper of the wind had been her comforters. She was deeply rooted here, more so than she was ever to become again throughout her long life. Nantucket became a sort of paradise lost to her. She would return again and again, but never was it quite so wonderful as she remembered it. And she would raise generations of children, grandchildren, and great-grandchildren on her tales of the special warmth and felicity of doing things "Nantucket way."

CHAPTER
III

SCHOOLING

NOTHING IN Lucretia's experience had prepared her for the bustling city of Boston. Its population was almost thirty thousand when the Coffins arrived in 1804, a far cry from little Nantucket Town. From its wharves giant sailing vessels plied the seven seas. Along its waterfront were many large countinghouses. Her father and his partner occupied space in one of these. Behind lay the maze of cobblestoned alleys of Boston's old city, scrambling up and down three hills, with the tower of Old North Church high against the sky.

From the bedroom window of the Coffins' house on Green Street, Lucretia could see both the Charles and Mystic rivers, and across to the low hills of Charlestown. Later the family moved to a larger and more expensive home on Round Lane. Boston was prospering, the newer sections of the city growing rapidly. Thomas Coffin was prospering along with the city, but he felt some conflict between his new wealth and his ideals of Quaker simplicity. When they first moved to Boston, he and Anna had enrolled their children in a private school; later they shifted them to a public school in order to guard them against "class pride." Lucretia always felt it had been a good experience. "It gave me a feeling of sympathy for the patient and struggling poor," she recalled.

Soon, however, the Coffin children had outgrown grammar school. It was Thomas Coffin's wish to provide each of his children, daughters and son alike, with a chance for higher education. Neither he nor Anna had gone beyond grammar school, but this was a new age. For Quaker children, however, it must be a religiously guarded education, in a school where they could be preserved from contamination with "the world's people." Choices were limited to two Quaker boarding schools. For Lucretia and Eliza the Coffins chose Nine Partners, established in 1796 in Dutchess County, New York. The following year they sent Thomas to Westtown, a similar school opened in 1799 in Chester County, Pennsylvania.

To prepare her daughters for Nine Partners, Anna Coffin was furnished with a list of the clothing they would need: "one or two plain bonnets, one cloak, not silk, two stuff or gingham gowns suitable for the season, made plain; three or four long checked aprons, one pair of scissors and one paper of pins." If fancy clothing were sent, it would be returned, she was warned.

The parting was hard, for this was the first time Lucretia and Eliza had ever left home. Moreover, it was uncertain when they would see their mother, sisters, and brother again. The trip was long and expensive, and the school discouraged visits home. Pupils were supposed to become part of the school family and stay until their education was complete. Going off to school was a little like setting out to sea. Fortunately the Coffin girls had the example of their seafaring father to inspire courage.

Set in the rolling hills of Dutchess County, Nine Partners was a large, barnlike building, ninety-nine feet long. The girls lived and were taught at one end of the building, the boys at the other. Their studies were identical, but each had separate classrooms, and each their own playground, separated by a high fence. On the top floor both ends had a large dormitory, where pupils slept on hard little cots, row upon row.

School was in session all year round at Nine Partners. New pupils like Lucretia and Eliza simply joined in, as though they had stepped upon a moving merry-go-round. The young scholars studied reading, writing, accounts, English grammar, and geography, and memorized large amounts of poetry.

At least twice a week the pupils all attended Quaker Meeting. Occasionally a visitor would come to the school to deliver an evening lecture on some improving subject. Otherwise there was no entertainment—no music, no dancing, no dramatics, no reading of fiction. Above all the young boys and girls were kept strictly apart.

Despite this separation of sexes the Quaker academies were

the first to attempt coeducation. At Westtown the boys were offered Latin, and the girls had hours of needlework, but in general the idea was stressed that the educational opportunities should be equal. As a result Quaker girls as a group were among the first to receive any sort of higher education in the United States. Their pioneering in such professions as medicine as well as in the field of equal rights may have been a result.

Lucretia Coffin thrived in the spartan environment of Nine Partners. Its sparseness was familiar to her, and the chance to meet young Quakers from up and down the Eastern Seaboard enlarged her horizons. She was still moving exclusively in the narrow world of Quakerism, but it was a larger world than Nantucket Quakerism. As a student she could now test herself against her contemporaries, and to her delight she found she was often the most able. One by one her intellectual strengths were unfolding—a quick, retentive memory; a probing brilliant mind; an ability to reason logically. She lacked a soaring imagination, but she had the gift of empathy; she could easily put herself in the place of another and feel his or her pain or joy. From her Quaker background she, all her life, entertained a rather narrow-minded prejudice against fiction and drama, but she loved didactic poetry and memorized it voluminously. At Nine Partners she committed the whole of William Cowper's *The Task* to memory, and drew upon it throughout her life.

Her sharp wit delighted her classmates, except for the unfortunate few who found themselves the brunt of it. She was an excellent mimic of the sober Quaker elders. Pretending to have been sent by the Meeting to discipline an offending member, she reported in Quaker singsong, "Friends, we have visited Tabitha Field—and—we labored with her—and we think we *mellowed* her some."

Lucretia's greatest problem at Nine Partners was the rules and regulations that governed every aspect of a pupil's life. For talkative Lucretia, the rule of silence was hardest to obey. She was often in trouble and was often punished for talking in class. She knew she had to learn to bridle her long tongue, and she tried to be obedient. Some of the other rules, however, she considered petty and arbitrary, and she did not hesitate to argue with the teachers about them. This plunged her into still further trouble.

One day a rumor spread quickly through the school that one of the younger boys was being punished severely for a minor infraction. Lucretia liked the boy and thought his punishment was unfair. Girls were strictly forbidden to cross over to the boys' side of the school, but they knew hidden doorways and back stairs. Lucretia somehow persuaded the meek and terrified Eliza to make the dangerous journey with her. Finding the closet into which the boy had been locked without his supper, they slipped him slices of bread and butter under the door, then managed to return to the girls' side without getting caught.

The fires of adolescence, working within Lucretia, had heightened both her sensitivity to the underdog and the anger against injustice deeply embedded in her from her Nantucket childhood. During this impressionable period she read for the first time *An Essay on Slavery* by Thomas Clarkson, a British abolitionist. Although his language was restrained, Clarkson spared no details in describing the horrors of the Middle Passage—the sexual abuse of the women, the torture of defiant slaves, the human cargoes thrown overboard in order to earn insurance money. Lucretia was enraged. The Wakefield account she had earlier memorized faded in comparison. Here was a wrong crying to heaven to be righted.

Lucretia Coffin was not alone in her awakening anger against slavery. In both the United States and Great Britain many young men and women were responding to Clarkson's plea, and abolitionist societies were being organized throughout the land. The idea of gradually freeing the slaves by raising money to buy them one by one from the slave owners was being advanced as a possible solution. Meanwhile it was necessary to stop the importation of slaves as a first step. The abolition of the African slave trade was now before the United States Congress, and many abolitionists were lobbying for its passage.

At Nine Partners at this time a particular visitor, a tall, gaunt man with a beaked nose and piercing eyes, would occasionally electrify the calm of Quaker Meeting with his fiery denunciations of the sin of slavery, of spilled blood and human degradations and defilements. This was Elias Hicks, one of the founders of Nine Partners and a member of the School Committee. A simple Quaker farmer of the old school, believing in the direct relationship between God and conscience, Hicks felt led to shake his beloved Society of Friends awake to its present duty in regard to slavery. Having been the first to protest the institution, the Quakers had slowly rid themselves of slaveholding and in the 1780s had played a role in lobbying against the continuation of slavery in the Northern states. Now, however, some had retired from the struggle, content to keep their own skirts clean. Hicks was determined to return them to the path of manifest duty. At Nine Partners he had a willing audience. Elsewhere he was beginning to earn a reputation for extremism. Lucretia's ardent heart responded to his anger.

James Mott, Sr., the superintendent of the school, was also a determined abolitionist and often spoke against slavery in Meeting. Lucretia was impressed with his words, but even more so with his refusal to use slave products. He dressed in linen rather than cotton, used maple sugar instead of cane sugar in his coffee, and refused to write on paper with a cotton content. As she came to know Mott, she learned to admire him in other ways too. A retired merchant and miller, he was serving the school gratis because its "pecuniary difficulties" prevented paying a headmaster. He was a deeply religious man, a Public Friend who had once preached on Nantucket Island. Despite the welter of rules and regulations governing life at Nine Partners, he had advanced ideas about using punishment sparingly and motivating students to learn by relying on example and a high degree of expectation. His book, *Observations on Education*, published in 1797, came out against corporal punishment and in support of equal education for women. Lucretia read the book and agreed with him warmly on both counts.

A classmate of Lucretia's was Sarah Mott, the superintendent's granddaughter. As soon as Lucretia enrolled at Nine Partners, they formed a friendship. When the school decided to grant the pupils a few unusual days of vacation, Sarah invited Lucretia home to Mamaroneck on the north shore of Long Island Sound, where the Mott clan had recently settled. The sight of the soaring gulls and the smell of salt must have made it seem almost like home to Lucretia. She immediately liked the Mott family, Adam and Anne, Sarah's parents, and Mary, Abigail, Richard, and James, her sisters and brothers.

James Mott, the younger, was a tall, blond, serious young

man, who rarely said much. She had glimpsed him before in the
halls of Nine Partners, for he was a teacher at the boys' end, but
this was her first opportunity to get to know him. He was eighteen to her thirteen, an immense difference, but she liked his
looks and his dignity, which reminded her of his grandfather
and also of her own father, Thomas Coffin. She saw little of
James during the brief visit, for she and Sarah helped Anna
Mott in the farmhouse kitchen, while he divided his time between his father's fields and his uncle Richard Mott's mill, but
Lucretia admired what she saw.

Back at school Lucretia settled down to her books with redoubled earnestness. By 1808 when she was just fifteen, she had
completed all the courses Nine Partners had to offer. There was
no such thing as graduation; one simply stepped off the merry-
go-round and went home. In Lucretia's case, however, the
school staff was loath to part with her. Rarely had there been
such a scholar on the girls' side. They decided to offer her a job
as assistant to the girls' head teacher, Deborah Rodgers, earning
her room and board but no pay. Deborah was a warm, strong
practical woman, rather like Anna Coffin. Lucretia
admired her very much. She was also a skilled teacher of grammar, a subject in which Lucretia had always excelled. Lucretia
decided to accept the offer, although she wanted to visit home
first. In the two years since she had left, the baby, Lydia, had
died, but there was a new little sister, Martha, to meet.

On her return from Boston, Lucretia found changes in the
faculty. James Mott, Sr., had left, to be replaced by a resident
couple as superintendents. The enrollment was up to fifty-eight,
higher than it had been before, and several additional assistant
teachers had been hired. Somehow she must have seen the
schools' books, for she learned something else that enraged her.
The young James Mott, that tall blond fellow, was being paid
one hundred pounds a year, whereas much older and more
experienced Deborah was getting only forty pounds a year.
Their positions and duties were actually the same, and the girls
paid the same tuition as the boys. There was only one explanation: Deborah was paid less solely because she was a woman.

Talk about injustice! Lucretia had been accustomed to regarding women as the equal of men, not only in the life on the

island of Nantucket but also in the Society of Friends. If there were subtle differences in their status—and there were—she had not so far noticed them. Nor had Lucretia been aware that in society at large a woman had virtually no legal rights or status. She was under the care of her father until she was turned over to her husband, she did not control her own property, and she had little voice in the decisions that affected her life. She was always exploited as a worker, for she had no bargaining position. All these things nineteenth-century America accepted as matters of course. Until this moment Lucretia had not realized the existence of inequality purely on the basis of sex. Now it hit her in the face. That she herself was not being paid at all did not worry her; she was, after all, just an apprentice. But someday she would be a full-fledged teacher like Deborah, and when that day came, she would demand equal pay for equal work. "The injustice of this distinction was so apparent that I early resolved to claim for myself all that an impartial Creator had bestowed," she wrote of the episode.

She did not blame young James Mott for getting a larger salary than Deborah Rodgers. He was, after all, simply the innocent beneficiary of an unjust system. Now that she was no longer a student but a teacher, she found she was often in his company. He did not talk much, but she could chatter enough for the two of them, and he seemed to approve of almost everything she said.

Young Lucretia Coffin must have been lovely. Her eyes were hazel and deeply set under finely arched brows. Her skin was white, her cheeks pink, her mouth rosy. Though small and slender, she had a rounded figure and a narrow waist. Some people found her cameo features severe in repose, but she was often laughing and chattering, lit by an inner fire. Even when she was quiet, an amused smile lurked at the corners of her mouth.

A year passed. Lucretia was offered the job of full assistant to Deborah and was promised free tuition for Eliza as well as room and board if she would stay. Several of the teachers, James among them, had decided to study French on the side. If Lucretia would stay, she could join them. Lucretia accepted quickly. Sitting on the stiff and prickly horsehair chairs in the stuffy front parlor of the school, a handful of teachers began each night to pick their way through a book of French grammar and prose. The French lessons lasted only six weeks, but it was perhaps at this time that Lucretia Coffin and James Mott fell in love.

They were in many ways opposites. He was tall and blond, she was short and dark. He was taciturn and serious; she was talkative and merry. He was rather gloomy at times; she was full of hope. Some people found him cold; she was generally perceived as warm and friendly. He was cautious; she was impetuous and sometimes gullible. They both seemed to delight in these differences. She found his silence restful and his strength a rock against which she could anchor. He delighted in her ability to put into words the thoughts he could not express, and her vivacity warmed him and made him feel alive. He, too, was a heavily burdened second child, his sickly older sister having died in infancy, and for similar reasons shared Lucretia's powerful sense of injustice. Left to himself, however, he was apt to conclude that nothing could be done about it. It was Lucretia's enthusiasm and sense of mission that drove them both into action.

While this relationship was deepening and taking its own special form, events outside the little world of Nine Partners were moving at a rapid rate. In Europe, Napoleon was on the march, and the consequent U.S. embargo on foreign trade was having a depressing effect on the economy. Relations with Great Britain were deteriorating in a series of events that led up to the War of 1812. There were Indian troubles.

In these uncertain times restless Thomas Coffin decided to make yet another great gamble and put all his capital into a factory for the manufacture of cut nails, a new product of the Industrial Revolution. The factory he purchased was located at French Creek, outside Philadelphia, and here he moved his entire family in 1809. At first the enterprise was a great success, bringing in as much as $100,000 a year. Thomas enrolled Mary and Eliza at Westtown along with Thomas junior, and sent for Lucretia to come home. There was no longer any need for her to work for a living.

Lucretia came, but she had a proposition for her father. Would he take young James Mott into partnership with him?

The two had not yet been before Quaker Meeting to declare their intentions, but they had an understanding, as well as the blessing of both sets of parents. Under the circumstances Thomas was glad to be able to offer the younger man a chance. A few months after Lucretia moved to Philadelphia, James came to board with the Coffins. Plans for the wedding could now begin, and all their prospects seemed bright.

CHAPTER
IV

MARRIAGE
AND EARLY STRUGGLES

TROTTING FROM shop to shop with her mother, getting ready for her wedding, Lucretia got her first impressions of Philadelphia. It was twice the size of Boston and quite unlike it, with its neat gridiron of wide streets interspersed with parks and its endless rows of red brick houses. At the public market, farmers sold poultry and vegetables in season; along the main streets, oyster vendors pushed their barrows; and on street corners, hucksters sold the Philadelphians' favorite soup, "Pepperpot, smoking hot," by the cupful. Otherwise the city seemed serene and well ordered, still the "greene countrie town" of which William Penn, its founder, had dreamed.

In Boston you rarely saw a Quaker, but here there were many on the streets, and five downtown Quaker Meetings to accommodate them all. The Philadelphia Quakers seemed quite unlike the Nantucket Quakers with whom Lucretia had grown up. Many of them had become wealthy in banking and business. Although they clung to Quaker simplicity in dress, they wore "the best, though plain." They were far more reserved than their country cousins; the inner circle of born Philadelphia Quakers was hard to penetrate. Fortunately the Coffins already had Nantucket relatives in the city. They formed their own circle of Nantucketers in exile, and this remained the basic core of their life for many years.

At Southern District Monthly Meeting, which met at Second and Pine, James and Lucretia appeared in February to announce their intention of marriage, and here in March they were given Meeting sanction, a committee having waited upon them to be sure they were clear of previous commitments. The wedding was set for April 10, 1811, the guests were invited, Lucretia's pale gray wedding dress was given a last fitting, and a parchment scroll was prepared that each wedding guest was to sign.

The wedding itself was held as part of a regular Meeting for worship. James and Lucretia sat on the facing bench, on a special bridal seat that fitted between the men's side and the women's side. Before them the bare pine-paneled meetinghouse was filled with a blur of faces. After a period of silence, which seemed unbearably long but lasted only about five minutes, they rose, faced each other, and repeated the Quaker wedding promise, which each had memorized: "I, James Mott take thee, Lucretia Coffin, to be my wife, promising with divine assistance to be unto thee a loving and faithful husband so long as we both shall live," and then, "I, Lucretia Coffin, take thee, James Mott, to be my husband, promising with divine assistance to be unto thee a true and loving wife so long as we both shall live." After they resumed their seats, hardly daring to glance at each other, one of the overseers brought them the wedding certificate to sign, then read it aloud to the assembled group. Next came a longer period of worship, during which several of the ministers spoke from the silence. It was ended by two elders on the facing bench clasping hands.

"Is this really a wedding?" five-year-old Martha Coffin asked, wide-eyed.

Honeymoons were unheard of at this time. Lucretia and James spent their first night together in a room in the Coffin house newly spruced up for the bridal couple, and the next morning James set out with his father-in-law as usual for the cut-nail business. It was a custom of the times—and more important, a Nantucket custom—for a young couple to spend the first few months of their married life under the bride's roof. Perhaps it was regarded as a time of sexual adjustment. Lucretia never talked directly about sex—women in the nineteenth century didn't—but she was accepting and explicit about all other bodily functions and she loved life in all its aspects. Throughout the long years of her marriage she shared a double bed with James and bemoaned every night she was forced by illness or separation to sleep apart from her beloved.

Everyone who knew the Motts said it was a good marriage. They complemented each other in important ways. Although they were active in the same causes, there was no rivalry. Lucretia was the innovator, the spiritually gifted leader, James the writer of letters and petitions, the chair of the meetings. He was an important figure in his own right; had he not been married to Lucretia Mott he might have become more famous. The fact that he was able to accept her preeminence in a day when society frowned on such an arrangement and few male egos could endure the consequent bruising is a testimony to the largeness of his spirit and the depth of their love. In their private life, in everything that mattered, they were equal partners. Lucretia looked up to and respected James and was tender of his dignity. If their enemies sometimes called him Mr. Lucretia Mott, neither of them seemed to care.

To make her contribution to nineteenth-century America, Lucretia Mott drew on hidden reservoirs of strength—the strength of a sturdy sense of personal identity, a good relationship to a strong mother, a creative and growing marriage relationship, deepening spiritual sensitivity. Even so, it took every ounce of energy and endurance she had to fight the uphill battles against prejudice of all kinds to which she committed her life. If she had had less support, if her relationship to James had been draining, she might never have found creative outlets for her drive, her energy, and her anger.

In August 1811 the young Motts moved to a neat new house of their own at 48 Union Street. Lucretia tacked down new carpets and hung curtains with zest. In this house she and James would start their own family. Now at last, as a matron of eighteen, she had a chance to make those blackberry puddings and codfish dinners she had practiced so faithfully in Nantucket.

Hovering over their new happiness, however, was a black cloud. Business conditions were seriously depressed, and the cut-nail factory was beginning to fail. By October the income from it was not sufficient to support two households. Since the new house on Union Street was roomy, the six Coffins moved in with the newlyweds. James and Lucretia were not to be alone again for another twelve years.

By Christmas Lucretia knew she was pregnant, and on

August 3, 1812, her first child, Anna, was born at home. Lucretia was attended by her mother and a midwife. There were pains of course, "suffering of which only a woman knows," but then there was the great joy of holding the "fat little pet" and feeling the first tentative tug of her lips at breast. Afterward Lucretia felt wonderful. It was the custom of the day for women to remain closely confined in their bedrooms for four to six weeks after giving birth, but Lucretia would have none of it. She took a ride in a carriage less than a week after Anna's birth and was "classified among the Indians for so rash an act," she remembered later. She also horrified proper Philadelphia by refusing to employ a nursemaid, though good girls were available at one dollar a week. Nursemaids were not the custom on Nantucket; besides, the Motts couldn't afford the extra expenditure.

The War of 1812 was now being fought along the Canadian border, but business was worse than ever. James was a worrier. When Lucretia discovered she was pregnant again, he decided to move his family back to the Mott homestead in Mamaroneck, New York, and find a job in Uncle Richard Mott's cotton mill, where he had worked during brief recesses from Nine Partners.

It was here, in her mother-in-law's house, that Lucretia gave birth to her first son, on July 23, 1814. He was named Thomas Coffin Mott, after his grandfather, and there was general family rejoicing. Lucretia was to insist later that an equal fanfare must greet the birth of baby girls, but now, at twenty-one, she couldn't resist feeling rather proud.

Events outside the circle of home continued to be ominous. The war with Great Britain was escalating. The United States forces were under siege at Fort Erie, and British troops were on the march toward Washington and Baltimore. At Mamaroneck the news was received with consternation and sorrow. The Mott family not only shared the traditional Quaker testimony against war, they were pacifists as well. Grandfather Mott was one of the first to write a book condemning war. News of the capture and burning of the new capital city at Washington filled the papers and added to the gloom.

The British blockade curtailed the cotton business. Uncle Richard had to tell young James he could no longer use him.

Fortunately James heard of a job he could have in a wholesale plow store back in Philadelphia. In October the little family packed up and moved once more.

The life of Quaker Philadelphia was proceeding serenely, war or no war. Lucretia's beloved younger sister Eliza had been keeping company for some time with Benjamin Yarnell, son of one of the most respected of Quaker Philadelphia families. Now they had been to Meeting to declare their intentions and were to be married in November. Lucretia was home in time to help with the quilting and the seaming and the baking, and to be present at the wedding.

Anna needed Lucretia at her side. At this very moment, just as her third daughter was being received into the heart of Philadelphia Quakerism, the Coffin family was in disgrace. The cut-nail business had failed and been sold to satisfy creditors. In addition, Thomas Coffin had lent money to a friend who had defaulted. The Coffins were some nine thousand dollars in debt. Thomas's business partners were disputing his accounting, and the story was all over town.

Lucretia's feelings were torn. She could not help sympathizing with her poor father, who was clearly suffering and desperately searching for a way out of his difficulties. On the other hand this was not the first time he had disregarded her mother's sage advice; Anna had begged her husband not to advance the loan. It wasn't fair that women should suffer the consequences of decisions in which they had no voice. "Ever taught to confide and trust in men in pecuniary matters, they risk more than they ought to where they have no exercise of judgment," she concluded.

Worse was to follow. Thomas Coffin's resistance to disease may have been weakened by worry; early in 1815 he fell ill with typhus, the only member of the family to contract it, and in a few short days he died. Lucretia had admired her father as a heroic figure throughout her childhood. On the other hand, he was always going off and leaving her beloved mother in straitened circumstances. Now he had done it again, and finally. Along with her grief for his loss was anxiety: How was Anna Coffin to manage, a poor widow of forty-five with four children to support? What was to become of the debt?

But Anna now showed that Nantucket backbone Lucretia so admired. She decided to open a shop, just as she had done on Nantucket. And she announced that she was assuming her husband's full debt and would pay it off gradually. James Mott had signed a note for three thousand dollars to clear his father-in-law's name. One of Anna's first acts as a widow was to tear up that note.

James himself was once more out of work. In desperation, he decided he, too, would open a store. But Anna Coffin seemed to have a knack for merchandising that he did not possess. Her shop was soon a thriving enterprise, while his, just two doors down the street, did poorly. Lucretia saw that the strain and worry were making him physically ill. When he was offered a job in a bank in New York, she urged him to take it, even though it might mean another move and more wear and tear on their household things.

Meanwhile a resolution had been forming in the back of her mind. Why shouldn't she help too? Anna at two and a half was a bright child and was beginning to learn to spell a little. Tommy, at nine months, had said his first words. She had loved being with them, but she had to confess that the life of a full-time housekeeper was a bit confining. James frequently came home exhausted at night just when she was ready for some human company. Why shouldn't she copy her mother and work to augment the family income?

There was even a job open for her. Rebecca Bunker, a middle-aged niece of her mother's, had been hired to open a school in connection with the Pine Street Meeting. She needed an assistant. If Lucretia would join her, they might even teach a little French to their pupils.

James was settling down to his job in New York and beginning to make plans for Lucretia to join him. But why should a wife always follow her husband? Lucretia talked with a Philadelphia merchant who was willing to offer James the same salary he was receiving in New York. She then wrote her husband outlining all the reasons she thought he ought to take the Philadelphia job. "I shall rest satisfied with thy better judgement," she told him tactfully, "But I should not mind being thought changeable, if I were thee."

James was glad to follow his wife's plan and return to Philadelphia. Lucretia soon began teaching at the new school. She and Rebecca Bunker started with just four pupils but soon had ten, each paying ten dollars a quarter.

During the time she had been home with the babies, Lucretia had satisfied her love of reading. She always read while she nursed the children, pulling a rocking chair close to the bed so that she could prop up her book on a pillow. One of the books she had reread was Grandfather Mott's *Observations on Education*. At home with her own children, and now at school, she tried to carry his ideas into practice. Love and kindness were to be the governing rules, with little or no punishment. When a child disobeyed, Lucretia tried to let him know how disappointed she was merely by her facial expression or the tone of her voice. It seemed to her that it worked. Often she would find that the child, if left alone, would later come to her with an apology.

With both James and Lucretia earning salaries, and Anna Coffin's shop doing well, their times of troubles seemed to be over, but suddenly, in April 1817, tragedy struck. Both Lucretia and her beautiful rosy, healthy Tommy came down with an undiagnosed fever. Both ran high temperatures, but Lucretia's broke within a few days. Tommy's did not. The stricken parents hovered over his bedside as he fought for breath. At the very last he opened his eyes and said "I love thee, Mother." Then he was gone.

Ill and weak herself, Lucretia was totally crushed by this blow. She had known death before—seeing two baby sisters and her own father die—but this struck at the very heart of her being. For days she was so pale and quiet that her family worried about her. After a while she seemed to regain her health and her usual good spirits, but she never completely recovered from Tommy's death and could never speak of it without tears coming into her eyes. Six years later she gave birth to another son and called him Thomas Coffin Mott, but she was never as close to him as she had been to her original Tommy. She complained once or twice that he was "cool," but perhaps it was she who never quite gave him the place in her heart that was forever reserved for the boy she had lost.

"The ways of Providence are mysterious," visiting Friends

told her, or "God has taken him for His own." Lucretia listened politely but was inwardly dubious. The Spirit she knew in her inner being was not capricious. No, God's natural laws operated everywhere, and uniformly. To believe otherwise was to believe that the very universe was arbitrary and unfair. Deaths such as Tommy's must be due to ignorance of God's laws or failure to observe them. Someday someone would learn what caused and what could cure the fever that had taken her beloved son.

She knew she was right, but the explanation did nothing to fill the aching void. She began to read books on religion, above all the Bible, with which she was already thoroughly familiar, searching it now for fresh riches. She found much that was rewarding, but also much that her reason rejected. The God she knew in her heart of hearts could never have commanded acts of cruelty or injustice, condoned slavery or the unfair treatment of women. God spoke directly to men and women today, just as he had spoken to the prophets of biblical times. They had been only human and subject to error. "Far safer...to admit man fallible than judge God to be changeable," she concluded.

At this impressionable time she began to read the sermons of William Ellery Channing, the founder of American Unitarianism. His plea for humanitarian concern and for the role of reason in religion struck a responsive chord in her. Channing said that duty was the greatest gift of God to human beings of whatever station in life, and that obedience to the Inward Monitor would lead a man or woman to perfection. This was exactly what she believed, Lucretia felt. But sometimes it was hard to accept and obey when the heart was sore.

At Twelfth Street Meeting, which they now attended, she sat in the silence seeking to accept her loss and to find her own path of duty. One First-day, about a year after Tommy died, she was in the midst of this search when suddenly she found herself on her feet, her own voice filling the quiet meetinghouse in firm, clear tones of prayer: "As all our efforts to resist temptation and overcome the world prove fruitless, unless aided by Thy Holy Spirit, enable us to approach Thy Throne, and ask of Thee the blessing of Thy preservation from all evil, that we may be wholly devoted to Thee and Thy glorious cause."

It was what the Quakers call "an appearance in the

ministry.'' Members of the Twelfth Street Meeting liked Lucretia's sweet, clear voice and her earnestness, and were stirred by the spiritual power behind her simple words. They encouraged her to speak if she again felt a message had been given her. After this first time Lucretia was less frightened.

She spoke again and again, finding it easier each time. Her messages were in essence simple ones: the importance of obedience, the need for strength from beyond, the priority of religious experience over cult and creed. She found, however, that even in the grip of inspiration she could draw from her reading and present her ideas logically. It was begun to be said in Philadelphia that James Mott's young wife had a genuine gift. In January 1821 she was formally recognized as a minister, a tribute rarely paid to a young woman still in her twenties.

The death of Tommy, and her deepening religious experience, had sobered Lucretia Mott somewhat, but she retained a saving sense of humor. She needed it, for her ministry was sometimes over the heads of members of her Meeting and therefore misunderstood. One day speaking in Meeting she repeated a favorite quotation: ''Men are to be judged by their likeness to Christ, rather than their notions of Christ.'' A few days later two women elders came to call. Lucretia received them in her cheery front parlor. After a few opening remarks they sat in silence. Then one ventured to tell Lucretia that the Meeting had been tried by something she said last First-day, something about ''notions of Christ.'' When Lucretia repeated for them the full quotation, and told them that it was from the writings of William Penn, they sat in silence for a few more moments, then left. Every time she told the story, Lucretia couldn't help smiling over the expression on their faces.

But the critics were not always so easily routed. From the very beginning of her ministry Lucretia was a controversial figure, outspoken in challenging Quaker rules of discipline whenever she felt them to be unfair. Shortly after she had first been made a recorded minister of Twelfth Street Monthly Meeting, she learned that the elders were preparing to disown a poor widow for ''conniving'' at the marriage of her daughter to a man who was an attender but not a formal member of the Meeting. It had always seemed to Lucretia that the rules against marrying out of

Meeting were applied too harshly. How was the Society of Friends to hold on to its membership if it kept up this steady pace of disownments? The widow was being cast out on a mere technicality, and Lucretia dared to speak up against the procedure. Beyond protesting, there was nothing she could do about it for the present, but someday she would return to the issue.

James Mott had meanwhile been made clerk of Twelfth Street Meeting. Cautious himself by nature, he might have become a conservative Philadelphia Quaker if it had not been for his fiery wife and his devotion to her. As it was, he found himself, along with Lucretia, involved in yet another controversy, this time with the weighty elders of Philadelphia Yearly Meeting, the overall body encompassing Quaker meetings in Pennsylvania, New Jersey, and Delaware.

Several years earlier two radical reformers, Frances Wright and Robert Owen, had given some lectures in Wilmington, Delaware, on education and on knowledge. Fanny Wright, a Scotswoman, was notorious because she spoke to mixed, or "promiscuous," audiences and because she was said to condone free love. When some liberal members of Wilmington Monthly Meeting not only attended the lectures but took their children to hear "that woman" speak, they were disciplined and disowned. Rather than submitting weakly, they appealed their disownment to Philadelphia Yearly Meeting, and the case was widely discussed.

Lucretia thought their disownment was outrageous. How could you punish people simply for their willingness to listen to new ideas? What danger did new ideas hold anyway? Everyone knew that the Truth would prevail over error. She protested vigorously and persuaded the milder James to join with her. For a while there was talk of disciplining, perhaps even disowning, the young Motts. "My husband and self came close to 'losing our place' by uttering our indignant protest against their intolerance," she wrote friends.

In addition to these public battles, the Motts had much in their private lives to preoccupy them. Their own family was growing, Maria having been born in 1818, the second Thomas Coffin Mott in 1823, Elizabeth in 1825, and Martha, nicknamed

Pattie, in 1828. Once more Lucretia read books while she nursed babies. She read the complete works of William Penn, a large folio copy that she propped up on a pillow next to her chair. She also read Mary Wollstonecraft's *Vindication of the Rights of Woman*, and found herself in complete agreement with this first champion of equal rights.

James was now in the wholesale business and doing moderately well for the times. Lucretia was exceedingly thrifty. She turned carpets, hemmed old sheets, restuffed pillows. Their household expenses rarely exceeded one thousand dollars a year. It worried both Lucretia and James that he was often called upon to handle cotton, that slave product, but James had had enough of financial floundering and uncertainty. He was determined to continue earning an adequate living, conscience or no.

Their new prosperity made it possible for them finally to set up their own establishment. In 1824 they moved to a house on Sansom Street. Anna Coffin had given up her shop and was running a successful boardinghouse. Her children were now all independent, except for the handicapped Sarah: Eliza was busy with a household of babies; Thomas Mayhew Coffin, although unmarried, was in a thriving partnership in whale oil; Mary had married a Quaker pharmacist, Solomon Temple, and had a baby girl. The youngest, Martha, was away at Kimberton Boarding School in Chester County.

Just after the two households separated, however, a series of tragedies occurred. First the handicapped older sister, Sarah, fell, and died shortly thereafter. Nothing was said in the family circles. She died as she had lived, surrounded by a shroud of silence.

Next Mary Temple died giving birth to her second child, a boy. When Lucretia was only ten years old she had been given complete charge of this younger sister. Now she was at her bedside when the end came, feeling responsible still. Mary turned her dying face to the wall with a look of sadness that Lucretia could never forget.

Martha, now eighteen, came home from Kimberton to be with her bereaved mother and promply fell head over heels in love with one of her mother's boarders, a dashing army captain,

Peter Pelham, from Kentucky. Against Anna's strongest objec-
tions the two eloped to Florida and were married in November
1824. Now Anna was entirely alone, except for the two
motherless Temple children. Little Anna Temple thrived, but
the baby boy, Samuel, sickened and died. Just when matters
had reached this lowest point, the elders of the Meeting arrived
to inform Anna that Martha was being disowned for marrying
out of Meeting. Lucretia's determination that something must
be done about this foolish rule took deeper root.

Martha wrote from Tampa that she was expecting a baby and
was coming home to have it. She arrived in May 1825, and the
baby, Marianne, was born in August. Now that her mother had
some company, Lucretia decided to take Anna Temple into her
own family; the little girl would have the companionship of the
four young Motts. All five children promptly got the measles. In
January word came from Tampa that Peter Pelham had
suddenly died of a fever, leaving Martha a widow at nineteen.

In the nineteenth century death was a close and constant
companion of any family. Lucretia afterward felt that all these
bereavements had taught her not to set store by earthly plea-
sures. She turned instead to a deepening spiritual life and a
continuing search for the path of duty.

She was especially haunted at this time by scenes of slavery.
In 1818 she had accompanied a woman Quaker minister on a
trip to Virginia and had there seen slaves working in the fields or
bound together in chains on the roads. These sights, combined
with those described in the writing of Clarkson, were almost
more than she could bear. Right in Philadelphia there were
often disturbances on the city streets as slaves visiting the city
with their Southern masters tried to escape. Despite the aid of
local blacks and abolitionists, they were too often caught and
dragged away, chained. Sometimes, too, a crowd would gather
as a slave kidnaper tried to hustle a free black out of the city,
intending to take him South and pass him off as an escaped
slave. Isaac Hopper, a close friend of the Mott family, was involved in many slave rescues and told harrowing tales whenever
he visited the house on Sansom Street.

And then there was the condition of the free blacks, who lived
only a few blocks from the Motts. A few were wealthy and

educated men and women, running their own businesses, but most lived in poverty and suffered from extreme discrimination. Lucretia blamed their situation on the existence of the institution of slavery. James was a member of the Pennsylvania Abolition Society, a venerable institution organized in Philadelphia in 1775. Assigned to the Education Committee, he helped to supervise a school for black children called Clarkson Hall. From this experience he often came home with stories of children sent to school too hungry to learn. Lucretia looked at her own well-fed children and was touched to the quick. The institution of slavery was clearly a great evil, fastened even more strongly on the nation by the Missouri Compromise. But what was one person to do about it?

Then one day in Meeting for worship it came to her with sudden clarity that there was one step she must take. She must stop using all products of slave labor. Elias Hicks and James Mott, Sr., had set her an example long ago. There were presently in Philadelphia enough abolitionists who used "free produce" to support a free-produce store. Lucretia had admired these men and women without stopping to think that she herself might actually practice the same boycott. Now, however, she saw that it was her duty and that she must obey. No more sugar, no more cotton, no more writing paper with rag content, no more molasses. It was not going to be easy. Lucretia loved that new delicacy, ice cream, and her children were fond of candy. Moreover, what was she to do with a husband who dealt in cotton? Never mind, it was on her alone the duty had been laid, and it was she who must be faithful.

Lucretia's family, however, soon found themselves drawn into her crusade, as they so often were. Lucretia discovered that special sweets for children could be bought through stores that carried free-produce goods. These candies did not taste very good, but each had an inspiring little motto enclosed:

> *Take this, my friend, you must not fear to eat.*
> *No slave hath toiled to cultivate this sweet.*

James struggled with his conscience over his cotton business. How could he give it up and risk plunging his family into poverty again? But how could he not give it up when he so wholeheartedly agreed with Lucretia? He decided at least to join her in a personal boycott of slave products. In 1826 he helped to form the Philadelphia Free Produce Society which encouraged the establishment of free-produce stores and helped to educate the public on the importance of the boycott. It was not until 1830 that he was finally clear that he must stop dealing with cotton in his business. He switched to wool, and after a few anxious months discovered to his delight that he was doing just as well as ever.

Lucretia not only refused to use slave products, she preached in Meeting about it. This got her into trouble with the elders, who felt she ought to stick to more spiritual subjects. It also made her widely known as a female abolitionist. When Mary Lloyd, a London Quaker, addressed a letter to "an unknown but fellow member of the same Christian society," describing the antislavery activites of female Bible societies in Great Britain and urging her American sisters to form similar groups, the letter was delivered to Lucretia. She did not act upon the idea for eight years, but when she did, she started a chain reaction that had important effects upon the antislavery movement and the woman's rights movement in both England and the United States.

FRIENDS' BRICK MEETING HOUSE AT NINE PARTNERS.

Friends School and Meeting House at Nine Partners, in Dutchess County, New York, where Lucretia Mott was first a pupil, later a teacher (Courtesy of Friends Historical Library, Swarthmore College)

Anna Folger Coffin, Lucretia Mott's mother *(top, left)* (Courtesy of Friends Historical Library, Swarthmore College)

Portrait of Lucretia Mott by Joseph Kyle, circa 1841, now in the National Gallery, Washington D.C. *(top, right)* (Courtesy of Friends Historical Library, Swarthmore College)

Cherry Street Meeting House (Hicksite) at Fifth and Cherry Streets, Philadelphia *(center)*. The legend reads, "A Fourth Day Morning View of Friends Meeting House on Cherry Street, Philadelphia. This building which is about 42 feet front on Cherry Street by 100 feet deep was commenced on the 19th of 11th Month 1827 and completely finished so that Meeting was held therein on First day the 3rd of 2nd Month, 1828 — A period of only 66 working days in the most inclement season of the year.— Such despatch has been hitherto unknown in this or perhaps any other city." (Courtesy of Friends Historical Library, Swarthmore College)

Elias Hicks *(bottom, right)* (Quaker Collection, Haverford College Library)

Abby Kelley Foster, in an 1846 daguerreotype by Robert Douglass, brother of black abolitionist Sara Douglass *(top, left)* (American Antiquarian Society)

Isaac Hopper, "the intrepid little abolitionist" and Quaker bookseller *(top, right)* (Quaker Collection, Haverford College)

James and Lucretia Mott, from a daguerreotype about 1842 *(bottom)* (Courtesy of Friends Historical Library, Swarthmore College)

The burning of Pennsylvania Hall on May 17, 1838, by a Philadelphia mob objecting to the inclusion of black women at the Anti-Slavery Convention of American Women being held there *(top)* (Quaker Collection, Haverford College)

The Executive Committee of the Pennsylvania Anti-Slavery Society, 1839 *(bottom)*. Back row, from left: Mary Grew, Edward M. Davis, Haworth Wetherald, Abby Kimber, Miller McKim, Sarah Pugh. Seated, from left: Cyrus Burleigh, Margaret Jones Burleigh, Benjamin Bacon, Robert Purvis, Lucretia Mott, James Mott (Courtesy Friends Historical Library, Swarthmore College)

CHAPTER
V

A WRENCHING BREAK

LUCRETIA MOTT was not alone in her conflicts with the elders of Philadelphia Yearly Meeting. Throughout Delaware, New Jersey, and Pennsylvania Quaker men and women were increasingly troubled by the growing power and authority of the weighty and wealthy Philadelphia elders. In the loose, democratic structure of the Society of Friends, each yearly meeting is independent, but many felt that Philadelphia Yearly Meeting was attempting to extend its control beyond its own borders while tightening the rules of discipline for its own member meetings. The leader of this heavy-handedness was a man named Jonathon Evans. Lucretia referred to him bitingly as "the pope of the day."

Protest against the power of the elders came to center around their treatment of Elias Hicks, the prophetlike minister who had preached against slavery at Nine Partners School. Hicks visited the Philadelphia area as a Public Friend in 1819, 1822, and 1826. Lucretia and James were proud to entertain him in their home and to accompany him on his visits to area Meetings. Philadelphia Quakers needed to hear his sermons against slavery, they believed, as well as his call for a return to old-fashioned Quakerism and the primacy of the Christ within.

Hicks was now in his seventies, a tall, gaunt old man with burning black eyes and long white hair. His speech had become more fiery with each passing year. He reminded Friends that the early Quakers had celebrated each day as equally holy, and called the growing tendency to observe the Sabbath "Jewish superstition." He also lashed out against the new evangelicalism now becoming fashionable among the worldly city Friends. This talk of being washed in the blood of the Lamb, of salvation through redemption, was not for the Children of the Light, he thundered. It was the inward Christ that mattered, not the outward events of his birth and death. "To the Christ that was never crucified, the Christ that was never slain, to the Christ that cannot die, I commend you with my whole soul," he prayed in Meeting.

To the Philadelphia elders it all sounded very much like a rejection of the Scriptures and a denial of the divinity of Christ. They decided to try to discipline Hicks and prevent his preaching in the Philadelphia Yearly Meeting area. Hicks, however, refused to meet with them. Many local Quakers, who did not entirely understand or approve of Hick's preaching, nevertheless believed in his right to speak in Meeting as the Spirit moved. In the country Meetings particularly a democratic spirit prevailed. Ideals of equality, left over from the French Revolution, were still seeping into the national consciousness. Andrew Jackson's campaign for the presidency in 1824 had further bolstered the national revolt against the propertied classes. The country Quakers were tired of the superior attitudes of their wealthy city cousins. Gradually a faction led by a Quaker teacher, John Comly, developed over Hick's right to speak. The serene life of Philadelphia Quakers was shattered by bitter factional fighting.

At Yearly Meeting in the spring of 1827, tensions erupted in an angry dispute over appointing the clerk. John Comly was supported by a large number of representatives, but the Orthodox insisted on continuing Samuel Bettle, the clerk of the previous year. Both sides were intransigent, and the majority finally joined Comly in "a quiet retreat from the scene of confusion." Both groups regarded themselves as the legitimate Society of Friends and laid claim to the same meetinghouses and schools.

Lucretia and James deplored the petty bickering. Allowing a "party spirit" to rule them was all right for young people, perhaps, but not for the pillars of the Society, they thought. James, however, admired Hicks too much, and objected too strongly to his critics, to remain impartial, and soon decided to join the Hicksites. Lucretia was less sure. Although she personally agreed with Hicks, and supported his right to speak, she saw small-mindedness and bitterness on both sides of the controversy. Were the new Hicksites really going to reduce the power of the elders? She wasn't convinced. Her sister, Eliza Yarnell, remained staunchly Orthodox, and Anne Mott, her mother-in-law, unexpectedly took the orthodox side as well. She did not pay her usual visits, nor did she answer either James's or Lucretia's letters for months on end. When she did write, her tone was frosty. Lucretia knew how deeply her husband was attached to his mother, and shared in the hurt.

Lucretia's very prominence in the Society of Friends caused added difficulty. Others could change sides without much outcry, but the Orthodox hated to lose Lucretia with her gift in the ministry, and the Hicksites coveted her. Changing would mean that the doors of her beloved Twelfth Street Meeting, where she had found solace after Tommy's death, would be forever closed against her. Lucretia would be denounced by the ministers and disowned by the elders. Her deep-seated need to win approval made her quail at the prospect. Yet how could she even contemplate being on the opposite side from James, whose strength and support she needed? And how was he to manage without her, who was his voice and life? By late fall she made her decision and was meeting with the city Hicksites in temporary quarters at the beautiful red brick Carpenters Hall.

Denunciations rained down upon her. It was a time of suffering she never forgot. Years later she told a young minister facing a similar break that it had been like death "to find that she must part with old friends for the truth, and to have meeting houses closed to her in which she loved to meet them, and to suffer reproach that she might be true to her own soul." To walk in the Light, she was discovering, was to pursue a hard and lonely road.

Like a widening fissure in the earth, the separation that had begun in Philadelphia spread up and down the entire Eastern Seaboard. Neighbors refused to speak, families quarreled. Grandfather James Mott had written the young couple many helpful letters. Now Anne Mott demanded that James and Lucretia send them back, fearing that they might make it appear that the late James Mott, Sr., sided with Hicks.

Westtown School remained under the control of the Orthodox. In 1826 Lucretia had prepared her daughter Anna to go to
Westtown; now it was necessary to bring her home again. But
Lucretia was not ready for Anna's education to end, and Maria
at ten seemed to have outgrown grammar school. Fortunately
she knew just where to send both girls. Her mother, Anna Coffin, had recently moved to Aurora, New York, to run a girls'
school on a nearby farm in partnership with Susan Marriott, an
Englishwoman. Cousin Rebecca Bunker was head teacher, and
Martha Coffin Pelham taught art. Anna Coffin had enrolled
Anna Temple, so the Mott girls had plenty of family for company. They also had a chance to milk the cow and feed the
chickens, and hear the rooster crow at dawn, joys that as city
girls they had missed.

The Hicksite-Orthodox schism soon reached Aurora. Anna
Coffin took the Hicksite position and was disowned by Scipio
Meeting. Martha, having lost her membership as a result of her
marriage to Peter Pelham, was through with the Society of
Friends. In addition to studying art she began to read novels and
to wear gay colors. Soon she was keeping company with a dash-
ing lawyer, David Wright, just now setting up his practice in the
Auburn area.

With so much of her immediate family in upper New York
State, Lucretia found her life suddenly much simplified. Only
two children were at home: Thomas and Elizabeth. The house
seemed practically empty. The Motts had always entertained
numerous visitors to the city at Yearly Meeting time; now they
began to invite "strangers" who came to Philadelphia on anti-
slavery business to stay with them at Sansom Street. Soon it was
known up and down the East Coast that all reformers would
find a hearty welcome at the Motts'.

James was earning as much as twenty-five hundred dollars a
year, but Lucretia still resisted household help. She had discovered that she had a remarkable talent for simplifying housework
when she really put her mind to it; and while she was home with
the babies, it was an outlet for her energies. She liked to get up
in the morning and bake a dozen pies or preserve two dozen jars
of pickled herring before the rest of the family was even stirring.
She gave up the fancy stitching that occupied the time of so

many women of the day, but while she talked or attended meetings, her hands were busy knitting or sewing. She kept a careful record of every penny she spent and began a lifelong habit of giving what she saved to charity. Destitute blacks could always count on something to eat and perhaps a few coins at Lucretia's door.

But the world outside her home pulled at Lucretia. The Hicksite branch of the Society of Friends was much in need of her talents both as organizer and consolidator and as minister, and for the next few years she gave most of her excess energy to its service. She began on a small scale by visiting all the families who were members of the new downtown Hicksite Monthly Meeting. As Elizabeth Coggeshall had done on Nantucket twenty-five years before, Lucretia went from household to household to sit in the best parlor with family members, bowing her head in silence until she was moved to speak. This first mission was a great success. She might have immediately gone on to more ambitious projects if she hadn't discovered she was pregnant again, at the advanced age of thirty-five.

Pattie was born in October 1828. For the next two years Lucretia stayed close to home, confining her ministry to the Philadelphia area. In May 1830 she was chosen as clerk of Philadelphia Women's Yearly Meeting.

Within the first few days of her appointment she was faced with a major dilemma. A messenger from the Men's Meeting brought her a copy of a letter prepared by John Comly, its clerk, and addressed to London Yearly Meeting. The purpose of the letter was to defend the Hicksite Society of Friends against the charge of heresy. Since Quakerism had been born in England in the seventeenth century, London felt itself to be the final arbiter in matters of doctrine. The evangelical movement had first affected the British Friends, and it was they who had converted the Philadelphians. They therefore had sided strongly with the Orthodox group and refused to recognize the Hicksite majority. A previous epistle sent in 1828 had been returned by London to the Hicksite Friends unopened.

Between sessions Lucretia Mott read the text of the second letter with a sinking heart. In addition to declaring that the Hicksites were not infidels or deists, it declared that "the history of the birth, life, acts, death and resurrection of the Holy Jesus, as in the volume of the book it is written of him, we reverently believe.'' This was a repudiation of Hicks and a creedal statement such as she could never approve.

What was she to do? As clerk of Women's Yearly Meeting it was her duty to read the statement to the group and, if it met with their approval, to sign it, whether she agreed or not. She had little hope that the women would reject what the men had accepted. In matters like these, the Quaker women were accustomed to going along with the men as slavishly as Grandfather Folger's sheep. Could she rouse them against the letter by speaking her mind? In the depths of her heart she was beginning to know that the majority were ready to make any compromise to win the approval of the authority figure, London Yearly Meeting. Well, she knew what it was to long for approbation. But she also knew the driving force of a voice within that pushed her in the opposite direction.

As soon as the Meeting reconvened, Lucretia read the epistle to the women, enunciating it clearly in her sweet schoolmistress voice. Then turning over the clerkship of the Meeting to the recording clerk, she stepped down to the floor and, to the amazement of the women, spoke against the letter.

It contained sentiments utterly opposed to her own convictions and to the inherent spirit of Quakerism, she told the shocked meeting. While as clerk it might be proper and necessary for her to sign it on behalf of the meeting, still, as an individual she could not approve it, objecting as she did to any statement in the nature of a declaration of faith other than in the Divine Light in the soul.

There was an uneasy rustling among the women. Some secretly agreed with Lucretia but did not dare voice their true feelings. Quakers do not vote; when the time came to approve the epistle, there was only a gentle murmur of assent throughout the crowded room.

With a heavy heart Lucretia reread the rough draft Comly had sent her. She must sign it now, but at least perhaps she could make a few changes in the wording, changes both Meetings would approve the next day. With her firm, clear hand she went over the text, correcting, revising. She struck out the word *opponents* and replaced it with *adversaries*. In place of *brother-ly* she wrote *friendly*. In several spots Comly had used the expression *brethren*; she made it *brethren and sisters*. Some acknowledgment had to be made that women comprised more than half of the Yearly Meeting!

Comly did not like the changes, nor the fact that Lucretia Mott had spoken against the letter. It did not help matters that London Yearly Meeting shortly returned the letter with the word *mendacity* written over it. Lucretia had predicted it would do no good. Who likes to be proved wrong? Thereafter he watched her closely and turned an attentive ear when he heard whispers about her.

There were such whispers, for Lucretia's increasing activism in the antislavery cause and her outspoken views about the rights of women were beginning to bother many Hicksites. They thought her gullible, ready to follow any new enthusiasm. Her beloved John Comly gave her little opportunity to explain things, Lucretia complained in confidence to a friend. Still, she would have "to learn to bear evil report even should we be made of no reputation thereby."

Others in the Yearly Meeting, however, admired Lucretia, and not a few were afraid of her sharp tongue. She remained a powerful figure in Quaker circles. Year after year in the 1830s she was made clerk of Women's Yearly Meeting and placed on important committees. During her tenure she influenced the women to go on record as opposed to "purchasing goods pro-duced through slavery." She also played a crucial role in con-ducting a thorough study of all the school-aged children within the Yearly Meeting and the schools they attended. The results suggested that more Quaker schools were needed and that the Hicksites must have their own seminary in which to train teachers. Especially women teachers, Lucretia thought. Some-day she must do something about this.

Meanwhile she had begun to travel in the ministry, leaving the younger children under the care of their Coffin grandmother, who had returned to Philadelphia to live with the Motts, or with her own daughter, Anna, now a blooming girl of eighteen. On her first trip, made in the summer of 1830, she took time for a visit to her sister Martha, now married to David Wright in

Aurora, New York. To the horror of most Philadelphians she insisted on making the four-day trip to Aurora without a chaperone. "You may meet Lucretia Mott," Mary Biddle of Philadelphia wrote Clement Biddle. "She and little Mary Yarnell set out this morning for Aurora, and consistent with the idea of the former respecting the independence of the female character, she proposed being her own caretaker from New York to the end of the journey."

Increasingly, Lucretia undertook journeys in the ministry to areas where the conflict was particularly fierce, such as Muncy, in the mountains of north-central Pennsylvania, and Salem, in south Jersey. She was by now sufficiently partisan to enter with a certain zest into the brisk competition between Hicksites and Orthodox for members.

For the next fifteen months she also traveled throughout the Delaware Valley area. Whenever possible, James accompanied her on these jaunts, driving her from town to town in an open buggy. They did not talk much; nevertheless, they both valued the long, peaceful hours they spent together in wordless communication. When they arrived at their destination, and Lucretia felt moved to speak, she was strengthened by the knowledge that James was somewhere in the room.

The wool business prevented James from leaving Philadelphia for extended periods, however. In April 1833 Lucretia started on an ambitious trip through New York State that was to end at her beloved Nantucket. She was accompanied by Phebe Post Willis, a cousin of James's and Lucretia's friend and confidante. The two women adventurously set off for New England alone, taking the steamboat from New York to Providence. This was Lucretia's first return to her island home since she was a child of eleven. As soon as they were out on Long Island Sound, smelling the salt and hearing the cries of the gulls, Lucretia's spirits must have lifted. Although she was seasick on the voyage from Woods Hole, she rejoiced at the sight of Nantucket Town huddling about its harbor, the silver-shingled cottages, the single church tower, the wide, windswept sky.

The Friends of Nantucket had also suffered from the separation. Although the Hicksites were in the majority, they seemed leaderless. Lucretia preached earnestly to the little flock, many of them related to her by family ties. Some of her relatives had chosen to remain Orthodox, but she was relieved to find that in personal relationships they were still cordial. She left for "the continent" delighted and refreshed by the visit but troubled by the state of the Society on her native island. Some other Friends ought to follow up on her visit soon.

Back in Philadelphia, having visited Bedford, Lynn, Salem, Providence, and New York City, Lucretia continued to feel a little uneasy about the speed with which she had traveled. When she reported in her Monthly Meeting that she had fulfilled her mission, a Friend in the next seat reminded her after Meeting that "Saul had said he had done all when the best was kept back." Lucretia told her tartly that "I would allow her to go and finish all that I omitted." In a more serious vein she tried several times to see Edward Hicks, a Bucks County sign painter and Quaker preacher (now famous for his paintings entitled *Peaceable Kingdom*). Hicks had obtained a minute from his Meeting giving him permission to make a religious visit to New England, and Lucretia wanted to instruct him on whom he should see and what he should say. Hicks, however, was a true Quaker quietist, believing that he should make no plans and take no action unless under the direct leading of the Spirit. The Spirit did not seem to be directing him to go to New England after all. In fact, it did not direct him to be home when Lucretia came calling. It was the beginning of an antagonism between the two. He thought she was "conniving." She decided he was an "oddity."

A few days after her return from New England, Lucretia and James had driven out to Byberry to tell John Comly about her trip. It was, Lucretia wrote Phebe, an "*uncommonly* pleasant visit." Lucretia was still torn between wanting to hold on to John Comly's approval and obeying that inner voice that was urging her on to ever more radical and controversial positions. It was a conflict to be repeated over and over again. She solved it during the early 1830s by working hard to "bear ill repute" and by being more traditionally "religious" than at other times in her life.

She was forty now, an age when most of her contemporaries had settled into peaceful grandmotherhood. She would be a grandmother herself soon. Anna was engaged to marry Edward Hopper, a young lawyer, son of Isaac Hopper, the abolitionist. Even Maria, who was going to a school kept by Rebecca Bunker in Mount Holly, was beginning to have beaux. At home Lucretia's duties were lessening, with the three younger children at school and help in the house, at last, to do the heavy cleaning and the laundry.

Yet Lucretia showed no signs of slowing down. In the world outside her cocoon new winds were blowing. The romanticism of the nineteenth century was coming into flower in a literary burst in New England, in the birth of the transcendentalist movement in and around Boston, and in the development of a whole host of radical reforms: antislavery, nonresistance, communitarianism. In the summer of 1833 Mary Lyon visited Emma Willard's Female Academy in Troy, New York, and began to dream about Mount Holyoke; Catherine Beecher was writing about female education; the founders of Oberlin College were discussing the admission of women. "Mighty powers are at work in the world, and who shall stay them?" Dr. Channing had said. Lucretia agreed and frequently quoted him. To both Channing and Lucretia, the power of change was the power of good, for progress itself was positive. Now Lucretia, after long years of preparation, was about to be swept up in the changes.

CHAPTER
VI

THE
ANTISLAVERY CRUSADE

IN AUGUST of 1830 Lucretia and James Mott entertained a young "stranger" at their Sansom Street home. He was William Lloyd Garrison, a twenty-five-year-old journalist from Boston who had been working in Baltimore on an antislavery newspaper, the *Genius of Universal Emancipation.* The editor of the paper, Benjamin Lundy, was a friend of the Motts and had urged the fiery Garrison to visit them on his way back to Boston.

At the Mott dinner table Garrison poured out a tale of woe. He had just completed seven weeks in prison as the result of a libel suit brought against him by a prominent slave trader for an intemperate editorial Garrison had written for the *Genius.* Garrison was not penitent; in fact, he thought the libel suit proved the growth in power of the faction supporting slavery in the United States, and its ability to silence critics through the courts. In the course of his year in Baltimore with Lundy he had become much more radical. The *Genius* supported the Colonization Society, a group that planned to buy slaves and send them back to Africa. This scheme was supposed to bring the so-called benefits of a white civilization to the black continent while gradually ridding the United States of slavery with pain to no one. Lundy believed that the colonization idea was politically expedient, although he had his doubts about it. While in Baltimore, Garrison had learned from black friends that they had no desire to return to Africa, a land they had never seen. Instead they wanted to stay in the United States and share in the prosperity of the new land. Colonization, he concluded, strengthened the public fear that blacks and whites could never live side by side, furthermore, it denied education to free blacks and "lulled the whole country into a deep sleep."

Lucretia had supported the Colonization Society, but now she listened with deep interest as William Garrison talked about his growing conviction that there was only one answer to slavery: immediate emancipation. Any scheme that called for the compensation of the slaveholders acknowledged their right to hold human beings as property in the first place. The abolitionists must become far more militant, for the Slave Power was now immense. Would the Motts help to awaken the people of Philadelphia to this need?

The Motts would. Lucretia bustled about, securing the Franklin Institute for Garrison to give his talks and assembling an audience, largely Quaker. The night of the first lecture, however, Garrison disappointed her by reading, instead of delivering, his speech, and mumbling at that.

"William, if thee expects to set forth thy cause by word of mouth thee must lay aside thy paper and trust in the leading of the Spirit," she told him.

Garrison resolved to take her advice. He was deeply impressed with the little Quaker lady, who seemed to him not only sweet tempered but extraordinarily intelligent for a woman. Garrison wrote later that the interviews helped to free him from "sectarian prejudices." It was the beginning of a lifelong friendship. Garrisonian ideas were very much in keeping with those that Lucretia was evolving out of her own religious convictions. She was sometimes influenced by him and often agreed with him, though she frequently thought he was too strident in his tone.

Back in Boston from his Philadelphia visit, Garrison set to work establishing his own antislavery newspaper to advocate immediate emancipation. On January 1, 1831, the first issue of the *Liberator* was published. "I am in earnest, I will not equivocate, I will not excuse, I will not retreat a single inch, and I will be heard," the single-minded young editor declared.

On the first of August, 1833, Great Britain abolished slavery in the West Indies. Many British Quakers had worked on the reform movement that took credit for this victory. Garrison had meanwhile found enough converts to his cause to found the

New England Anti-Slavery Society and to develop substantial backing in New York. Inspired by the success of the campaign in Great Britain, he decided to call a convention in December 1833 to form a national organization. He chose Quaker Philadelphia as its site.

The convention opened on the morning of December 4 in the Adelphi Building, at Fifth below Walnut. James was one of some sixty delegates present. Lucretia, having just returned from a trip to Delaware as a Quaker minister, was busy seeing to the comfort of several out-of-town delegates who had arrived at the house on Sansom Street with letters of introduction.

The house was crowded already. Its regular occupants now numbered ten, and Martha Wright had recently arrived from Aurora, New York, to visit, bringing several small children. Lucretia nevertheless managed to double up enough family members to give each visitor a bedroom of his own. On these occasions she not only made up the beds with fresh linen but hung fresh curtains at the windows. Sometimes she confessed that in her hurry she forgot to see that all the curtains matched.

Garrison was staying at a hotel. As soon as Lucretia had things organized at home, she called on him and invited him to come to tea the next day and bring along any friends he might wish to include. She issued a few more such invitations, then took time to count up her guests. There would be fifty! With the help of her sister, mother, and daughters she spent the morning of December 4 shopping and baking. For high teas like this one she liked to serve oysters, spiced tongue and pickled herring, strawberries or gooseberries in season, and homemade breads and cakes. In between times she arranged her front parlor, laying on the table an array of antislavery pamphlets and a seal, featuring a kneeling female slave with the message, "Am I not a Woman and a Sister?" at its base. Thomas Yarnell, Lucretia's nephew, quipped that he supposed that had been placed there to make an *impression.* The antislavery symbol popular with most abolitionists was a kneeling male slave asking "Am I not a Man and a Brother?" Half the slave population was excluded.

The tea was a success. The next morning James and his guests returned to the convention while Lucretia stayed home to clean up and prepare for the next evening's tea. Just as she and Mar-

tha were sitting down to their morning letter writing, Thomas
Whitson, a Lancaster County abolitionist, arrived with an invitation for the ladies of the household to come to the meeting as
specially invited guests.

Nothing could have pleased Lucretia more. But it didn't seem
fair that only women of the Coffin-Mott family were invited.
Would it be all right if she took a few minutes to spread the
word to some of her friends? There wasn't time, Thomas Whitson told her. A few other women had already been asked, and
the gentlemen were eager for their guests to come right away.
Accordingly Lucretia hurried to notify her mother and her
daughter, Anna Hopper, and to get ready for the trip downtown. Martha, who preferred to finish her letter to David, her
husband, watched in some amusement as the three "clapped on
their bonnets" and hurried out of the house.

At Adelphi Lucretia and the two Annas were shown to special
seats. Here they found three other Quaker women, and the six
prepared to sit quietly and listen to the proceedings. It had not
occurred to any of them, not even to Lucretia Mott, with her
advanced views of woman's rights, that women should actually
participate in the deliberations.

They had been invited to hear a preliminary wording of the
Declaration of Sentiments. "We plant ourselves on the truths of
Divine Revelation and on the Declaration of Independence as
an Everlasting Rock," the document said. Lucretia smiled to
herself. Surely the author had meant that Divine Revelation was
the Everlasting Rock? Someone would certainly mention the
error. But no one did, and to her own great surprise she found
herself on her feet, asking permission of the chairman to say a
few words. That gentleman, Beriah Green of the Oneida Institute, agreed, and Lucretia suggested it would be better to
transpose the phrase. One of the younger delegates, sitting up
front, turned around wondering what woman knew the meaning of the word *transpose*. Beriah Green thanked Lucretia and
said he hoped she would speak again if so moved.

Lucretia thanked him for his courtesy and sat down. She had
intended to keep quiet, but there was a small grammatical error
on the next page, and this, too, she rose to correct. The next day
when the final document was read, she was deeply moved by its

ringing message, including a pledge to struggle not only against slavery but also against prejudice and to use only moral means in the fight. It seemed to her a beautifully worded and compelling statement, and she was surprised when it was announced that several prominent abolitionists had already been approached to sign it and had refused. She once more found herself on her feet, arguing that right principles were stronger than great names. "If our principles are right, why should we be cowards? Why should we wait for those who never had the courage to maintain the inalienable rights of the slave?"

"Go on, go on," several delegates urged her, but she had said her say and again sat down.

There was more discussion of the uses of the document. Finally it was time to sign it. They must think carefully, a Philadelphian warned his fellow delegates. Each man must realize that his signature on this piece of parchment might cost him loss of business, perhaps social ostracism. There was a long moment of silence in the little hall. Then, although Lucretia did not stand, her voice was clearly heard. "James, put down thy name!"

James signed, and the other delegates rose and solemnly marched forward to sign also. Many of them were quite young, and until Lucretia's calm assurance, had been frightened by the warnings they had heard. One of these was James Miller McKim, a twenty-three-year-old Presbyterian divinity student from Carlisle, Pennsylvania. It was he who had turned to see what woman knew the meaning of the word *transpose*. At the end of the session he spoke to Lucretia, and she immediately invited him to stay. The delegate from Maine was leaving; one of her bedchambers would be empty.

McKim was the only white member of his local antislavery society, which had appointed him delegate to the convention. He knew and shared the strong feelings of his black friends against the institution, but this was the first time he had met the abolitionists with their bewildering array of ideas, not only against slavery but in support of woman's rights, nonresistance, and natural religion. It was all at variance with the structured theology he was studying. He confessed to Lucretia that he felt as though "all his props" had been knocked away. Lucretia immediately took him under her wing, lent him books, introduced him to Quaker Meeting. Miller developed a strong attachment to the handsome older woman.

It was reciprocated. The young man with his dark good looks and earnest, searching attitude touched a deep chord in Lucretia. In part her feeling was motherly. Miller was eighteen years younger than she, not much older than Tommy would have been if he had lived. She found particularly moving the fact that he was an orphan, responsible for five younger brothers and sisters. She longed to comfort him, to free his mind from the shackles of dogmatism, to introduce him to the joys of free inquiry.

But there was something more. The one real lack in her relationship with James was intellectual discussion. James was an intelligent man, a profound man in many ways, a man who shared her every conviction. But he wasn't a man who liked to talk about theology, religion, or any other abstract subject. Lucretia loved to debate endlessly on points of religion, to quote the Bible to back up her positions at the same time she questioned large chunks of it. Miller was more than her match. He had the Presbyterian love of words and concepts and an argumentative streak that made it impossible for him to give ground. The two discussed, debated, and argued endlessly, beginning the day of the antislavery convention and continuing for almost forty years. He filled a void in her life that no one else could.

The relationship between these two had a curiously intense quality from the start. Lucretia wrote to both her sister Martha and her friend Phebe about Miller, calling him "the darling subject of my pen." After he left her house, she corresponded with him regularly, advising him on his reading, his vocation, his romances, and encouraging him to come to Philadelphia as often as possible.

During the first few days when Miller was on Sansom Street, Lucretia had taken a giant step into her future. The antislavery convention had recommended the formation of female antislavery societies everywhere, and Lucretia thought it important to organize one in Philadelphia immediately while enthusiasm was high. Accordingly she called together a meeting for the evening of December 9 at a local dame school and invited all the Philadelphia female abolitionists. Although Lucretia had had experience running meetings within the Society of Friends, she knew nothing about presenting resolutions or taking a vote. She did not feel capable of chairing the meeting, and she was quite sure no other woman in Philadelphia would be able to do so. Instead she asked James McCrummel, a black minister, to preside, and Samuel May of Brooklyn, Connecticut, a Unitarian minister, to address the women.

The thirty women who gathered that night at Catherine McDermott's schoolhouse had no idea that they were making history. They named themselves the Philadelphia Female Anti-Slavery Society, selected a committee to draft a constitution, chose Lucretia Mott as corresponding clerk, and decided to meet five days later to establish the new organization. By the end of the meeting they were ready to decide they could thereafter dispense with help from gentlemen.

At the second meeting Lucretia Mott read the new constitution, which she had helped to draft. "We deem it our duty, as professing Christians, to manifest our abhorrence of the flagrant injustice and deep sin of slavery by united and vigorous exertions," the preamble declared. The entire constitution was read, modified, and adopted on the spot. Lucretia's was the first signature.

The little band of pioneer women was mainly Quaker, but there was a sprinkling of Presbyterians and Unitarians. Among them was Abba Alcott, wife of Bronson and mother of Louisa May. The group was also integrated, or "amalgamated," to use the nineteenth-century term. Charlotte and Margaretta Forten, daughters of the wealthy black sailmaker, James Forten, were present, as well as Hattie Forten Purvis, wife of Robert Purvis, a handsome and well-to-do country gentleman from Byberry. Sarah McCrummel, the wife of the black minister, signed, as did Grace Bustill Douglass, a black Quaker who kept a Quaker millinery shop next to her father's thriving bakeshop. Later Sarah Mapps Douglass, a schoolmistress and Grace's daughter, became one of the society's most active members.

These black women were all middle class and thoroughly respectable. Nevertheless, the mere fact that they were holding regular meetings with white women was enough to send a shock wave through Philadelphia's body politic. From its moment of birth the little society of female abolitionists was suspect; soon their meetings would lead to violence. Rather than frightening the women, this public reaction strengthened their resolve. If their timid efforts to do good led to such public fear, they might just as well act as boldly and radically as they could.

For Lucretia Mott, friendships with the Fortens, Douglasses, and Hattie Purvis opened another door into a world she had known little about. Her feelings about slavery and racial prejudice had been strong, but they had been based only on observation. Now she had close friends who actually experienced the pain of discrimination, whose relatives had known slavery, whose homes were endangered when there was rioting in the streets.

There was one thing she could do right away and that was to break down segregated social patterns. Enthusiastically, Lucretia began to have her black friends to the house. To her surprise and distress this upset Anna Coffin. Her mother, Lucretia noted, believed in integration in principle; she just found it hard to bear in practice. There was, strange to say, an "aristocratic streak" in the older woman. "Her principles and long cherished predilections & prejudices are sadly at war with each other," Lucretia wrote Martha. "She would far prefer others acting out our principles than my doing so."

Thanks to the presence of black members, the Female Society found itself very much involved in the life of the black community in Philadelphia. When Sarah Douglass's school was unable to support itself, the society took it under its wing for a spell. When black children were denied the right to participate in a Sunday celebration at Independence Hall, the society protested. When a Vigilance Committee was developed to help escaping slaves and warn free blacks of the approach of kidnapers, members of the society were actively involved. Since most of the blacks were quite poor, the society developed an early welfare system. In 1839 the Female Society divided the city into sections and assigned each member a section to respond to the needs of black people. In 1840 members' assignments were to visit and report on black schools. Lucretia herself began a lifelong practice of preaching quite regularly in the black churches.

As time went on, the Female Society moved more and more into areas of public protest and government petitioning. It has been correctly called one of the first women's political groups. Through it, women learned to exercise talents they did not know they possessed. It rapidly became the springboard for the woman's rights movement.

Through the Female Society Lucretia Mott began to discover the gentle yet firm leadership of which she was capable and to have confidence in her own vision.

Lucretia's most enthusiastic supporter and co-worker was as usual her husband. As a founding member of the American Anti-Slavery Society, James Mott's name was one of the twelve hundred attached to a call for a convention to found a regional society for Delaware, eastern Pennsylvania, and New Jersey. Lucretia attended the meeting in Harrisburg as a delegate of the Philadelphia Female Anti-Slavery Society. The thought that men and women might work together in the same society had not yet crossed anyone's mind, but behind the scenes Lucretia was influential. She and James felt the new organization needed a newspaper and persuaded their old friend, Benjamin Lundy (whom they had rescued from jail for bankruptcy), to edit the *National Enquirer and Constitutional Advocate of Universal Liberty.* Lundy, however, was too opposed to Garrison and too set in his ways to work under the direction of the new group. A year later the Motts helped to ease him out and replace him with an unknown poet and journalist from New England, young John Greenleaf Whittier.

Public opposition to the growing antislavery movement soon took an ugly turn. The South was thoroughly alarmed by the sudden rash of antislavery tracts that began to pour over its borders. Would these not lead to rebellions such as that led by Nat Turner in 1831? Steps were taken to ban the deluge of propaganda. Northern businessmen and workingmen were equally outraged. In Boston William Lloyd Garrison was heckled. In New York City on the night of July 9, 1834, a mob collected outside the Chatham Street Chapel, where an antislavery meeting was in progress and stormed down Pearl Street. Isaac Hopper, the intrepid little abolitionist, having moved to New York, now stood outside his antislavery bookstore to defend it in person. The mob passed him by, but surged on to the home and warehouse of Arthur Tappan and Lewis Tappan, his brother, and here broke windows and chopped at doors. Scattered by faint-hearted police, they regrouped and went to the black section of town, where they burned houses and churches.

Scarcely had the Philadelphia abolitionists read this shocking news than violence was in their own territory. An antiblack riot occurred in Columbia, Pennsylvania; then a few days later in Philadelphia itself. Here trouble began one hot night in August when white men and boys attacked a group of blacks on South Street, near Eighth. The next night the mob collected at Seventh and Bainbridge and wrecked a black church before starting methodically to vandalize a row of black homes. On the third night, when the mob started to tear down a second church, the blacks, realizing they were going to get no assistance from anyone, gathered in self-defense. The police finally arrived on the scene; but their halfhearted intervention only helped to fan the flames. Altogether thirty-one homes and two churches were destroyed.

The Motts were out of town during the riots, attending antislavery meetings in Lancaster County with their friend Thomas Whitson. On their return they went immediately to inspect the shocking damage to the black neighborhoods, only six city blocks from their home. The sight of the charred churches convinced them that this was not a riot provoked by the blacks themselves, as the city newspapers were comfortably assuring citizens it was.

The impact of the riots was to frighten many abolitionists into inaction. While this atmosphere of fear still reigned, Prudence Crandall, a Connecticut schoolmistress, came to Philadelphia to look into establishing a school for black students. In her hometown of Canterbury, Connecticut, she had tried to establish such a school the year before, only to have the incensed townspeople throw filth into her well, set fire to her house, and demand the immediate passage of a Connecticut law barring such activity. Under the hastily contrived law she had been sent to prison and locked into a jail cell with a condemned murderer. A higher court finally reversed her conviction on a technicality, but the townspeople continued to make life unbearable for Prudence and her pupils.

Prudence, now married to the Reverend Calvin Philleo, decided to move her school to a more congenial climate. Philadelphia seemed a logical spot. She and Calvin stayed with the Motts during a week in early September 1834, and Lucretia took Prudence to call on "some fifty of our most respected colored families" to solicit scholars. Many pupils signed up, but several timid Philadelphia abolitionists, frightened by the riots, persuaded Prudence to hold off until after the fall elections.

The coming of fall did nothing to relieve their fears, however. The Society of Friends as a whole was nervous about the new radical antislavery movement with its violent rhetoric and its sympathy for rebellious blacks. The majority of Quakers, whether Hicksite or Orthodox, did not want to be involved, and they did not want their members to become active. It was suggested instead that if Quakers wanted to work against slavery, they form their own Quaker antislavery societies. Most of all, the Friends did not want individual members to preach against slavery in Meeting. The subject was too exciting; it was bound to cause discord.

By the fall of 1834 Lucretia was writing to Phebe Willis that attempts were being made to bar the subject from Meeting. "I can never willingly submit," she said. "William Penn said he hated obedience upon authority without conviction." She told the alarmed elders of her Meeting that she knew the subject was controversial and that she would try to use caution. But the very surge of energy that brought her to her feet demanded that she speak on the subject nearest to her heart, and that subject was now the abolition of slavery.

The problem was compounded as Lucretia continued to make trips in the ministry. In all these meetings she spoke as the spirit moved, and it almost always moved her to address the problem of slavery. In addition she had begun taking stacks of antislavery literature to distribute at the meetings, a practice that she followed until the Civil War. Elders in New York were as eager to keep the subject of slavery from coming up as were those in Philadelphia. One of the most vivid early memories of

Anna White, a Shaker leader, was of listening to an antislavery address by Lucretia Mott, then seeing the little woman "abruptly silenced by the guardians of Quaker Orthodoxy." In Connecticut a somewhat gentler elder told Lucretia that "he never liked to hear preachers, when they had something unpleasant to communicate, try to throw the blame off themselves by laying it upon the Lord." Lucretia, who sometimes struggled with her conscience over the frequency of her antislavery remarks, thought this was acceptable eldering.

There was no let up in the constant criticism. Her friendship with Miller McKim was scrutinized closely, and John Comly was heard to say that "she was bringing hireling ministers into the area." (The Quakers disapproved of all paid ministry.) When Lucretia and James struck up an acquaintance with William Furness, a Philadelphia Unitarian minister and abolitionist, this also displeased the Friends. Was she becoming a Unitarian?

As a way of making money the Philadelphia Female Anti-Slavery Society began the annual custom of having a sale or fair. Members met weekly to sew pillows and reticules with antislavery slogans and to make dolls and rag rugs for the fair. Sister organizations in Boston, New York, and as far away as Great Britain gathered up bundles of goods to be sold. Anna Mott Hopper, Lucretia's grave older daughter, was often in charge.

This annual fair was regarded by the majority of Quakers as frivolous, and rumors abounded in regard to it. Lucretia was selling engravings of herself! Buttons off the coat of a great man! Sacred objects! One by one Lucretia patiently responded to the criticisms, while at the same time defending the fairs not only as harmless but as positively beneficial. They gave many women and young people an opportunity to be involved in antislavery work, and they raised healthy sums of money—sometimes more than $2,000—for the cause.

Lucretia Mott was alternately amused and annoyed by all the carping. She did not trim her sails; instead she kept right on with all her antislavery activities and became increasingly critical of modern Quakerism. Would an outside observer to Yearly Meeting suspect that the Society of Friends held testimonies against intemperance, war, and slavery? No, "a deathlike silence reigns. . . . Our strength seems mainly exerted in holding up to view the necessity of going to meeting and wearing a plain garb.''

Instead of compromising she started a new campaign.

The Philadelphia Female Anti-Slavery Society had strengthened her faith in the capacities of women. This made her more aware of inequalities in her own Society. Though the Women's Meeting had the duty of dealing with a woman who had offended against the discipline, it was up to the men, not the women, to make the final decision as to whether or not the offender was to be disowned. Lucretia thought this was not only unjust but totally illogical. She spoke about it several times in the Women's Business Meeting but found she did not have enough support among the women to change the rules. ''Our foolish women set their faces so against any change—hugging their chains so hard I despair of any advance in our day,'' she wrote Phebe. ''I am often reminded of Cowper's apt lines:

> 'Such dupes are men (women) to custom & so prone
> To reverence what is ancient, and can plead
> A course of long observance for its use
> That even servitude, the worst of ills,
> Because delivered from sire to son,
> Is kept and guarded as a sacred thing.' ''

With the organization of the antislavery societies Lucretia herself had shed some chains. She was less eager to please such persons as John Comly and was more attuned now to the rhythms of the nineteenth-century passion for reform. There was a world outside of Quakerism and a role for her in that world. The demands of the day as well as her own inner drives were conspiring to thrust her onto a larger stage.

VII

THE
HOUSE ON
NORTH NINTH STREET

THE PACE Lucretia Mott set herself, the amount of anger she had to bottle up in order to preserve a calm exterior, the sheer stress of battle soon began to take a toll. Shortly after the organization of the American Anti-Slavery Society she began to suffer from dyspepsia, pains in her stomach so sharp that she was almost "bent double." A Philadelphia doctor suggested that she indulge in more pleasure and relaxation, dissipate a little and leave antislavery efforts alone for a while. Lucretia told him smartly that she would be willing to do so if his wife would take her place in the antislavery crusade. She had no intention of slowing down, so she accepted her stomach trouble more or less stoically.

In 1836 Dr. Joseph Parrish put her on her first diet. She was to eat principally beef and mutton, with stale bread and no vegetables, and to drink cream and lime water for breakfast and supper. During the day she was to take a wineglass of camomile tea with ginger and fennel seed and a little ammonia or spirits of hartshorn added. An alternative pick-me-up was to be made with the yolks of eggs beaten with a little ginger and sugar and boiled water gradually poured into it. She tried this regimen for a while, then, finding it did little good, went on to another.

Lucretia was never introspective. As she gaily wrote Miller McKim, she had not even time for "such inspection into my own state as the deranged nature of it requires." But she was interested in phrenology, an early, groping attempt to understand human psychology and to find an explanation for deviant behavior beyond simple depravity. It seemed to her self-evident that the development of the brain would affect the size and shape of the head. The women of Nantucket had been given adequate opportunity to develop intellectually, and one could see it. "Look at the heads of these women, they can mingle with men, they are not triflers, they have intelligent subjects of conversation." Anna Coffin, her mother, had a particularly large, broad brow.

In 1838 George Combe, a Scottish phrenologist, visited Philadelphia. Through Harriet Martineau, he and his wife had an introduction to the Motts. Combe offered to do a study of Lucretia's head. She could hardly refuse. According to Combe, Lucretia's temperament was "nervous, bilious;" her "combativeness" was large, her self-esteem "moderate," and her "love of approbation" very large. She was censorious, conscientious, quick to see the ridiculous.

Nervous and bilious or not, Lucretia kept the pace. More and more strangers visiting Philadelphia stopped with the Motts: William Lloyd Garrison in 1835; John Quincy Adams, former U.S. President and now congressman from Massachusetts, in 1836; Harriet Martineau, the British writer and abolitionist, that same year; the Combes in 1838. Charles Burleigh, the eccentric abolitionist known for his flowing red beard, made his home with the Motts for a while and called Lucretia mother, perhaps to her amusement. Miller McKim was in and out.

In October 1836 Maria Mott married Edward M. Davis, a local merchant, abolitionist, and Hicksite. According to Nantucket custom, the two started married life with the Motts. The snug house on Sansom Street was finally bursting at the seams. In 1837 the Motts bought a larger house at 136 North Ninth Street, above Cherry. Now they had a dining room big enough to seat fifty, and on the upstairs floors enough bedrooms to house the basic family of eight or ten plus any number of out-of-town guests. Lucretia was free to invite even more strangers to stay. The result was that she sometimes managed a veritable hotel.

When people commented on Lucretia Mott's remarkable ability to entertain with apparent ease, she always said it was because she had learned not to be fussy. "When people are so over particular as to have to be in the kitchen and at their domestic concerns all the time, visitors cannot enjoy the added tax on the visited."

At the ever-expandable Mott dinner table the conversation was lively and apt to cover any of the numerous topics of the day: antislavery, mesmerism, the water cure, the Texas question, tight lacing, spiritualism, politics, poetry. Lucretia liked to keep her guests sitting at the table after each meal, pouring tea and coffee and watching the stimulants take effect. James sat at the far end of the table, occasionally catching her eye, putting in a word here, a word there to keep the conversational wheels rolling. While she listened, Lucretia's hands were always busy with her knitting or with sewing rags into balls for rugs.

Making rag rugs was one of Lucretia's specialties. She tore rags into strips, sewed them together, and wound them into balls. When she had enough balls, she took them to a weaver to be woven into rugs. Every female member of the huge Coffin clan eventually had several of Lucretia's rugs on her floor. She liked to use bright colors. Once when Lucretia was down to nothing but tans and grays, Elizabeth Cady Stanton, a friend of her latter years, sent her a large package of brightly colored rags.

This unceasing activity won Lucretia a reputation as being a housewife without equal. In a day when it was feared that if a woman had any interests outside of her family, the family was bound to suffer, her dual role as housewife and reformer was constantly praised. "She is proof that it is possible for woman to widen her sphere without deserting it, or neglecting the duties which appropriately devolve upon her at home," one editor wrote rather unctuously.

Lucretia was proud of her ability to manage. Still, she confessed that things occasionally got ahead of her. Sometimes James would put on a clean shirt, only to find its buttons missing. He was, she reported to her sister, "remarkably bearing...the most striking evidence of dissatisfaction is in finding the buttonless shirt thrown on the bed and another put on its place."

Her favorite task was laying down carpets. She not only frequently changed the carpets in her own house but also insisted on doing it for all other members of the Coffin clan. The choosing of colors and the cutting and tacking of carpeting for parlor and dining room and bedchamber was a positive pleasure for her, as well as a creative outlet. It may well be that she pounded a few stubborn critics on the head in the course of pounding in those nails.

Housekeeping in general seems to have served Lucretia as a physical outlet. Whenever she was particularly worried or angry, she threw herself with redoubled energy into baking, scrubbing, ironing, preserving. In a day when nice middle-class ladies were allowed no exercise, Lucretia found in her housework and her dozens of errands about the streets of Philadelphia the release she craved. Housework did not drain her; it recharged her batteries for more battles of the mind.

Lucretia's deep immersion in the lives of her children and her closest friends gave her sanctuary, a little Nantucket Island in a sea of troubles. She drew nourishment from her relationships. The more controversy swirled around her head, the more she turned to family and friends, reaching out naturally for their support while she gave them her own full time and attention.

The Mott family itself was growing. Anna Mott Hopper lost a baby boy a few days after his birth in 1836, but had a healthy baby girl, Lucretia, in the spring of 1838. At about the same time Maria Davis gave birth to her first child, Anna. Lucretia was present for all these deliveries. She always found childbirth moving and wrote in vivid and graphic detail to her relatives about the duration of the labor, the size of the baby, the coming on of the mother's milk.

Anna Coffin, who also lived at 136, was the undisputed head of the Coffin clan in the Philadelphia area. Once a week the whole Coffin and Folger connection met in one or another of their homes, taking turns alphabetically. Distant cousins claimed connection in order to be included. Whenever Martha Wright visited or a deputation arrived from Nantucket, there would be a round of lively family parties.

In between times, Anna kept in touch with her relatives by writing "family sheets," round robins that went to Nantucket, New Bedford, Ohio, Aurora, New York, and back. The family sheets contained intimate details of the housekeeping arrangements and health of each member of the family, the engagements, weddings, confinements, and funerals, the successes and failures. It was everybody's right to know as much as possible about everyone else's business.

Beyond the immediate family circle, the Motts saw most of

the Philadelphia abolitionists at least weekly. Sarah Pugh, a Quaker schoolmistress, and Mary Grew, a graduate of the Hartford Female Seminary and a journalist, both joined the Philadelphia Female Anti-Slavery Society and were drawn into the inner circle at 136 North Ninth. James Forten and his daughters, as well as the Douglasses, were often invited for dinner when there were strangers to entertain.

And then there was Miller McKim. Lucretia's deep interest in the young man had continued. Thinking that Unitarianism might solve his religious quest, she introduced him to William Furness, of the First Unitarian Church of Philadelphia. It didn't work, however, and Lucretia found herself defending Unitarianism against Miller's attacks. "I want thee to have done with calling Unitarianism rationalities—'icy philosophizing'—thee doesn't know what thou mayest be thyself," she chided him.

Sufficiently shaken by new ideas of the ninteenth-century reformers, Lucretia's Quakerism, and the combination of Unitarian and trancendentalist ideas she exposed him to, Miller gave up all thought of entering the Presbyterian ministry. Instead he enrolled for a semester in medical school, then quit and tried teaching. Finally Lucretia persuaded him to take a job as agent of the Pennsylvania Anti-Slavery Society, with an office on North Fifth Street, not far from the Motts.

There was another way of keeping Miller close, and that was to marry him to a nice Quaker girl. Lucretia enthusiastically promoted his interest in a Lancaster County woman, Sarah Speakman, although she told Miller she was not going to plead guilty to the role of matchmaker. Sarah's father was concerned about her marrying out of Meeting, and Lucretia was able to calm some of his fears by assuring him that Miller was no longer a strict Presbyterian, that he had undergone a decided change in his religious convictions. The father finally relented, and Sarah and Miller were married in 1840.

The McKims were invited to the house whenever there was a party at 136 North Ninth. Many times, however, such evenings would end with a heated argument between Lucretia and Miller. The two could never see eye to eye, but could never give up the attempt to convert the other.

James was doing moderately well in the wool business, but Lucretia Mott had to keep to a strict budget in order to afford all her entertaining and still have money to give away to charity. She shopped around for bargains, bought and preserved food in season, turned sheets, reversed James's collars, mended clothing and towels. In a small book she kept track of every penny she spent.

Members of Lucretia's inner circle loved to tease her about her economies. Once, when she and Sarah McKim were talking, Lucretia observed a feather floating above the younger woman's head. The story has come down through the McKim family. "Without a pause in her conversation, she captured the piece of down, took scissors, needles and thread from a reticule at her waist, unstitched a seam in the cushion on which she was seated, tucked the feather in and repaired it before Grandma McKim's fascinated eyes."

They teased her, too, about her endless committees and her various diets. She took the teasing in good stride, for she felt their supportive love. If she were sometimes bossy and, as the phrenologist said, censorious—objecting very strongly, for example, to Martha Wright going to the theater while she was visiting in Philadelphia—they seemed to have accepted these traits without rebelling. She was never devious or manipulative; she simply let her family know what she expected of them and was not shocked if they argued back. Her life at home continued to be a source of nourishment and strength, preparing her for the escalating battles that lay in store for her public self.

CHAPTER
VIII
PROMISCUOUS
AUDIENCES

In May 1837 Lucretia Mott and her oldest daughter, Anna, went to New York City to attend the First Anti-Slavery Convention of American Women. This national gathering had been organized by Lucretia with the help of Maria Chapman, the beautiful and aristocratic leader of the Anti-Slavery women of Boston and William Lloyd Garrison's strong supporter. After four years of experience, the women were feeling confident. The male abolitionists had many suggestions for the convention, but the participants brushed these all aside and ran an efficient and fruitful three-day meeting. In the course of the convention they pledged themselves to launch a campaign for one million signatures on a petition to end slavery in the District of Columbia. They also decided to publish two pamphlets by Philadelphia members: *An Appeal to the Women of the Nominally Free States* by Angelina Grimké and *An Address to Free Colored Americans* by her sister, Sarah Grimké.

Daughters of a wealthy slave-owning family in South Carolina, the Grimké sisters had joined the Society of Friends and had moved to Philadelphia in order to separate themselves from the slave system. In March 1835 Angelina attended a lecture that George Thompson, a British abolitionist, delivered to the Philadelphia Female Anti-Slavery Society. Deeply moved, she decided to enlist in the battle for immediate emancipation. Her first step was to join the Female Society in the spring. Later that summer, disturbed by the growing violence against the abolitionists, she wrote Garrison a fervent personal letter urging him never to give way under pressure. "The ground on which you stand is holy ground." Without asking Angelina's permission to do so, Garrison immediately published the letter in the *Liberator*. Overnight the name Grimké became famous in anti-slavery circles outside of Philadelphia, and there were increasing calls upon Angelina to speak. In the fall of 1836 she was invited to become an agent of the American Anti-Slavery Society.

Angelina was not pretty, but when she spoke, she became impassioned and quickly moved her audiences. Having seen slavery firsthand on her father's plantation, she could, in addition, speak from experience about its horrors. At first Angelina spoke only to female audiences, according to the custom of the day. So popular were her lectures, however, that when she spoke in New York, a few men began to slip into the back of the halls and churches. There was immediate talk. Was she becoming a second Fanny Wright?

To defend her good name, her sister, Sarah Grimké, who had not entirely approved of the antislavery lecturing, decided to join Angelina in New York, while the Philadelphia Female Anti-Slavery Society under Lucretia's leadership passed a minute of support declaring that "when our brothers and sisters are crushed and bleeding under the arm of tyranny we must do with our might what our hands find to do, for their deliverance, pausing only to inquire 'what is right?' not 'what is universally acceptable?' "

This was the birth of the nineteenth-century woman's rights movement in the United States, springing from the abolitionist cause. Lucretia Mott greeted the development with delight. Ever since Nine Partners days she had been looking for a way to fight for sexual equality. Her battles, to date, had been confined to the Society of Friends, where lip service was given to the cause but women were still inferior in business decisions. Now a whole new world was opening up. Lucretia's faith that there was that of God in everyone, that women were as sacred as men, blacks as whites, children as their elders, made the link between feminism and the antislavery cause a natural one. She had followed her leading and proceeded as the way opened in establishing the Philadelphia Female Anti-Slavery Society. Now the rightness of that leading seemed to be apparent. There was light on the way ahead.

Encouraged by the approval of their sister delegates, the

Grimké sisters set off to New England to continue their antislavery lectures. In Boston their meetings were attended by a few men, and in Lynn, Massachusetts, where they spoke under the auspices of the Friends Meeting, the gathering was declared open to all. When news of this "promiscuous" meeting reached the ears of New England clergymen, there was a strong and immediate reaction. A few days later the sisters were denied the use of a church in Danvers for their lecture, and thereafter their arrival in each of a number of New England towns signaled alarm, protest, problems about obtaining halls, the gathering of a mob, and sometimes the throwing of stones and rotten tomatoes. In July the Congregational General Assembly issued a directive called a "Pastoral Letter" warning congregations against itinerant female lecturers and urging women to remember Saint Paul's injunction that they should keep quiet in churches and adhere to their own natural roles as clinging vines.

The "Pastoral Letter" stirred up controversy within the antislavery ranks. Some abolitionists feared the mixing of the antislavery and the woman's rights issues and declared themselves opposed to the Grimkés' speaking. Some even signed a second directive, a "Clerical Appeal," denouncing Garrison's attack on the clergy. Maria Chapman wrote a satirical poem about the ensuing war of words.

> *Confusion has seized us, and all things go wrong*
> *The women have leaped from their spheres*
> *And instead of fixed stars, shoot as comets along*
> *And are setting the world by the ears.*
> *In courses erratic they're wheeling through space*
> *In brainless confusion and meaningless chase.*
>
> *They've taken a notion to speak for themselves*
> *And are wielding the tongue and the pen*
> *They've mounted the rostrum, the termagant elves*
> *And—oh horrid—are talking to men!*
> *With faces unbalanced in our presence they come*
> *To harangue us, they say in behalf of the dumb.*

But not all women rushed to the Grimkés' aid. Catherine Beecher, Angelina's former teacher at Hartford Seminary, had earlier urged in an essay that women not be organized into abolition societies, since their subordination to men was according to divine law.

From Philadelphia, Lucretia Mott followed the blazing path of the Grimké sisters with delight. When Angelina Grimké was invited to address the Massachusetts legislature on the issue of slavery, she wrote Miller that the Grimkés were doing a noble part in the great work of correcting "the low estimate of woman's labors." Then cautiously she quoted a third party as having said that perhaps "the unfettering of the female intellect from the thralldom of prejudice would prove of even more value than the original object of the anti-slavery movement."

Meanwhile she had work to do at home: signatures to gather for the great antislavery petition; sermons to preach at the black churches; arrangements to be made for the Second Anti-Slavery Convention of American Women, to be held in May 1838 in Philadelphia. It was very much hoped that the new Pennsylvania Hall, being built by the abolitionists and reformers on Sixth between Mulberry and Sassafras, would be open for the occasion.

Lucretia and James had begun raising money for the new hall in December 1836. The violence against abolitionists had caused one public building after another to close its doors to antislavery meetings. Even the churches and Quaker meetings were afraid to admit them. Fortunately there were enough well-to-do businessmen among the abolitionists to raise the sum of forty thousand dollars for a building.

The resulting hall was handsome, with the pillared facade of a Greek temple. Its first floor contained a small auditorium, committee rooms, offices (including the office of John Greenleaf Whittier, now editor of the *Pennsylvania Freeman*), and free-produce stores; the second floor consisted of a large hall with galleries. The whole was lit with modern gas, and there were ventilators in the ceiling to permit a flow of fresh air. As a final touch the building was decorated in blue and white, the chairs upholstered in blue plush and the sofas in blue damask.

Lucretia had of course packed the house on Ninth Street for the opening week of meetings. Mary S. Parker came from the Boston Female Anti-Slavery Society, along with Maria Chapman and her sister, Anne Weston. Seven other guests gathered at the Motts', including William Lloyd Garrison and, as Maria Davis wrote Edward, "two coloreds."

On the morning of May 14, the dedication ceremonies for

Pennsylvania Hall began with a series of speeches. John Green-leaf Whittier had written a special poem for the occasion. On Tuesday the Anti-Slavery Convention of American Women opened its sessions in the new hall. The women agreed upon resolutions calling for the boycotting of slave produce and for an end of slavery in the District of Columbia. They could not, however, agree on the most pressing question, the right or duty of antislavery women to speak to promiscuous audiences. So strong were the feelings on both sides that it was necessary to hold a special meeting on Wednesday evening, not under the official sponsorship of the convention, where women who wished to would be able to speak.

All week there had been angry mutterings throughout the city about the "amalgamators." The abolitionists were felt to be dangerous radicals, intent on overthrowing every human institution. Working-class men and women, barely able to survive on meager wages, felt themselves especially threatened. The financial panic of 1837, severely felt in Philadelphia, had heightened their fear. The thought of interracial marriage was particularly abhorrent. The fact that both black and white guests attended the wedding of Angelina Grimké to Theodore Weld, an abolitionist minister, that week inflamed popular prejudices. Maria wrote Edward that a black boy at Mother's had sat "perched by the parlor window, watching the passersby who were shocked at all their prophesies of amalgamation appearing to be thus fulfilled."

The sight of black women hurrying in and out of Pennsylvania Hall as they attended the convention was particularly irritating to hostile onlookers. Each day there had been crowds of men on the corner of Sassafras watching the convention. By Wednesday night there was an angry, jeering mob.

The opposition evidently stimulated the abolitionists. Garrison spoke first, giving the crowd "the cause of human rights in good old Saxon language." At one point in his speech the mob surged into the hall, but Maria Chapman was able to restore order. Angelina Grimké Weld came next, and with shining eyes and brilliant cheeks gave one of her best appeals for the end of slavery. Deeply moved, young Abby Kelley of Lynn, Massachusetts, swept to the podium and poured out her heart in her maiden speech. "You will have to be an antislavery lecturer," Theodore Weld told her. "If you don't God will smite you."

At the end of the evening Lucretia Mott came to the front. Ill health during the past two years had made her thinner; she was down to ninety-two pounds, and her face was beginning to show signs of her forty-five years. But her step was as sprightly as that of a young girl, and her voice as clear. The audience relaxed at the very sight of her, so calm, so sensible, so in command. Tonight she had to explain that the meeting had lacked the sanction of the convention, because the women had not been able to agree among themselves about the propriety of women addressing promiscuous audiences. "Let us hope," she concluded drily, "that such false notions of delicacy and propriety do not long obtain in this enlightened country."

During the night of May sixteenth notices were posted all over the city calling upon all citizens with due regard for property and the preservation of the Constitution to "interfere, forcefully if they must" with the convention. The mob Thursday was huge and ugly. Daniel Neall, the president of the hall, visited the mayor with a delegation and asked for protection. They were told, however, that the turbulence was the fault of the abolitionists for holding the convention in the first place. The mayor had only one suggestion: Ask the black women to stop attending the meetings. Lucretia delivered the message on Thursday afternoon but said she did not agree with it and that she hoped none of the women would be put off "by a little appearance of danger." Then she arranged for the women to leave the hall two by two, a white woman in arm with a black one.

The danger, however, was not only apparent, it was real. By night the mob had swelled to seventeen thousand. The mayor, thoroughly alarmed, asked Neall for the key to Pennsylvania Hall, locked it, announced to the crowd that he had stopped the proceedings, appealed mildly for peace, and then went home, leaving the premises unguarded. The mob promptly burst open the doors, collected all the books and benches, and set fire to them, breaking the gas pipes to increase the conflagration. By nine P.M. flames were shooting skyward. John Greenleaf Whittier, determined to save the galley proofs of next day's *Pennsylvania Freeman*, disguised himself in Dr. Joseph Parrish's white overcoat and wig and ran into the burning building along with the looting crowd, managing to retrieve his precious papers without attracting attention. Nothing else, however, was saved. The fire companies played their hoses on the surrounding buildings but allowed the fire to gut Pennsylvania Hall unchecked. By dawn it was a smoking ruin. The mob, still not appeased, began to look for fresh targets.

The Motts and their large company returned to the house on Ninth Street, almost sure that an attack was imminent. Against his better judgment James Mott saw Maria Chapman and Anne Weston off on their return trip to Boston. Garrison, too, left town. Charles Burleigh and Miller McKim helped to move some of the Motts' clothes and furniture to a neighbor's, and Miller accompanied grandmother Anna Coffin, Pattie, and Elizabeth to Maria Davis's house.

Young Thomas Mott refused to leave his parents, but loitered near the front steps, listening for the mob. At one point he rushed in, excited, to report, "They're coming!" The crowd, however, poured up Race Street past Ninth, led by a friend of James and Lucretia's, who shouted, "On to the Motts!" and pointed in the wrong direction.

In her own front parlor Lucretia sat chatting with her friends with a composure that amazed them. Afterward she confessed that she had not felt quite as serene as she had seemed. It had been "a searching time." But in the hour of danger she had felt herself strengthened and uplifted, ready for whatever the night might bring. Providentially, it finally brought a few hours of rest.

Others were not so lucky. The mob, having given up on prominent abolitionists, turned south and attacked Mother Bethel Church on Sixth and Lombard, then the nearby Shelter for Colored Orphans. Once more, Philadelphia police carefully stayed away from scenes of violence.

In the morning the antislavery women held the final session of their convention at Sarah Pugh's little schoolhouse. Here they pledged themselves to meet again in Philadelphia the next year. Rather than give way to the ugly public prejudice expressed the previous night, their resolution stated, they would *expand* their social relations with their black friends.

No sooner was the meeting over than Dr. Parrish came to the Motts with an earnest request that the resolution be stricken from the minutes. Lucretia and James tried to calm his fears of further rioting. They themselves felt purged by the experience. "The color prejudice lurking within me was entirely destroyed by the night of Pennsylvania Hall," James Mott afterward wrote.

The events of Pennsylvania Hall served to heighten the tensions within the American Anti-Slavery Society over the "woman question." Inspired by her maiden speech, Abby Kelley went straight to Boston to take part in the New England Anti-Slavery Society. Here she spoke from the floor and accepted a position on a committee, causing a protest and the resignation of six clergymen. Just as Angelina Grimké Weld retired into domesticity, taking her sister Sarah with her, Abby began her career as a female antislavery lecturer. Her meetings were repeatedly mobbed, the clergy thundered against her, and she was often called a true Jezebel from the pulpit. In 1839 she played a key role in the decision of the American Anti-Slavery Society to admit women as members, and in 1840 her appointment to a committee led the society to split into two factions.

Lucretia Mott was delighted to see women taking their place along with men in the antislavery societies. She herself became an officer of the Pennsylvania Anti-Slavery Society in January 1839. In *Godey's Ladies Book*, editor Sarah Josepha Hale attacked her for her advanced views on the role of women, as well as her heretical notions. Yet it did not occur to Lucretia that working side by side with men should be considered as an alternative to the women's organizations. She was surprised and flustered when she received a passionate letter from young Abby Kelley suggesting that there be no more separate antislavery conventions of American women. Otherwise were they not following the same principles if they excluded men?

What answer could Lucretia give? There was logic to Abby's position. Yet the Philadelphia Female Anti-Slavery Society had been a source of support and strength for many women. Lucretia had watched many shy ones bloom and gain confidence from the experience of conducting their own business. Perplexed, she consulted several of the reformers who "have the cause of human rights at heart.'' No one, however, could give her an answer. She finally sat down and wrote a long letter to Abby. She, too, wanted full equality, she said, and there was no better way to get ready for it than for those who had seen the light to take every opportunity to speak in public. At the same time, she thought it was all right to permit women to meet together for special purposes, just as women had always done in the Society of Friends. Among Quakers, the separate women's meetings had been useful ''in bringing our sex forward, exercising their talents, and preparing them for united action with men, as soon as we can convince them that this is both our right and our duty.''

Similarly, she continued, within the antislavery movement the separate conventions had educated many women to a fuller understanding of their powers. If some were still in the dark on the subject of equal rights, it was up to the enlightened ones to labor with them and convince them that ''in Christ there is neither male nor female,'' not to withdraw and leave their sisters to serve alone. If Abby would come to the 1839 convention, Lucretia thought they might go over the whole matter together. If she, Lucretia, were wrong in her position, she would then be ready to abandon it.

Abby did not answer the letter, nor did she come to the convention. Lydia Maria Child, the writer, also declined. Lucretia was soon too busy to worry about the matter further. Frightened by the burning of Pennsylvania Hall, Philadelphians viewed the approaching convention with a jaundiced eye. Lucretia approached all seven downtown Friends Meetings with a request to use their space and was turned down by each, including her own beloved Cherry Street Meeting. The churches were equally opposed, only the Universalist Church offering space, which was far too small. The Society was finally forced to meet in a stable, the hall of the Pennsylvania Riding School.

One May morning, several days before the convention was to take place, Mayor Isaac Roach called on Lucretia Mott at her home on North Ninth Street. He wanted to prevent the outrages that had occurred the previous year, he said. Therefore he had a few questions and suggestions. Was the meeting to be confined only to women? And if women, only to white women? He did not think much of the Riding Hall idea. Why not hold the meetings in Clarkson Hall, the property of the Pennsylvania Abolition Society? If they would do that and avoid "unnecessary walking with colored people," he thought that it would be possible to keep the peace.

Lucretia was furious. She told him tartly that Clarkson Hall was not nearly large enough and that the women did not anticipate danger and had not asked his protection. They would not be meeting at night because, "to the shame of Philadelphia," the only building they could procure had a barn roof and could not be lighted for such a meeting. As for avoiding walking with blacks, Lucretia said that that was impossible. Social equality was a fixed principle of the women. She herself had several invited guests "of that complexion," and she would naturally be accompanying them to and from the meetings.

Mayor Roach found nothing to say in response to this quiet but thorough tongue lashing. He bid her good day, but called once more, just after the convention had begun. How long did the women intend to continue to meet? He had several special officers on duty and he would like to send them home. Do so, Lucretia told him. She had absolutely no idea how long the meetings would continue. The women had never asked, and did not want, his aid.

After all the worry, the meetings passed quietly and uneventfully. Attendance was smaller than the previous year because many of the women from New England were not present. They were locked in a bitter factional fight. Mary S. Parker, who had presided at Pennsylvania Hall in 1838, thought the "woman question" and abolitionism should be kept separate. Maria Chapman opposed her. Maria poured out her anger in a letter to Lucretia, which arrived during the meetings in the Riding Hall. As soon as the convention was over and her guests had gone home, Lucretia wrote back, urging Maria to avoid "harsh epithets" and to keep as near to Mary Parker and others as possible. They must continue to hope—even against hope—that the other faction would see the error of their ways.

The schism, however, did not heal. It spread, instead, throughout the whole antislavery movement and split the American Anti-Slavery Society into two factions in 1840. The problem was more complicated than the "woman question" alone. Garrison had believed from the beginning that men and women of diverse views could unite in the antislavery crusade without needing to quarrel over their other differences. He himself was an absolute pacifist, or nonresistant, and an opponent of sectarian religion, and he was intrigued, if not wholly committed, to the "no Human Government" views of his friend John Noyes, who preached a Christian anarchy. Garrison believed that abolitionists should neither vote, hold office, serve on juries, nor in any other fashion recognize a state that was in effect supporting slavery with a bayonet. He gave these and other points of view ample coverage in the *Liberator*, to the horror of more conservative abolitionists, who feared the public would identify their cause with his "ultra" views.

Although she agreed with the Garrisonians on most issues, Lucretia Mott objected to their stridency. She wrote Maria Chapman some months later to suggest that it did not help to air all the details of the quarrel and that she wished Garrison would "record them more sparingly in his paper." Meanwhile she desired that "my dear friends . . . not be driven from the ground of Non-Resistance." Amid a flood of denunciations she tried to play the thankless role of peacemaker.

From her Quaker mother, Lucretia had learned the art of "eldering," saying forthrightly to a person what part of his or her behavior needed correcting. Lucretia seemed always able to chide her friends without expressing hostility. This quality in her was highly prized by both her friends and her children. You knew exactly where you stood with Lucretia Mott.

In the fall of 1838, after the burning of Pennsylvania Hall, Garrison called together a group to form the New England Non-Resistance Society. Its Declaration of Sentiments, which Garrison wrote, rejected not only force but all government based on force. Public reaction was strong—and negative. Even Quakers were not quite sure they believed in nonresistance. It was eight years before Thoreau wrote his famous essay on civil disobedience, seventy before Tolstoi published *The Law of Love and the Law of Violence*, seventy-seven before Gandhi began to develop his theories of *satyagraha* while living in South Africa. Nonresistance sounded like the idea of a total fanatic.

Lucretia and James were visiting friends and relatives on Long Island at the time of the new Society's first meeting and did not attend. In the fall of 1838, after the excitement of Pennsylvania Hall, Lucretia was in a mild state of depression. Maria and Edward had left for a year in Europe, and James had lost money heavily when a factory in which he had an interest burned to the ground. They were poor again. Lucretia at forty-five may have been facing menopause. She wrote Phebe that she could find no comfort either in or out of Meeting, "and as to preaching I felt as if I could never open my mouth again."

By the spring of 1839, however, Lucretia had regained her usual good spirits in time for the women's convention, and at the time of turning leaves she traveled by stagecoach to Boston to take part in the first anniversary meeting of the Non-Resistance Society.

Early in the proceedings a controversial resolution was introduced: "That while we are applying our principles to civil government we will not be unmindful of their application to ourselves in the regulation of our own tempers and in the government of our families, leading to the abrogation of all infliction and penalties and to the substitution of the law of peace and love."

This was an advanced view. Even the radical pacifist Henry Wright thought that some physical restraint of infants might be necessary. Lucretia, however, was convinced that punishment was an ineffective way of teaching a child to obey; there were better methods. If children seemed to demand punishment, it was probably because the parents were unprepared to make their expectations known. "They overlook the fact that a child, like all other human beings, has inalienable rights. It is the master that is not prepared for emancipation and it is the parent who is not prepared to give up punishment."

Lucretia's attendance at the Non-Resistance Society resulted in further criticism within the Society of Friends. She was once more substituting good causes for true religion, it was charged, and mingling with "the World's people." In New York City a Quaker minister, George White, began to preach heatedly against reforms and reformers. "He would rather be a slave than an abolitionist," he once declared. A man of somewhat

shady background, having once been bankrupt and now own-
ing, it was rumored, several grog shops, he nevertheless won a
wide and admiring audience to his campaign. More and more he
appeared to have two targets, Isaac Hopper in New York and
Lucretia Mott in Philadelphia.

In November he came to Philadelphia and arranged to have
the three Hicksite Meetings gather to hear him preach at Cherry
Street. Here he made sweeping denunciations of modern abolitionists, nonresistance, and "imperious women." He repeated
the same charges at Caln and Western Quarterly Meetings. It
was clearly his purpose to have Lucretia disowned from the
Society of Friends, and she was sufficiently alarmed about it to
write to her cousin, Nathaniel Barney, who was prominent in
New York Hicksite affairs, to ask him to prepare to serve as
peacemaker. Hurt as she always was by the willingness of so
many Friends to listen to criticism, she continued to preach both
nonresistance and abolition as she traveled among Friends
Meetings.

In February 1840 her travels took her to Delaware. With her
for part of the trip was Daniel Neall, the president of Pennsylvania Hall, and his new wife, Anna Coffin's cousin Rebecca
Bunker. In Smyrna, stones were thrown at their carriage. They
disregarded the incident and proceeded to a local Friend's home
for tea. They had just finished eating when there was a knock at
the door. When their host answered, he was greeted by a small
group of raw-looking men, who demanded that Daniel Neall
come with them. When Daniel refused, more men arrived and
forced their way into the house. Rebecca shook from head to
foot.

"I pled hard with them to take me as I was the offender if
offense had been committed and give him up to his wife—but
they declining said 'you are a woman and we have nothing to
say to you'—to which I answered 'I ask no courtesy at your
hands on account of my sex,' " Lucretia wrote to Maria Chapman. When the men refused her offer and took Daniel Neall
away, she followed them, continuing to argue, so intent on what
she was doing that she forgot to be afraid for herself. With
Lucretia watching, the men rather shamefacedly smeared a little
tar on Daniel's coat, attached a few feathers, and gave him a

token ride on a rail. They then turned him over, virtually unharmed, to the little Quaker woman.

The story of this event was repeated over and over in Non-Resistance circles as an example of the application of Christian principles. Lucretia hadn't thought at the time she was proving anything; she was simply concerned enough about both Rebecca and Daniel to be willing to take the latter's place if necessary. The elderly Nealls were after all a part of the extended Coffin clan.

In Philadelphia the antislavery split was polarizing, and it was painfully clear that it was going to interfere with personal relationships. In 1840 Thomas Earle became a candidate for vice-president of the United States for the new Liberty party, organized by the anti-Garrisonians. His wife, Mary Hussey Earle, and Lucretia had never gotten on well since they were cousins on Nantucket Island, but she was a part of the Coffin circle. Now, however, her manner became frosty. John Greenleaf Whittier went over to the opposition and criticized Abby Kelley for "blowing up" the American Anti-Slavery Society. Theodore Weld allied himself with the sectarian group, and Angelina and Sarah appeared to be going along.

Lucretia continued to try to make peace, absorbing into her own frail physical economy the tensions of the schism. Little wonder that she once more became ill with dyspepsia.

There was one standard cure for ill health in the 1840s—a sea voyage. It was especially appropriate for Lucretia, who loved the smell of the salt water. Providentially an opportunity arose in the spring of 1840 that could provide Lucretia both with a change of air and an excuse to placate her driving conscience for such a change. She and James were named delegates from Pennsylvania to the World's Anti-Slavery Convention, to be held in London in June.

CHAPTER
IX

THE
LONDON CONVENTION

ON MAY 7, 1840, Lucretia and James Mott set sail on the packet *Roscoe*, bound for London and the adventure of a lifetime. At first they had thought they could not afford such a trip, but a wealthy relative had heard about their selection and sent a check making it possible. The Friends of Cherry Street Meeting, their concern for Lucretia's health evidently triumphing over their annoyance with her, had given the Motts a traveling minute stating they were traveling among Friends with permission of the Meeting. Libby and Pattie were under the care of their older sisters. There was nothing, for once, to worry about.

Although a bit seasick, Lucretia was enthusiastic about everything. Other members of the ship's party were "most companionable," she noted laconically in the little diary she was keeping of this great adventure. The cabin fare was abundant, half the company teetotalers, the others drinking not to excess, the conversation spirited.

The other members of the Pennsylvania delegation were all women: Mary Grew, Sarah Pugh, Elizabeth Neall, and Abby Kimber. They were all in their twenties, and Lucretia called them "the girls." New England, too, was sending women in its delegation. News of this unprecedented move had already reached Great Britain, and the reaction had been decidedly negative. "The woman question" had not yet raised its controversial head in reform circles. The British female abolitionists continued to hold their meetings separately and had no thought of being present at the coming convention. "So if any do come from America, they will have to encounter strong feeling against it, which exists here, standing alone," Joseph Sturge, a British abolitionist, warned in a public letter.

Tensions among American abolitionists had come to a head at the May meeting of the American Anti-Slavery Society. When Abby Kelley was placed on the business committee, a large number of clerics and others opposed to Garrison withdrew, forming the New Organization. Once the moderates left the convention, the remainder, called the Old Organization, quickly named Lucretia Mott a delegate from the national convention, as well as a member of the Executive Committee. Thus while she was on the high seas, out of touch with events, she was formally recognized as the leading female abolitionist.

Arriving in Liverpool on the night of May 27, the Motts and their company took a leisurely ten days to reach London, stopping en route at Chester, Manchester, and Birmingham. On the way they dutifully saw the sights and presented their letters of introduction to British reformers, most of whom were either Unitarians or ex-Quakers.

Throughout the trip Lucretia was busy recording first impressions. Everything was new: the manner of enclosing bread in napkins for dinner, the little egg spoons served with boiled eggs, the fact that the hotels provided nightcaps for gentlemen, the communicative coachmen who conducted them through the countryside, the large, strong dray horses they saw in the streets. Wherever she went, Lucretia's attention was fastened on the way people lived, the things they ate, their poverty or affluence. Mere sightseeing was lost on her. In Manchester they visited a cotton factory, where the girls and women were paid half the wages of men, and a pin factory, where Lucretia thought she had never seen little girls' fingers move so fast.

They visited Blenheim Palace in Woodstock. Lucretia found the symmetry of the castle gratifying to her "organ of order," but preferred walking across the grounds to touring the interior. At Oxford they saw Christ Church and the Bodleian, where Lucretia was pleased to find a piece of sculpture by a woman. The party next took a coach to Slough, then a short railroad to Windsor, where they stayed at the Crown Inn and visited the castle. Lucretia attended the chapel service but couldn't understand the indistinct speaking and thought the boys' "chauntings bordering on the ridiculous." She also didn't like to see the banners waving overhead, "war and church united."

James was even more critical. In a short book, *Three Months in Great Britain*, written after the trip, he described Windsor as "one of the many monuments to the extravagance and folly of the British nobility and aristocracy which oppressed the laborer, taking from him in the shape of imposts and taxes so much of his earnings as to leave but a scarce subsistence for himself." They met, he complained, very few people who saw the effects of the palaces and parks on the population. This insight was one of many that put the Motts ahead of their time.

The final leg of the trip to London they completed on top of a coach, seeing a band of Gypsies and observing the fine roads. It was raining, and London's buildings were far darker than the red brick of Philadelphia. Finally they turned into a dark court and dismounted at an old inn, Saracen's Head, where they had booked lodging. The forbidding look of the place, with its scowling visages, caused Lucretia to exclaim in dismay, "So this is London!" They would have to find other lodgings, she insisted. The girls got cake from a nearby confectioner's shop for their dinner, while one of their guides scurried about until he located comfortable quarters in a rooming house at No. 6 Queen Street Place, Southwark Bridge, Cheapside, where a number of other abolitionists were staying.

The next morning Joseph Sturge arrived to breakfast with them and to beg Lucretia to submit to the British Society's decision not to admit women. "We endeavored to shew him the inconsistency of excluding Women Delegates—but soon found he had prejudged & made up his mind to stand with our New Organization; therefore all reasoning was lost upon him, and our appeals in vain," Lucretia recorded in her diary.

There was still a week to go until the convention started. Lucretia thought she might yet succeed in persuading the British abolitionists to reverse their decision. She soon learned, however, that her cause was hopeless. Not only were representatives of the New Organization from the United States present in force, prepared to attack her and her female colleagues, but she had a second set of adversaries to deal with. The British Friends had received an epistle from the Orthodox Friends in America warning them to be on their guard against the Motts.

The letter, Lucretia subsequently learned, was written by Stephen Grellet, and was actually read in London Yearly Meeting. Although the London Friends feared her chiefly for her heresy, it seemed apparent that they were also determined to use their not inconsiderable influence on the convention to prevent her from being seated.

Almost thirteen years had passed since the separation among American Friends, but British Friends felt as strongly as ever that the Hicksites were heretics. They perhaps remembered Lucretia particularly as the signer of the rejected Epistle of 1830. Now they had heard that she was a radical even among the Hicksites, mingling freely with Unitarian ministers and preaching more and more forcefully a simple gospel of love and good works that to many ears was nothing less than a denial of the divinity of Christ. Even if they felt themselves strong enough to tolerate such heresy, some London Friends were at first afraid to invite her to their homes for fear of her effect on their children.

Lucretia Mott nevertheless fought gamely for woman's rights. At an evening gathering in the offices of the British and Foreign Anti-Slavery Society she reminded those present that a woman, the British Friend Elizabeth Heyrick, had first proposed the doctrine of immediate emancipation, and she promised them that when a world's convention met in the United States, women would not be excluded. Later, with the help of Sarah Pugh, she prepared a protest on behalf of the excluded women delegates from Pennsylvania. On the very eve of the convention she argued with a small delegation of British abolitionists sent to ask her once more not to offer herself as a delegate.

At their lodgings James and Lucretia had found themselves in a hotbed of all male New Organization delegates: James Birney, the Liberty party candidate for president; Henry Stanton (with his new bride, round-faced, high-spirited Elizabeth Cady Stanton); Nathaniel Colver and Elon Galusha, Baptist clergymen from the United States; as well as four Baptists from Jamaica and one from Barbados. Colver had already distinguished himself as an opponent of woman's rights during the New England struggles, and Lucretia was almost immediately embroiled in a running feud with him. On the first night of her stay in London he invited her to go with him to his Baptist meeting and speak. It is hard to tell whether the invitation was sincere or not. Lucretia evidently thought not, and refused. Colver on his return treated her "rather rudely." A few days later, when the company was informed that the women were officially rejected, Lucretia teasingly asked "Colver and Galusha if they had heard that a similar course was to be pursued toward the new organization—alarmed them."

The battle came to a white pitch the night before the convention. "Colver rather bold in his suggestion—answered & of course offended him," Lucretia recorded in her diary. "Prescod of Jamaica (colored) thought it would lower the dignity of the convention and bring ridicule on the whole thing if ladies were admitted—he was told that similar reasons were urged in Pennsylvania for the exclusion of colored people from our meetings—but had we yielded on such flimsy argument, we might as well have abandoned the enterprise. Colver thought Women constitutionally unfit for public or business meetings— he was told that the colored man too was said to be *constitutionally* unfit to mingle with the white man. He left the room angry."

While all this sparring was going on at their lodgings, Lucretia and James were the centers of a social whirl. Everyone in reform circles had heard by now about the American woman, and although many differed with her, they were all eager to meet her. When the Motts went to meeting in Grace Church, no one spoke to them, but in private a number of Friends wanted to become acquainted. Elizabeth Pease, abolitionist and author, called and talked orthodoxy, but introduced Lucretia to her parents. Anne Knight, an author of poetry for children and a budding advocate for woman's rights, met Lucretia and became her close companion. Jacob Post, a Quaker friend of Isaac Hopper's, invited the Motts to dinner. The Starbucks, distant relatives of Lucretia through Nantucket ties, entertained the Motts also, but explained they were now members of the Church of England. Even Anna Braithwaite, one of the Quaker ministers sent to Philadelphia in 1826 to counteract Elias Hicks, decided to be hospitable. Each day they made new friends and received more invitations.

On Friday, June 12, the World Convention opened at Freemason's Hall on Great Queen Street. The delegates sat in the main section of the hall, directly under the podium. Visitors and observers were in the wings. Lucretia and the other women delegates were conducted to special seats "behind the bar," a railing separating the back of the hall from the front. Here they were introduced to many leading British abolitionists before the meeting was called to order.

After opening silence, the veteran abolitionist Thomas Clarkson appeared, accompanied by his daughter-in-law and his grandson. It was a moving moment; many in the hall, like Lucretia, had first been converted to active abolitionism by his writings. Now he had grown old and white-haired in the struggle. The good feeling engendered by his arrival, however, was soon dissipated as the group got down to the business at hand: a discussion of the admission of women delegates.

Wendell Phillips, a handsome and aristocratic young Harvard graduate, led the fight for the admission of women, arguing that the convention itself should set its own rules and decide who could be delegates. Adding a fine edge to his usual eloquence was the fact that his own wife, Ann, had come as a delegate from Massachusetts and was sitting with Lucretia. Several Americans supported Phillips, as well as Dr. John Bowring, editor of the *Westminster Review*, who said he found the female delegation from the United States "one of the most interesting and encouraging and the most delightful symptoms of the times." A British solicitor, William Ashhurst, also spoke up for the admission of women, pointing out that it was ridiculous to call it a world convention and then exclude half the world.

Opposed, however, were the vast majority of the delegates, including most of the British Friends present, as Lucretia noted bitterly in a letter home. Henry Grew, Mary Grew's father, opposed the resolution on biblical grounds, much to his daughter's dismay. Many members of the New Organization added their voices. Saint Paul's admonitions, the necessity of honoring English usage, and the "proper sphere" of women were all thrown into the argument against the admission of women. The debate was long and noisy, but when the question was at last called, Wendell Phillips found nine tenths of the members against him. Of the New Organization, only Henry Stanton, egged on by his young wife, Elizabeth Cady, was in favor of admitting women.

Lucretia Mott wondered if she ought to continue at all under the circumstances, but several British friends persuaded her that her very presence, plus the fact that she had crossed the ocean to be there, was a help to the cause of women. "Seeing how the thing is viewed on this side of the Atlantic, how altogether unprecedented it is for women to be admitted even by courtesy as visitors in business meetings, we were disposed to regard it as one great step in the history of world reform," Lucretia wrote her children. She was prophetic. Not only was Elizabeth Cady Stanton, who sat beside her behind the bar, freshly inspired to a lifetime devotion to woman's suffrage, but Anne Knight, also a constant attendant, became the first champion of woman's rights in Great Britain.

Perhaps feeling some guilt for their actions, the British abolitionists thereafter treated Lucretia like royalty. An armchair was provided from which she had a perfect view of the proceedings. Members of the British and Foreign Anti-Slavery Society came forward, two or three at a time, to pay their respects to her, and to introduce the notables present. Daniel O'Connell, the great Irish orator, "made himself quite agreeable." Amelia Opie, an English poet, stopped by to tell Lucretia that she and her friends were "held in high estimation and have raised yourselves by coming." William Ball, a Quaker member of the aristocracy, introduced himself. Thomas Clarkson called at her lodgings and allowed the younger women delegates to cut locks of his white hair as mementos. Lady Anne Isabella Byron, who had been the estranged wife of the late poet, became a devoted attendant. Lucretia wrote home with pride about all these well-known people she was meeting, although she also remarked that she was disgusted by the way the convention sought the sanction of great names. "I am sick of this man-worship. It is crushing its millions in this as in other lands."

Arriving five days after the convention started, Garrison himself decided he could take no part in the proceedings that had rejected women, and joined Lucretia and her bevy of admirers behind the bar. His presence helped swell her reputation as "the lioness of the convention," as an Irish journalist called her.

Lucretia enjoyed the approbation, but she chided O'Connell for offering "flattering compliments which we could not receive in place of rights denied." Instead, she continued to devote her energies to finding ways to protest the injustice of the exclusion of women. Through Joseph Sturge and George Stacey she tried to arrange for a meeting with British women abolitionists to discuss the situation. The women were afraid to meet with Lucretia Mott lest other subjects be alluded to. Lucretia finally invited a company of antislavery women to her lodgings. It was a "stiff-poor affair," she confided to her diary, "found little confidence in women's action either separately or conjointly with men, except as drudges." She also helped Wendell Phillips and others prepare a protest that was submitted on the last day of the convention, only to be tabled on motion of Nathaniel Colver. She persuaded both Daniel O'Connell and William Howitt to write letters expressing their displeasure with the action of the convention against women, then arranged for the letters to be published. And whenever she was called on to speak in public, she managed to mention the unjust exclusion of women.

Nevertheless, in the eyes of some, she had compromised. Abby Kelley wrote to Garrison to ask if Lucretia Mott had "sacrificed principle at the altar of peace." Lucretia admitted that her stance might be viewed in that light, but she had known before she left Philadelphia that her credentials might not be received, and she had taken the chance.

Years later Elizabeth Cady Stanton recalled that she asked Lucretia what would happen if the Spirit had moved her to speak despite the vote of excommunication. "Where the Spirit of God is, there is liberty," Lucretia replied.

Apparently the Spirit did not so lead. Outside the convention, however, Lucretia made a number of speeches and preached at a Unitarian church in a manner that inspired Elizabeth Cady Stanton. At the final soiree at the close of the convention she was formally invited to speak. John Scobie, secretary of the British and Foreign Anti-Slavery Society, attempted to prevent her by rising to address the group on another matter, but Lucretia remained standing, and the delegates shouted Scobie down. Lucretia's subject was free produce, and in the course of the speech she referred to herself as a Quaker. After she had finished speaking, Josiah Forster, a British Friend, arose to explain that she was really not a Quaker, but he was quieted with shouts of "Shame! " and "Down!"

Forster in fact followed the Motts around, making a "correction" whenever they referred to themselves as Quakers, although James and Lucretia always prefaced their remarks by explaining that they belonged to a branch of the Society of Friends not in unity with those in Great Britain. Forster also did his best to prevent Lucretia's speaking in public. He reminded Anne Knight of an old hen. He even managed to get the roll call of the convention changed and an asterisk after James Mott's name with the notation "erroneously described as a member of the Society of Friends."

The Motts met fear of their heresy everywhere. Even Anne Knight admitted to a mutual friend that she thought Lucretia heretical for her rejection of the atonement, but loved her for her works' sake. Robert Hayden, the English painter, had planned to put Lucretia's portrait in the forefront of a painting he had been commissioned to do of the World Convention but refused to do so when he found she had "infidel notions." William Howitt wrote Lucretia that he felt sure that she had been excluded from the convention not for being a woman but for being a heretic.

Elizabeth Fry, the British prison reformer, shared the prejudice. Lucretia had of course heard about Elizabeth Fry and was happy to be taken by some British women to a meeting of the Prison Society, where she saw her giving a report. A few days later Elizabeth Fry was at the antislavery convention, but again the two did not meet. After the close of the convention itself the British and Foreign Anti-Slavery Society held a special meeting at Exeter Hall. Here Elizabeth Fry came, in company with the duchess of Sutherland. Their appearance was greeted with applause, and they were escorted to prominent seats on the platform among hundreds of men.

Lucretia whispered to one of her female escorts that she thought it was rather inconsistent to place Elizabeth upon the platform when there had been so much fuss about urging the American women to keep to their proper sphere. The remark was evidently repeated to Elizabeth Fry, for when the two met at last at a social occasion, Elizabeth hastened to tell Lucretia how out of place she had felt at the antislavery meeting and how she had been given this prominence against her will. She then apologized for not having spoken to Lucretia at the prison meeting. Lucretia accepted the apology and turned the subject to Elizabeth's younger brother, Joseph John Gurney, who was traveling among Quakers in the United States preaching an evangelical message to Orthodox meetings while he urged more active stands on the slavery issue. In Philadelphia he had been received coldly. Lucretia told Elizabeth she was sorry she had not tried to see him and encourage him, despite their religious differences.

This might have been the beginning of a friendship between the two women, but Elizabeth remained frightened of Lucretia's heresy. After tea was served, she offered a prayer for the American visitors "that our mission might be a blessing in breaking the fetters of the poor captive, but above all blessed to ourselves in bringing us to the unsearchable riches of Christ." Elizabeth Cady Stanton thought the prayer was aimed directly at Lucretia. She urged Lucretia to pray for Elizabeth Fry, that her eyes might be opened to her bigotry and uncharitableness! Lucretia refused.

Two days later Samuel Gurney, a rich banker and another of Elizabeth Fry's younger brothers, entertained the delegation. It was he who had earlier given a party but excluded the Motts because he feared their influence on his children. Now, however, he had relented to such an extent that he introduced his daughter to Lucretia and suggested that they stroll together on the lawn. At supper he placed her on his right hand. Lucretia took the occasion to reprove him for serving wine to young people!

Both Elizabeth Cady Stanton and Wendell Phillips recalled, years later, that Elizabeth Fry had conspicuously avoided meeting Lucretia on this occasion, going indoors when she was out, and out when she was in. Lucretia herself never mentioned this, and Mary Grew did not remember the snubbing. Nevertheless, it is clear that Elizabeth Fry did not make good the opportunity to learn to know the American Quaker woman who was to become as famous as she.

After the close of the convention the Motts spent another three weeks in London, being entertained, seeing the sights, and meeting celebrities. They had two meetings with Robert Owen. Lucretia thought him "altogether visionary" and noted that his head was "poor in development." They also called on Thomas Carlyle, but had an unsatisfactory visit. Carlyle explained he was far more interested in the condition of the poor in Great

Britain than he was in the problem of slavery. Lady Byron, who had taken a great liking to Lucretia, sent her books to read, took her to see a school in which she herself was interested, and introduced her to friends. Lucretia also went faithfully with James and friends to see such founts of culture as the British Museum, but found it tiring.

A visit to the Zoological Gardens became an occasion for a discussion of clothing. Standing before a cage of brilliantly plumed birds, one of the men pointed out to Lucretia that God evidently believed in bright colors. "Yes but immortal beings do not depend on feathers for their attractions," she replied tartly. "Moreover, if it is fitting that woman should dress in every color of the rainbow, why not man also?"

Finally, on July 11 the Motts left London and, after spending a few days in Birmingham and Manchester, took ship for Ireland. During the London Convention they had met a family of Irish Friends, the Webbs, well known as reformers and abolitionists. The two couples were immediately attracted to each other, and the Webbs urged the Motts to visit Dublin. They spent a week enjoying the sights, walking in the Killarney Hills, and being entertained by local Friends and reformers. Lucretia found the food delicious—plenty of gooseberries, strawberries, and rich cream—but objected to the use of wine at table. It was altogether a pleasant and relaxing time, marred only by the conditions of the poor, which the Motts found worse than elsewhere in their travels.

"Saw the poor in hovels—their degradation—their wretchedness—conversed with some of them—returned to R. Webb's for tea—talked on the condition of the poor compared with our slavery," Lucretia wrote in her diary.

From Dublin the Motts traveled to Belfast, where they visited the editor of the *Irish Friend*, and then took ship for Glasgow for two weeks of sightseeing and visiting in Scotland. They attended Friends Meeting but found it disappointing, the longest message being "tedious & dry, dwelling on the systems of the Schools of Divinity, which is so completely interwoven with the Quaker faith as to divest it of its original simplicity and beauty —mourned their degeneracy while they lamented our heresy," Lucretia wrote.

A Unitarian minister offered Lucretia the use of his pulpit the following Sunday, and she gladly accepted. Here she gave what was perhaps her first sermon on the rights of women, defending their right to speak in public, lamenting their unequal education, and calling for her sisters to "brush away the silken fetters that have bound them...and fit themselves to assume their proper position in being the natural companions, the friends, the instructors of the race." She spoke for nearly two hours and held a large audience in fixed attention.

At the beginning of this meeting James Mott had spoken briefly, introducing himself and Lucretia, explaining their mission, reading their minute from their home meeting, and explaining as usual that they belonged to a branch of the Society of Friends different from that of local Friends. Nevertheless, the Glasgow Quakers found it necessary to write a letter to the paper, stating that they did not wish to be identified with, or in any way responsible for, anything Lucretia Mott might have said at the meeting.

This was too much for James. He wrote a long, indignant letter to William Smeal, one of the signers of the letter to the paper. James accused the local Quakers of "cherishing a spirit of prejudice and bigotry incompatible with the benign religion of Jesus" and asked if "your doctrines are of such an evanescent character that they are in danger of vanishing before the sunshine of truth?" So stirred was he that when he wrote his book *Three Months in Great Britain*, he devoted much of it to a discussion of the prejudice held by British and Scottish Friends against the Hicksites and of his own fear of the decline of the Society of Friends in England.

Word of the newspaper attack fortunately did not catch up with the Motts until they reached London, and they continued on their way pleasantly. In Edinburgh they spent a relaxing two days with George Combe, the phrenologist, and his wife, Celia, renewing a friendship begun in Philadelphia in 1838. Combe did not formally examine James's head, but he told Lucretia later that when he visited Philadelphia in 1838, he had noted that James was a good and able man but he seemed occupied with business. "During his visit to us, his manifestation did justice to his brain, and he has left us all with the impression of talent and goodness worthy to be your mate."

Sarah Pugh and Abby Kimber had rejoined the Motts in

Edinburgh, and together they traveled in the Borders. On the coach to Melrose Abbey, they got into an argument over slavery with a vacationing Georgia planter. Although they didn't spare him, the Georgian accompanied them as far as Abbotsford, home of Sir Walter Scott. Here a rather crabby guide hurried them through the mansion. Lucretia, however, managed to strike up a conversation with a woman who turned out to be the widow of Tom Purdie, Scott's beloved companion and gamekeeper. Mrs. Purdie gave them fresh bread from her kitchen, tore out leaves from her husband's account books, and told them all about the present Scott family. In the midst of this conversation Lucretia went to find the Georgian so he also could meet Mrs. Purdie. The Southerner may not have been converted to the abolitionist cause, but he was touched by Lucretia's thoughtfulness.

It was people, not scenery, that Lucretia Mott enjoyed. Throughout the visit to Scotland she had been busy observing the everyday life of the people—barefoot women drawing handbarrows, shepherds with their long crooks, stone fences (as in Chester County), oatmeal stirabout and oaten cakes for breakfast. All these things interested her more than the wild Highland glens or a trip to Loch Lomond.

After a brief visit with Harriet Martineau at Tynemouth, the party returned to London. Here they rejoined the Stantons and other abolitionists and spent a final week visiting friends and sightseeing. Lucretia tried once more to interest herself in the British Museum, but instead found herself sitting near the entrance with Elizabeth Cady Stanton, answering the younger woman's fervent questions.

When she first arrived in London, Elizabeth Stanton had not known how she was going to feel about Lucretia, since her husband, Henry, was on the opposite side of the antislavery schism. She was, however, won over almost immediately and became Lucretia's ardent admirer. Watching the small Quaker woman parrying the attacks of the Baptist clergymen at their lodgings, listening to her expound her views on Mary Wollstonecraft and on woman's rights, hearing her preach from the pulpit of a Unitarian church in London, the younger woman was inspired to believe that her lifelong rebellion against male domination might after all have some fruition. "I found in this new friend a woman emancipated from all faith in man-made creeds, from all fear of his denunciations. Nothing was too sacred for her to question as to its rightfulness in principle and practice," Elizabeth recorded.

Finally it was time to return to the United States. The Motts took leave of their new friends with "full hearts" and boarded the *Patrick Henry* for an uneventful trip home. The summer in England had benefited Lucretia's health, just as her friends and family had hoped it might. Throughout the three months she had eaten everything she liked without suffering any ill consequences...except for one morning, when she tried shrimp for breakfast. She did not once complain of dyspepsia. Lucretia's good health may have resulted from the fact that she was under less psychological stress than she had been at home. Although she was attacked vigorously in London and Scotland, the attackers were "strangers," and Lucretia had therefore felt justified in fighting back rather than holding herself and her anger in check. Never before had she been quite so sharp as she was with Nathaniel Colver and Josiah Forster.

The London Convention was a turning point for Lucretia Mott. She was recognized now as a leading figure in both abolition and woman's rights. With recognition came the responsibility to continue the fight. The experience unleashed her; thereafter she did not attempt to hold back either anger or commitment. She did not waste energy debating with herself over her course; she went with the stream of her indignation and responded to the calls upon her time without reservation. By opening herself thus to her own feelings as well as to the demands of the times she ensured that she would continue to grow decade after decade.

The Motts returned to the United States sad that a world convention had not yet been held. But the exclusion of women from the meetings of the British and Foreign Anti-Slavery Society had even more important consequences. It started a train of events that was to lead, some eight years later, to a landmark in American history: the first woman's rights convention at Seneca Falls.

CHAPTER
X

TO KEEP
IN THE QUIET

THE LONDON Convention had reinforced Lucretia Mott's commitment to the struggle against slavery as well as for the rights of women. As soon as she had enjoyed a reunion with all the members of her large family and had reported to the Philadelphia Female Anti-Slavery Society, she was on the road again, with James at her side. She spoke to the state legislatures of Delaware, New Jersey, and Pennsylvania on the slavery issue. "A patient and respectful audience was granted while I pled the cause of the oppressed," she wrote a new English friend, Elizabeth Pease.

In Smyrna, Delaware, where Daniel Neall had been tarred and feathered, it was announced that Lucretia Mott would attend Meeting on Sunday and would probably speak. When Lucretia arose and began to speak against slavery, one man got up and stalked out of Meeting. Lucretia thought she recognized him as the leader of the gang who had captured Daniel Neall.

After Meeting, James discovered that someone—doubtless the man in question—had removed a linchpin from the wheel of the carriage. James replaced it and drove Lucretia back to the tavern, where a mob had collected. He asked the innkeeper if he would serve them dinner and feed the horses. That gentleman replied that due to the excitement he would be much obliged if the Motts would excuse him from answering their request. They were finally able to eat and to rest at the home of a friend, thirteen miles farther down the road, a trip of several hours.

The house on North Ninth was kept lively during the spring and summer of 1841 with the usual stream of visitors. John Greenleaf Whittier, traveling with the British abolitionist

Joseph Sturge, called but refused to break bread. Hospitable Lucretia was wounded. "They might have had Colver if we could have kept Stanton, Whittier, and Theodore Weld," she wrote the Webbs.

James was trying to repair his fallen fortunes. He had not recovered from the loss he had suffered in the factory fire, and hard times were depressing the wool business, along with most of the economy. Philadelphia had been losing its commercial and economic leadership ever since Andrew Jackson had forced the closing of the Second Bank of the United States in 1836. The nation as a whole had not yet recovered from the resulting panic of 1837. When business was brisk, James traveled widely buying up wool. (Lucretia loved to call it woolgathering.) Now, with little trade, he spent the long, hot, sticky summer in Philadelphia.

By fall, however, Lucretia was feeling the call to be on the road again, and James was sufficiently solvent to spare the expense. In October Edward Davis and Sarah Pugh accompanied Lucretia on a trip to Boston to attend the anniversary meeting of the New England Non-Resistance Society. En route they stopped in New York, where Lucretia preached at Meeting without the formality of a traveling minute.

The New York Quakers, she found, were in a state of turmoil. George White, the evangelical minister, was leading an effort to prevent all members of the Society from taking part in antislavery activities, and disciplining those who did. Isaac Hopper was a special target. Lucretia was indignant, and spoke strongly against intolerance. Her new fighting spirit, born in London, was flaming now. She gave a radical talk at Marlboro Chapel, in Boston, linking all the reforms of the day. "I long for the time," she declared, "when my sisters will rise, and occupy the sphere to which they are called by their high nature and destiny." No longer would they be the playthings of men, satisfied with trivial social and intellectual pursuits.

Back in Philadelphia she continued to frighten her fellow Quakers with her heretical views. One day a well-meaning elder dropped by the house on Ninth Street to report that he had been told that Lucretia had called the Bible "a blood rusted key." "I am very sorry thou wilt say such things," the elder complained.

Lucretia gently explained that she had simply quoted from a poem by James Russell Lowell:

> *Nor attempt the future's portal*
> *with the past's blood rusted key.*

The explanation only partially satisfied the complaining elder. Lucretia's new militancy in stating her liberal views had been noticed with alarm ever since her return from England. She had even appeared at Meeting in a new coal-scuttle bonnet, given to her by a British friend, with a higher crown and a few more pleats than American Quaker women were accustomed to wearing. The bonnet framed Lucretia's heart-shaped face, which was now filling out and becoming rosy as health returned, and she was secretly rather partial to it. Philadelphia Quakers, however, were so alarmed at this sign of her increasing worldliness that she was forced to put it away in the attic.

Despite the mounting criticism, she was still a powerful figure in Philadelphia Yearly Meeting. During the late fall she was sent along with two other Quaker ministers to visit all the meetings in central and western Pennsylvania. They traveled for five weeks, visiting nineteen counties, crossing the snow-covered mountains, and staying in the country inns as well as Quaker homes. Wherever she went, Lucretia tried to arrange a public meeting at which she could speak against slavery, as well as attending the Quaker meetings for worship.

Lucretia celebrated her forty-ninth birthday on January 3, 1842, and wrote piously that she hoped "the few remaining years allotted me may be devoted to the cause of suffering humanity and my own improvement." The death of two beloved friends, James Forten and Grace Douglass, both black abolitionists, had turned her thoughts toward her own mortality.

She was depressed as well by the fact that George White was gaining adherents in Philadelphia for his crusade against the abolitionists. He was now bold enough to bring a complaint against Lucretia Mott to her own Meeting. She had had no right to speak in New York Monthly Meeting last fall, he said, without a traveling minute. Fortunately the elder to whom the complaint was brought took it straight to Lucretia. She wrote back to New York Monthly Meeting, citing Quaker history "from William Penn to the present" to justify her right to speak.

Her concern about the attitude of New York Quakers toward Isaac Hopper was growing day by day. Isaac, his son-in-law James Gibbons, and an elderly Quaker, Charles Marriott, were now facing disownment by New York Yearly Meeting for having allowed an article to appear in the *National Anti-Slavery Standard* attacking George White. Lucretia used what influence she had in New York circles to fight the disownment, enlisting the support of friends and relatives in Hopper's cause. To her growing dismay she discovered, however, that both Mott and Willis relatives were lining up against him.

Worst of all was Phebe Willis. For a while Lucretia tried to avoid the subject in her letters to Phebe, fearing it would cause more trouble. Then in April she wrote a letter revealing her real feelings. She thought George White was deranged, and his followers deluded. "Let them go on and rend the Society into fragments, rather than force the advocates of justice and mercy to cease their pleadings for the right." So passionate was the letter that the prudent James wrote a note across the top urging Phebe not to circulate it.

New York Yearly Meeting upheld the disownment of Hopper in May 1842. In response, most of Isaac's children withdrew from the Society of Friends. Among them was Anna's husband, Edward, who resigned his membership in Cherry Street Meeting. It was the first break in Quaker membership in Lucretia and James's immediate family. They were sad, but supportive of Edward. Years later Lucretia said she thought Edward would rejoin the Society of Friends if New York would remove "that disgraceful Minute from your Record book." The minute, however, was never removed, and Hopper died in 1852 still excommunicated, Lucretia sorrowfully preaching at his graveside.

Another consequence of the disownment was the end of the correspondence between Lucretia and Phebe Willis, who had been her close friend and spiritual confidante for almost twelve years. Dependent on deep, sustaining relationships with her friends, Lucretia seemed destined to sustain painful breaks in these relationships as she survived schism after schism, both within the Society of Friends and in the larger reform movements in which she had her being.

The stiffening Quaker opposition to the radical abolitionists reflected the attitude of the larger society. Fed in part by the continuing depression, the public anger against the agitation continued to grow. A gag rule was in force, preventing the U.S. Congress from discussing citizens' petitions on the subject of slavery, and abolition literature was barred from circulation in the South. Abby Kelley, now the foremost female antislavery agent, met with mobs and riots whenever she tried to speak in Connecticut. John Tyler, a Virginia Democrat who succeeded to the presidency after the death of William Henry Harrison— Old Tippecanoe—was known for his stand on state's rights.

In this unfriendly climate Lucretia began to feel a leading to take her campaign against slavery to the South. In October 1842 she and James traveled to Baltimore Yearly Meeting. This time she had a traveling minute, but she was nevertheless met by a prominent Friend who said, "Now, Lucretia, let us have no battle array." She was hurt but undeterred. She held two large evening meetings that were quiet and orderly. J.E. Snodgrass, editor of the *Baltimore Sunday Visitor*, called Lucretia's speech "one of the richest oratorical treats I have ever had the pleasure of enjoying." Hearing that it was rumored in Philadelphia that he had been bribed to praise the speech, he replied that it was not he who was "bought up" but copies of his paper—bought up by men and women eager to read Lucretia's words.

After the Yearly Meeting was over, James and Lucretia traveled throughout Virginia, holding meetings and conversations with slave owners. They came away believing that such men and women were as open to reason as those Northerners who prefaced their remarks with "I am as much opposed to slavery as anyone else, but..." James wrote to Lucretia's cousin, "The slaveholders... will bear the truth spoken in gospel love, and in this love plain things may be said and will bring acknowledgement of this truth; of this we had full evidence."

Passing through Washington, the Motts were unable to gain a hearing for Lucretia at the House of Representatives. Lucretia found her conscience troubled about this omission. James accordingly wrote to John Quincy Adams, who had stayed with the Motts in Philadelphia, to inquire if Congressional Hall could be secured for his wife. The Congressmen, however, feared Lucretia's flaming abolitionism. Instead, it was arranged that she preach in the Unitarian Church early in January 1843.

Most of the Congressmen were just returning to the capital from the Christmas recess when Lucretia spoke accordingly. Surprisingly enough, over forty of them were present to hear her, as well as a large audience of government officials and journalists. The church was packed, with many people standing in the back and many turned away. Was this the famous radical they had heard so much about, this pretty little woman in Quaker gray? Lucretia took a deep breath, then spoke as she might have spoken to her own Monthly Meeting, letting the Spirit guide her from subject to subject—the need for more liberal religion as well as an end to war and slavery. Her audience was transfixed. One prominent slave owner was remarked to "twitch in his seat." Ralph Waldo Emerson wrote his wife that "it was like the rumble of an earthquake—the sensation that attended the speech and no man would have done so much and come away alive."

Lucretia felt that she had a direct leading to interest those in power in the subject of emancipation. This not only meant congressmen, it meant the man in the White House. After the talk in the Unitarian Church she persuaded James to accompany her up the hill to call on President John Tyler in person. Startled perhaps, Tyler received them and heard Lucretia's opening remarks. He told her he was interested in solving the problem of slavery, but the answer was colonization. James rose to his bait, reminding Tyler that the blacks have as much right as anyone to choose where they want to live. Tyler then asked slyly if the Motts would be willing to have them all in the North. "Yes, as many as want to come," Lucretia told him pertly. Taken aback by this assertive woman, Tyler said placatingly that he had liked a recent address by the Baltimore Yearly Meeting on the subject of slavery. Lucretia said she did not like it, because it was calculated to set the slave owners' consciences at ease. Tyler gave up and rose to say good-bye. "I would like to hand Mr. Calhoun over to you," he told Lucretia on parting. Calhoun, the leader of the South in the House, was a famous debater.

Lucretia left Washington convinced that "our hopes must not rest on those in power, but on the common people whose servants they are."

Having heard Lucretia's speech at the Unitarian Church in Washington, Ralph Waldo Emerson called on the Motts as soon as he reached Philadelphia and was charmed to find Lucretia a warm and considerate hostess. He wrote to his wife, Lydia, that she was "the best person in Philadelphia" and "the handsomest of women" as well as the leading Quaker. "I do not wonder that they are too proud of her and too much in awe of her to spare her, though they suspect her faith."

News of Lucretia Mott's successful public speech in a Unitarian church in fact cost her dearly in Philadelphia. Her enemies within the Society of Friends were growing bolder. At Philadelphia Yearly Meeting in the spring of 1843, she urged the women to assert their rights in yearly-meeting business. She was answered by an elder who said, "My friends, a body with two heads; what an anomaly!" Later in the day when the subject of slavery came up, she tried to strengthen the resolution and was again put in her place.

At the joint Meeting of Worship, Rachel Barker, a minister from Poughkeepsie, New York, rose and preached at Lucretia for over an hour, warning the young people present to avoid being led by false prophetesses into "the mixtures, the whirlwind, and the storm" of reform movements. They must instead keep in the quiet. Lucretia felt moved to answer the charges and preached back for another hour. "I did not spare her, stranger though she was. Every stale objection she urged...I was favored to meet, as if I had taken notes."

The following October George White himself came to Philadelphia and preached at Cherry Street Meeting against the reform movements. "No matter into what vice you have gone," he declaimed, "join not these associations...they are abominations in the sight of God." He singled out the American Anti-Slavery Society for special scorn. Many listened attentively. The noose around Lucretia tightened.

Should she simply resign from the Society of Friends? Her friend Abby Kelley had done so. The Webbs were soon to follow suit. Other friends were disowned or caught up in local schisms over the issue. The urge to keep in the quiet as opposed to the stirring call of antislavery agitation was opening old wounds and tearing the Society apart. Throughout the 1840s Lucretia worried about her proper course of action.

To resign was to leave the Society she loved in the hands of the conservatives. It also meant her children would have no religious base and might drift into membership in the Episcopal or Catholic Church, as some of her younger Coffin relatives had recently done. And it would deprive her of the opportunity to speak in Meeting, an experience she found continually refreshing and exhilarating.

The heart of the trouble, Lucretia thought, was the question of authority. When the Hicksites separated in 1827, it was in rebellion against the authority of the Yearly Meeting elders. Yet they had no sooner established their own meetings than they were once more appointing elders and ministers and giving them authority over the meeting.

During this difficult period an elderly New York Quaker had come to Philadelphia Yearly Meeting but had been refused permission to speak. In the spirit of Elias Hicks, he spoke anyway, protesting the ban and urging Friends to "seek Truth for authority, not authority for Truth." Lucretia agreed with him completely and made this her personal motto from then on.

To gain members, the Hicksites had made compromises on matters of authority and creed, Lucretia thought. As a result they had such leaders as George White. "When one compromise of principle is made for peace sake and to please men, we may expect darkness and opposition to follow," she wrote a friend. Yet to maintain her membership now, Lucretia had to make compromises. As a minister she was expected to attend the very meeting of ministers and elders whose power she feared. Critics such as Edward Hicks were not slow to point out this inconsistency.

The Quakers were not able to find grounds to disown Lucretia Mott, but they disciplined her by refusing to give her traveling minutes after October 1843. Though Lucretia continued to travel and speak in the ministry, she was frequently received coldly, ordered to sit down, and sometimes turned away. Her fighting spirit and her sense of mission kept her going, but she still loved approval and was easily hurt by the treatment she received. She expected more of the Society of Friends, as she demanded more of herself, and was deeply disappointed by what she saw as their failure to live up to their ideals.

During this long and trying period, Lucretia turned for sup-

port to her friends and family. She kept up her vast correspondence with her relatives, and she wrote frequently as well to her
new friends from London days. To the Webbs in Ireland she
poured out her anger at the behavior of the "pseudo Quakers"
toward Isaac Hopper and other antislavery Friends. At the same
time she tried to convert them to woman's rights. When Richard
Webb wrote that women should be allowed to participate in the
reform movements, she suggested the word *allowed* be omitted.
Women would never break their chains as long as freedom was
bestowed upon them, by sufferance. She also corresponded
with Elizabeth Cady Stanton, urging the younger woman to
learn more about liberal religion and applauding her efforts to
study medicine. She saw as much as she could of Sarah and
Miller McKim. Both the Philadelphia Female Anti-Slavery
Society and the Pennsylvania Anti-Slavery Society's executive
committees met in her front parlor and were a part of her
extended family. Whenever there were hurts outside of this circle, Lucretia retreated for strength within it.

Most of all, Lucretia Mott still depended heavily on her own
mother's moral support. Although headquartered with
Lucretia, Anna Coffin made frequent trips to Auburn, to help
Martha with housecleaning or the birth of a new baby, and
Lucretia admired her devotion in her letters to her sister.

During 1842 Anna Coffin traveled back to Nantucket for a
reunion with her remaining sisters. Although over seventy,
Anna Coffin was hale and hearty, sharp of eye and tongue.
Everyone expected her to live to a ripe old age. Unfortunately
this was not to be. In March 1844 she and Lucretia came down
with fever, vomiting, and "congestion of the lungs"—probably
a form of influenza. Members of the Coffin clan gathered to
take turns nursing the two invalids, but both grew steadily
worse. Although very sick, Lucretia was so anxious about her
mother that she could not sleep. Finally she persuaded James to
wrap her up in a blanket and carry her to her mother's bed.
Finding Anna Coffin much worse, she became very upset. The
older woman remained conscious and was able to say that the
ice cream she was fed was "elegant' or exclaim, when it was time
for her medicine, "A dog's leg." But during the night of March
25 she lapsed into a coma, and at 1 P.M. on March 26 she died.

Sick and weak herself, Lucretia Mott was crushed by the death of her mother. There had been so many losses in her life—the Nantucket Island of her birth, her father, her beloved Tommy, membership in the Twelfth Street Meeting, which had seen her spiritual awakening. At fifty-one Lucretia was still dependent on Anna's approval in many ways. Now that approval was gone forever. Some of her own desperate sense of loss is conveyed in a letter to her sister Martha a few days after Anna Coffin died. Martha must not feel that she had no mother, Lucretia said, for she and Eliza would visit every summer and make it up to her.

Anna Hopper added a note of her own, urging Aunt Martha to come immediately. The whole family was worried about Lucretia, who was still very weak and deeply agitated by her mother's death. A few days later inflammation of the brain (probably encephalitis) set in, and for several days Lucretia's life was regarded to be in danger. There were so many anxious inquiries about her that Miller McKim began to post notices on the door of the Anti-Slavery Society office announcing the latest news of her condition.

Martha came to nurse Lucretia, who fortunately soon rallied, sat up in bed, and asked for all the political news she had missed while sick. She was shortly well enough to face another family crisis. Martha's daughter, Marianne Pelham, confessed to her mother that although she was engaged to Rodman Wharton, a Philadelphia Quaker, she was really in love with her first cousin, Thomas Mott. James and Lucretia had warned Thomas to avoid such an entanglement two years earlier; and the two cousins had tried hard to stay apart and repress their feeling for each other. Now, however, Marianne felt she could not go on.

Martha told Lucretia that Marianne had felt sure the Motts would never permit such a marriage. "How little Marianne knew us to suppose we should oppose them if their hearts were so deeply interested," Lucretia responded. She and James thought the relationship was a misfortune but not of sufficient importance to weigh against the couple's happiness. When Cherry Street Meeting moved to disown Thomas for marrying out of Meeting and marrying a first cousin, it must have hurt her pride, but she made no comment.

By the first of May Lucretia was up and about, but the doctor felt that she must guard her nervous system carefully. In July she was able to visit Martha in Auburn, and while there to see Community Farm, a communitarian experiment organized by a small group of New York State abolitionists and reformers. On the first of August she celebrated the emancipation of the slaves in the British West Indies with her Philadelphia black friends. By fall she was sufficiently upset by the growing poverty in Philadelphia to plunge herself into a new cause.

This was the creation of an Association for the Relief of Poor Women (renamed the Northern Association in 1849). The sponsors raised money to provide a room where such women could gather and sew together, filling orders solicited from the more affluent. The pay was only twenty-five cents a day, but the needs in the city were so great that there were plenty of women eager to work at that wage. Thanks to Lucretia Mott's influence, both "colored" and white women were recruited. Elected president, Lucretia met with the board, selected applicants, supervised the workshop, solicited orders for sewing, raised money, and defended the project against the charge that she was coddling the poor women and making them dependent upon relief.

Nevertheless, Lucretia continued to feel the loss of her mother. In 1846 she wrote friends in England that she was still struggling to accept Anna's death. The deep ties, forged when Lucretia became her mother's mainstay on the island of Nantucket, were hard to sever. As she had at the time of Tommy's death, Lucretia sought to assuage her grief by turning to a deeper spiritual life and its fruits, a stronger commitment to social action.

Increasingly, too, she turned to James for support. The deep, symbiotic bonds between the two became stronger. He gave her added strength; she gave expression to his thoughts. When a group of Friends from London came to Philadelphia on their way to Indiana to deal with the antislavery faction of that Yearly Meeting, Lucretia felt a strong urge to call upon them. "But Jas Mott didn't incline to go with me and I had not the courage to go alone," she wrote Elizabeth Pease.

Although James occasionally demurred when he thought

Lucretia was too rash, he was usually willing to accompany her on her self-imposed missions. They talked things over in private; in public his support of her was absolute. Once when Lucretia rather sharply corrected a well-known minister, the Reverend Charles Ames, in a public meeting, the gentleman turned to James Mott for his opinion. "If she thinks thee wrong thee had better think it over again," Mott told him.

The death of Anna Coffin also meant that Lucretia assumed the matriarchy of the Coffin clan. No event in the family, from engagement to marriage, to the birth of a child, to a niece suffering with gathered breast or a milk leg, went without her active interest and involvement. She was not afraid to demand their love and support when she needed it; in turn, she responded generously and sensitively to the needs of the family circle as she perceived them. Although a few resisted her, most were caught up in her crusades by virtue of her sheer vitality and enthusiasm.

Baking the pies for a wedding or nursing a sick child added to Lucretia's always overcrowded calendar, but these duties seemed to refresh her rather than drain her energies. In becoming more like her mother, tart of tongue yet large-hearted, she grew in the strength of an established identity, a daughter of old Nantucket.

CHAPTER
XI

TO WALK
IN THE LIGHT

By 1845 the city of Philadelphia had outgrown its neat grid-work of downtown blocks and begun to fill up the open fields west of Broad Street and to stretch both north and south. The combined population of city and county, under 100,000 when Lucretia and James were married, now exceeded 300,000. A network of horse-drawn street railways took workers to their jobs. There were gaslights on the street, and a fine new waterworks supplied the city.

The Mott family was growing too. In the summer of 1845 Thomas Mott and Marianne Pelham were married, and a few months later Elizabeth, the third Mott daughter, married Thomas Cavender. The Hoppers had a new baby girl, Maria, and the Davises a baby son, Charles. All these happy events kept Lucretia from traveling in June and July.

By August, however, her family duties had lessened, and with James she set out for Ohio Yearly Meeting, held in Salem, in the eastern section of the state, not far from Pittsburgh. Salem had become a western center of antislavery agitation. Due to the efforts of Abby Kelley and the man she was to marry, Stephen Foster, a new newspaper, the *Anti-Slavery Bugle*, had just been established and was being edited by two young Quaker friends of the Motts.

To reach Salem in 1845 meant a four-day journey by railroad, canalboat, and stagecoach. Hot and cindery, Lucretia arrived in Salem in time to preach at Yearly Meeting on the subject of woman's rights. Later it was called the first such speech by a woman, for women, in the Midwest. Among the young women who heard the message for the first time on this occasion was

Mary Frame Thomas, later to become a pioneer woman physician and suffragist.

Back in Philadelphia, Lucretia helped the family get ready for the marriage of Phebe Earle. The house at 136 North Ninth had proved too small for the combined families, and the Davises had bought a home of their own on 140 North Ninth. At the same time James and Lucretia moved next door to 138 North Ninth. They arranged for workmen to cut a door through to the Davises on the second-floor level, so that the two large houses could be used as one in times of overload.

The move was planned for the early spring of 1846, and the Motts made it on schedule, though they were by this time deeply troubled by the turn of current events. War with Mexico seemed more likely with each passing day, while at the same time the United States and Great Britain were close to armed conflict over the U.S. claim to the Oregon territory, which the two countries had been administering jointly. American expansionists, crying "54-40 or Fight!" wanted to annex the whole of the territory up to that line of latitude. There was equally strong opposition in Great Britain to ceding any territory above 42 degrees and thereby losing the trade of the rich Columbia River basin.

With neither side willing to give ground in the spring of 1846, the choice between war and peace seemed to rest on an altered public opinion. In England a small group of peace-minded men and women, many of them Quakers, initiated a Friendly Address Committee, stimulating various groups in Great Britain to write their counterparts in the United States, urging joint public action for a peaceful settlement of the struggle.

"An Address from the Women of the City of Exeter," bearing some 1,623 signatures, was published in various Philadelphia newspapers. The first reply, drafted on June 10, was distasteful to Lucretia Mott and her friends for its sentimental tone and its appeal to the "bond of common blood" between the British and American women. A meeting was set for June 17 at which a new reply "which it is intended shall better assert the dignity and be more fitting the intelligence of the women of the present day" would be composed.

By this time the United States and Great Britain had reached a compromise, and the Senate on June 15 ratified a new treaty, setting the boundary at the forty-ninth parallel. The new letter, which Lucretia Mott read to the assembly, probably wrote, and was the first to sign, urged women to take increasing responsibility for peace: "We are gratified that the present difficulties between our countries are being amicably settled, but let us not forget that we have other brethren, urging upon us the duty to impress upon the heart of this generation the idea of the brotherhood of the race. The war waged by your government in India, and that of ours in Mexico, admonish us that it is now as ever important to instil the principles of justice, mercy, and peace."

Lucretia was one of five women appointed to collect signatures for this letter. Within two weeks the women had gathered 5,525 names and turned them over to the British consul in Philadelphia for mailing to the women of Exeter.

Martha came to visit Philadelphia in the fall. On the spur of the moment the two sisters decided to attend the convention of the Unitarian Church then being held. The minister of the host church, William Furness, was an active abolitionist and a friend of Lucretia's. When he saw her enter his church, he offered her a place on the speakers' platform. As usual, Lucretia could not resist an opportunity to speak. Martha described her talk as elegant.

Her remarks were published in the Philadelphia papers and caused a furor. Some of the Unitarians objected to the fact that a woman had preached in their church and sought assurances that this would never happen again. The Quakers, however, were even more outraged. *The Friends Intelligencer*, the weekly Hicksite journal, reported frostily: "Considerable uneasiness has been expressed by some Friends, on account of a statement which has been published, and somewhat extensively circulated, to the effect that a minister of the Society of Friends in this city appeared at a convention of 'Unitarian Christians' as an 'accredited agent from the Society of Friends.' " Lucretia, the editor explained, had lately "been engaged in appointing meetings among those not of our persuasion." Although Unitarians had introduced her as an "accredited" minister of the Society of Friends, Lucretia herself had not claimed to be a representative.

On the heels of Lucretia's daring act of preaching in the Unitarian Church, George White returned to Philadelphia for one of his periodic attacks on Lucretia. "It appeared to me to have made so deep an impression on the meeting that all the eloquence and sophistry of Lucretia Mott could not dissipate it, although she exerted herself to the utmost," Edward Hicks wrote in his memoirs.

Lucretia's enemies were now claiming that she was really a Unitarian. She, however, found Unitarianism too theological, rational, and cold for her own tastes. Speculation about the nature of God, whether He be One or Three, she linked to theology, a subject she thought of little value. What mattered was the practice of the religious life. In this she was in the tradition of George Fox, who disliked religious controversy for its "airy notions" and believed in the overriding importance of a direct experience of Christ. Lucretia felt herself to be in accord with Fox, William Penn, and Elias Hicks and believed she was struggling to return the Society of Friends to its true direction. "As to theology I am sick of disputes on that subject, though I can not say just as my husband does—that 'he doesn't care a fig about it'—for I want those I love should see their way out of the darkness and error with which they are surrounded," she wrote the Webbs.

The Webbs sent her a three-volume book by the Reverend Blanco White, a former Spanish priest who had been through a long spiritual search in which he first renounced Catholicism, then Anglicanism, then passed through a period of atheism, and finally came to rest as a Unitarian minister. The religious faith he evolved was largely experiential, resting on a direct relationship between God and man and on obedience to the Divine. All of this spoke to Lucretia's condition. She wrote enthusiastically that it was the "best radical or heretical book that has appeared in our age." She ordered a copy to study and to circulate among friends and filled several small notebooks with her comments. "I sympathized especially with Blanco White's lonely and sad feelings in having to give up one friend after another for the 'Son of man's' sake and that his honesty forbade all compromise and conservatism," she wrote the Webbs feelingly.

In the winter of 1846, Lucretia Mott gratefully turned from theological squabbles to give her attention to a new concern.

This was the terrible famine in Ireland and the resulting influx of half-starved, penniless immigrants into Philadelphia.

The Motts felt a special bond with Ireland after their visit to that country in 1840, and James entered into a fund-raising effort of Philadelphia Quakers to send money to the stricken land for famine relief. He was glad to do what he could, he wrote the Webbs, although he believed relief was merely palliative. "The axe should be laid to the root of the evil—oppression."

For her part, Lucretia devoted herself to the immediate problems of poverty in Philadelphia. Faced with an almost endless supply of cheap Irish labor, Philadelphia employers lowered wages and made no effort to improve working conditions. The situation of all working people was affected. In the textile industry the handloom weavers in Kensington and Southwark, now beginning to feel the competition from the new power-drive looms, became desperate. During the winter they struck for a decent wage. Although the strike was prolonged and the families were reduced to starvation, the owners did not give way. "With the oppressor there is power," Lucretia wrote bitterly to Elizabeth Pease. She and James did what they could, devoting First-day afternoons to visiting the families, laden with groceries. Nevertheless, they knew this was but a drop in the bucket of human misery.

One practical way Lucretia could help was to provide employment for young Irish women fresh from the old country—greenhorns, they were called—in her own house and in the homes of her friends and relatives. The practice, of course, was not without its personal advantages: Lucretia could count on an endless supply of help. On the other hand, training the greenhorns, who were unused to city ways, was a trial. In addition, Lucretia insisted on paying the highest, rather than the lowest, wages. At a time when prejudice against the Irish was common, Lucretia defended them stoutly. Once when Martha wrote to complain that several of her Irish servants had stolen from the kitchen, Lucretia scolded her for intolerance. "You'll not make me believe it is the Irish nature," she said. "Yours are exceptional cases."

With servants at home to do the ironing and start dinner, Lucretia was free to run her various errands, delivering baskets for the poor, finding jobs for her seamstresses, taking antislavery literature to the newspapers, calling on her sister and her cousins. Sometimes she figured she had walked seven miles by nightfall. The exercise was good for her. Her health was now better than ever, and she had gained weight. In fact, James wrote the Webbs she now weighed 140 pounds, as opposed to 110 when she went to London. Since she was scarcely five feet tall, this was a lot, but it was becoming. Her cheeks were rosy again, and her spirits high. At fifty-four she was still very much interested in her looks. When a Boston paper reported that spring that she was "a woman said to be sixty-five years of age," she was mortified and thought for a while of refusing all further public appearances.

Lucretia Mott had gone to Boston in May 1847 to attend the New England Anti-Slavery meetings. She always found the intellectual climate in Boston refreshing. The transcendentalists were interesting to her, although to her practical mind they were too sentimental and mystical. She liked Emerson as a friend but disagreed with some of his concepts. She knew Thoreau only slightly and would have been amused to know that, having heard her speak, he described her as expressing "transcendentalism of the mildest sort." She admired, and often quoted, the transcendentalist preacher Theodore Parker.

In July Lucretia spoke in Worcester, Massachusetts. Abby Kelley Foster wrote Stephen that Lucretia now endorsed all reforms "from laying aside the whip stick in families to that of thorough non-resistance, temperance, antislavery, women's rights, moral reform. I thought her decidedly more radical than when I saw her last," she concluded.

In late August Lucretia and James again journeyed to Salem, Ohio, to be present at Yearly Meeting. They then went on to Richmond, Indiana, where both Hicksites and Orthodox were holding their Yearly Meetings concurrently. James and Lucretia were met on the first day by some Hicksite elders, who urged Lucretia to return home, or if she remained, to refrain from speaking at the sessions of the Yearly Meeting. None of the local Quakers invited the Motts to stay with them—an almost unpardonable breach of hospitality in those days—and James and Lucretia were forced to take a room in a lodging house. They nevertheless persisted in attending Meetings, and Lucretia spoke several times during the silence. So coldly was she treated, however, and so often rebuked that the tension she suffered brought on an attack of neuralgia. James, worried about his wife, asked a local physician, a Friend, to treat her. This the doctor refused to do, saying to Lucretia, according to family legend, "Lucretia, I am so deeply afflicted by thy rebellious spirit, that I do not feel I can prescribe for thee."

James took Lucretia, who was in tears, back to their rooming house, and eventually she recovered sufficiently to return to the sessions. It would have been far easier to have given up and gone back to Philadelphia, but Lucretia felt it was her duty to endure the ostracism of these Indiana Friends, currently in the grip of an evangelical spirit, in order to remind them of their duty to the slave and of the simple Quakerism of an earlier day. She had a right, she felt, to expect a greater tolerance on the part of members of the Society she loved.

She paid a heavy price for this visit to Indiana, for the stress ultimately led to the return of the dyspepsia of which she had been free since London days. In spite of her poor health, however, Lucretia's fighting spirit was back. If they were going to call her a heretic, they were going to hear some radical thoughts. In January 1848 she and James and the faithful Edward M. Davis told William Lloyd Garrison that he might use their names in a call to an Anti-Sabbath Convention.

The goal of the Anti-Sabbath Convention was to end "penal enactments compelling the observation of the first day of the week as the Sabbath." The reformers, under Garrison's leadership, questioned the current strict observance of the Sabbath, which in their view deprived workingmen of any recreation on their one day of rest and made it unacceptable to pursue any reform activities. (Several years before, Abby Kelley and Stephen Foster had been arrested in Ohio for distributing antislavery literature on the Sabbath.) There was no real authority for the strict rules governing the Sabbath in the New Testament, they argued. Did not Jesus say that the Sabbath was made for man, and not man for the Sabbath?

Early Friends had also been anti-sabbatarians, in the sense that they believed every day of the week should be equally a day of worship. Lucretia Mott had always sewed on Sunday when she felt she must, although she generally kept her sewing neat so that it could be put away quickly if callers came by. In the early 1840s she had also decided to give up the practice of attending afternoon Meeting on First-days. Instead she spent the time visiting black families or poor women.

She was therefore in complete agreement with Garrison's objectives in holding the Anti-Sabbath Convention, although she wished his announcements of it would have been less strident. She not only attended but made several addresses, arguing that even if the Sabbath could be shown to have biblical sanction, it was still not binding on men and women of the present age. The Scriptures were but one of God's communications with human beings. His Truth was ever present and was subject to a "continuing revelation." Reformers, she argued, should bear a faithful testimony against what they believed to be wrong about the celebration of the Sabbath and not give the appearance of condoning it. She would no longer put her sewing away, not while "it is regarded a greater crime to do an innocent thing on the first day of the week—to use the needle for instance—than to put a human being on the auction block on the second day."

The Anti-Sabbath Convention naturally aroused a storm of controversy, and Lucretia Mott was attacked as one of the "spouters of heresy." Her reputation as a heretic was now national in scope. In the coming months she did nothing to diminish it.

Shortly after the trip to Boston she went to New York to attend the Annual Meeting of the American Anti-Slavery Society. Since this event generally conflicted with Philadelphia Yearly Meeting, she had not been able to attend for ten years. When Sydney Howard Gay (married to Elizabeth Neall), the new editor of the *Anti-Slavery Standard*, asked if he could announce her as a speaker, she said he might do as he liked. This was new for her; previously she had insisted on no announcements, so that she could be free to speak only if the Spirit led. She confessed in her letter to Sydney and Elizabeth that she was worried about her appearance. Last year the papers had said sixty-five, this year her eyes were red, and she expected them to say seventy-five.

In her speech, "The Law of Progress," she expressed for the first time her growing belief that there was only one Christ but many Messiahs, of whom Jesus had been one. Just as Jesus of Nazareth had led people forward from an Old Testament "law of retaliation" to the concept of loving their enemies, so reformers of the present day were carrying the revelation still further. "But a reformer now, the Jesus of the present age, on the Mount Zion of Peace, says, 'Ye have heard that it was said of them of old, thou shall war only in self-defense, but I say unto you, take not up the sword at all.' "And she called the modern abolitionist "the Jesus of the present age on the Mount Zion of Freedom." Reported in the press, this sermon was remembered and used as an example of her heresy for many years.

Nine months later she preached a third heretical sermon, which was widely reported. Philadelphia was the center for medical education in the United States at the time, and many of the medical students were from the South. A number of these were strongly opposed to the antislavery movement as well as to the training of women physicians, a cause in which Lucretia was becoming increasingly interested. Feeling that she might be able to sway their minds if she could speak to them, she accepted an invitation to address a special meeting early in 1849.

The large meeting room at the Cherry Street Meeting House was filled to overflowing. When Lucretia mentioned slavery, about thirty students got up to leave. Otherwise she had a rapt audience.

"I confess to you, my friends, that I am a worshipper after the way called heresy, a believer after the manner many deem infidel," she told them. "While at the same time my faith is firm in the blessed, the eternal doctrine preached by Jesus and by every child of God since the creation of the world, especially the great truth that God is the teacher of his people himself; the doctrine that Jesus most emphatically taught, that the kingdom is with man, that there is his sacred and divine temple."

Fifty-six now, Lucretia Mott was at the very height of her power as a Quaker minister. Sermons delivered in Cherry Street Meeting House in the fall of 1849 and the spring of 1850 were taken down by reporters and have been preserved. Everyone who heard her said that the spirit with which she spoke, the light that radiated from her, was as impressive as the words themselves. Nevertheless, these sermons reveal the range of her seeking mind.

Lucretia's major themes were essentially simple ones. She believed that the living spirit of religion must not be confused with the forms that had once cloaked it in the past, whether in written form, as in the Bible, or in customs and ceremonies. She liked to quote George Fox that "Christ has come to teach his people himself." With all the naïve fervor of the nineteenth-century faith in progress, she believed that a new spirit was at work in the world that would shortly bring an end to error and darkness and would cure most of the social ills. She often quoted Dr. Channing: "Mighty powers are at work in the world and who shall stay them?" These powers she attributed to the spirit of the living Christ. That spirit had inhabited Jesus of Nazareth but was equally alive today. "The messenger of the highest is now in our midst."

This spirit, Lucretia believed, demanded that men and women involve themselves actively in reform. The old Quaker quietism, in which one did nothing but allowed the Spirit to use one as it would, had been perverted, she believed, into an excuse for inaction. Men and women must seek the Light. "The great heresy is to await in a kind of indifference for the Light to come to us." By becoming vessels of the Holy Spirit in works of reform, modern men and women might become like Christ, messiahs sent from the Lord. "Let us not hesitate to aspire to be the messiahs of our age."

Christ was the Spirit of God made manifest to human beings. He had been available to men and women long before the Bible was written or Jesus lived. He was available today to people who lived in other cultures and other religions. He was the Light, the Truth that stirred within her and each person she addressed. He asked that they, too, become a vessel of the Holy Spirit, as Jesus had been.

To be like Jesus was to meet human need, both physical and spiritual. Jesus relieved suffering, but at the same time he directed sufferers to the Inner Fount. He himself never separated his inner spirit from his outward duties. The same flow was available to his followers. "Those who go forth ministering to the wants and necessities of their fellow human being experience a rich return, their souls being as a watered garden, as a spring that faileth not.''

Although Lucretia could not accept the whole of the Bible as inspired, she knew the whole of it by heart and drew extensive quotes from both the Old and New Testaments for her sermons, mingling them with selections from Penn, Fox, Hicks, Channing, Parker, and a few of her favorite poets. ''Truth speaks the same language in every age of the world and is equally valuable to us,'' she believed. Truth and Light were accumulative, the ''bold utterances of a Priestly or a Hicks'' were never in vain, as the world advanced from age to age toward the kingdom of God.

Orthodoxy and bigotry shut men and women from the Light. Lucretia longed to prune rote creed and superstition from minds, as she loved to prune bushes and trees, to let in heaven's Light. In that Light, which must always have been to her the clear, stark, uncompromising light of Nantucket, there was no room for prejudice to grow or oppression to flourish.

Love and reason were two Divine gifts, by which one could perceive the Inner Light. Lucretia did not regard herself as a mystic. Although she spoke only from divine inspiration and felt that once she was on her feet, the words were given to her to say, she believed this gift was not ''miraculous'' but simply arose from the ''Divine Implants'' of love and reason within her. She did not believe in intercessory prayer and prayed only for strength to follow manifest duty or for support when she spoke.

In her sermons she used logic and analogy and avoided the traditional Quaker singsong, speaking instead in a calm, sweet voice, which was part of her charm. In the 1840s she gave up the practice of kneeling in public prayer, but simply stood and addressed the Holy Spirit. At about the same time she decided to stop removing her bonnet when she rose to speak.

Yet for all her belief in reason, Lucretia Mott depended on a constant relationship between herself and the Divine Spirit. She did not need to set aside a special time for worship, she came to feel. She worshiped always. Worshiping meant seeking the Divine Will and practicing holy obedience. It also meant appre-

VALIANT FRIEND

THE LIFE OF LUCRETIA MOTT

WHENEVER SHE SAW INJUSTICE, HER INNER LIGHT MOVED HER TO SPEAK OUT:

Where God is, there must be true liberty.''(*London, 1840*)

I long for the day my sisters will rise, and occupy the phere to which they are called by their high nature and estiny.'' (*Boston, 1841*)

RESOLVED: That the speedy success of our cause depends pon the zealous and untiring efforts of both men and omen for the overthrow of the monopoly of the pulpit, and he securing for women an equal participation in the various rades, professions and commerce.'' (*Seneca Falls, 1848*)

'This is called a 'Woman's Rights Convention,' but the hrase 'Human Rights' would more appropriately express ts principles and its aims.'' (*Cleveland, 1853*)

'In the true marriage relationship the independence of the usband and wife is equal, their dependence mutual, and heir obligations reciprocal.'' (*Philadelphia, 1855*)

' . . . as the poor slave's alleged contentment with his ser-ile and cruel bondage only proves the depths of his degra-lation, so the assertion of woman that she has all the rights he wants, only proves how far the restrictions and dis-bilities to which she has been subjected have rendered her nsensible to the blessings of true liberty.'' (*New York, 1856*)

'There is no true peace that is not founded on justice and ight.'' (*Philadelphia, 1876*)

ISBN: 0-8027-0645-2

ciating the wise laws of nature and the divine spark in men and women.

"Is it not delightful to find so many fine minds and good people in the world? I am constantly combatting the 'human depravity' doctrine and preach instead the innate purity of man," she wrote Richard Webb.

Sadly enough it remained the Society of Friends that depressed her. Despite all her efforts, she seemed unable to budge it from dead center. At the end of one particularly dull yearly meeting she wrote the Webbs that the game wasn't worth the candle. "We were well nigh preached to death. Meeting going was advocated threadbare, gravestones denounced full measure; music, very wicked; while the slave had to sigh if not whistle for a hearing."

Yet she never gave up, and because she didn't, her influence is still felt in the Society of Friends today.

CHAPTER
XII

IT HAPPENED
AT SENECA FALLS

ON THE last day of the London Anti-Slavery Convention in 1840, as Elizabeth Cady Stanton later remembered it, she and Lucretia Mott walked back to their lodging, arm in arm. "Commenting on the incidents of the day, we resolved to hold a convention as soon as we returned home, and form a society to advocate the rights of women."

The proposed convention was long in coming. Elizabeth Cady Stanton was soon busy with a succession of baby boys and, as long as she lived on the outskirts of Boston, with a satisfying and intellectually stimulating life. Lucretia was equally busy fighting to keep her place in the Society of Friends, expanding her ministry, playing a role in a whole host of reform movements, and speaking for woman's rights. Yet the promise was not forgotten. Every time Lucretia came to Boston, she and Elizabeth discussed it further.

In the summer of 1848, with the headlines full of the revolutionary fervor sweeping Europe, the opportunity finally arose. In June, James and Lucretia Mott set out for northern New York State and a visit to the Seneca Indians on the Cattaraugus reservation. The Motts were members of the Indian Committee of New York and Philadelphia Yearly Meetings, which had for years been especially concerned about the Senecas. The Friends had set up a school and model farm on the reservation. Unhappily, they could not resist the temptation to try to convert the Indians to white man's ways. One suggestion was that women be taught to stay home and cook while the men worked in the fields. Lucretia protested that such a change should not be contemplated until a council of squaws was called. Her remarks

were regarded as facetious. Now she and James were at last
going to see conditions on the new reservation with their own
eyes.

There were only a few hundred Indians of the once proud
Seneca nation at Cattaraugus, many of their number having
died the winter before in an epidemic of typhus. They were
suffering now not only from poverty but from discord. Several
missionaries had been visiting the reservation and making
converts, with the result there was now a Christian and a Pagan
party. While James worried over needed repairs to the farm and
schoolhouse, Lucretia met with representatives of both groups
to hear their grievances. She was wise enough not to express her
point of view, but to recommend them to seek the wisdom of
"the Great Spirit." Having witnessed the Seneca Strawberry
Dance, she had been impressed with the deep religious fervor of
the Pagans. "It was far from me to say that our silent, voiceless
worship was better adapted to their condition," she wrote
Edmund Quincy.

The revolutionary spirit of the day was having its effect on the
Senecas, she observed in the same letter. "They too are learning
somewhat from the political agitations abroad, and as man is
wont, are imitating the movements of France and all Europe in
seeking a larger liberty—more independence."

After seeing the Indians, the Motts visited several settlements
of escaped slaves. Lucretia was impressed with the vigor and
courage of the blacks in clearing land for their farms and their
determination to educate their children. She found that they
knew little of the progress of the antislavery movement, since
postage was too expensive for them to subscribe to antislavery
periodicals, but she predicted it would not "long be necessary
for them to learn their lessons of liberty from the printed page.
The Spirit of freedom is arousing the world; and the press
universal will echo the glad sound."

On their way home James and Lucretia stopped at Auburn
for their annual summer visit with Martha and David Wright.
Lucretia also wanted to be sure to see her old friend Elizabeth
Cady Stanton, who had recently bought a house in nearby
Seneca Falls. When Jane Hunt, a Quaker woman who lived in
nearby Waterloo, came by to invite Lucretia and Martha to tea

on July 13 and said that Elizabeth was also coming, she was delighted.

Elizabeth was delighted too. After the excitement of Boston, she found life in the small country town dull, and the job of full-time housekeeper and mother was becoming depressing. A chance to see Lucretia was a chance to recall the exciting days in London and to talk about the subject closest to her heart, the status of women.

It was a small tea party. In addition to Lucretia, Martha, and Elizabeth, Jane Hunt had invited one other woman, Mary Ann McClintock, a local Quaker. The five sat around a mahogany tea table in the front parlor sharing experiences. Soon Elizabeth found herself pouring out an accumulated flood of grievances, in which her own unhappiness and her indignation at the position of women were mingled. She spoke, she recalled later, with such vehemence and indignation that "I stirred myself, as well as the rest of the party to do and dare anything." As twilight deepened, the women decided to put their long-discussed resolution into action. Still sitting at the tea table, they composed a call to a woman's rights convention to be published in the *Seneca County Courier* the next day:

SENECA FALLS CONVENTION

Woman's rights Convention—a Convention to discuss the social, civil, and religious conditions and rights of woman, will be held in the Wesleyan Chapel at Seneca Falls, N.Y. on Wednesday and Thursday, the 19th and 20th of July current [1848]; commencing at 10 o'clock A.M. During the first day the meeting will be exclusively for women, who are earnestly invited to attend. The Public generally are invited to be present on the second day when Lucretia Mott, of Philadelphia, and other ladies and gentlemen will address the convention.

Having announced the meeting rather precipitously, the women now found it necessary to plan what they were going to do. They met again on Sunday at Mary Ann McClintock's house in Waterloo to write their declarations and resolutions and to decide on the topic of speeches. Suddenly aghast at the step they had taken, they found it hard to come up with words in which to express their purpose. Then one of the group hit upon the idea of rewriting the Declaration of Independence as a way of encompassing their grievances and expressing the spirit of 1848:

> We hold these truths to be self-evident: that all men and women are created equal....The history of mankind is a history of repeated injuries and usurpations on the part of man toward woman, having in direct object the establishment of an absolute tyranny over her. To prove this, let facts be submitted to a candid world.... He has never permitted her to exercise her inalienable right to the elective franchise...he has compelled her to submit to laws, in the formation of which she had no voice...he has made her, if married, in the eyes of the law, civilly dead.

The completed document breathed life and fire. There was now not much to do but wait for the day of the convention and hope for a crowd. Lucretia feared there would be a small turnout. The good weather had ripened the hay, and local farmers were busy harvesting it. "But it will be a beginning and we may hope it will be followed in due time by one of a more general character," she wrote Elizabeth. James was sick and would not be able to be present until the second day. She and Martha would come from Auburn first and accept Elizabeth's invitation to stay with the Stantons. Meanwhile she had been to Auburn State Prison to hold a meeting with the prisoners. Had Elizabeth planned to have other reform meetings during the woman's rights convention?

By the nineteenth, James had sufficiently recovered, after all, to accompany Lucretia and Martha to Seneca Falls. Approaching the small town by horse and carriage, they were amazed to find the roads full of wagons. Evidently there was to be a larger crowd than Lucretia had feared. The chapel doors were locked, but a Yale student was hoisted through one of the windows and quickly undid the bolts. Immediately a large crowd surged in. Although the women had asked for women only, men were present as well. After a hasty consultation the small leadership group decided to let the men stay. In fact, they concluded, they needed James Mott. None of them felt equal to chairing such a large, mixed assembly.

Once the group was called to order by James, Lucretia, looking queenly in Quaker gray, opened the sessions by stating the purpose of the convention and reviewing the status of women around the world. Thereafter, throughout the two days, hers was the voice most frequently heard. She was, as one of the reporters stated, the guiding spirit of the meeting. Mary Ann McClintock and Elizabeth Stanton also made speeches, and Martha Wright read some satirical articles on the condition of women. The Declaration of Sentiments was read, reread, debated, and finally adopted.

Next came the presentation of resolutions. Among the most important of these were a call for the repeal of laws that placed women on an unequal status, a demand for equal standards of moral conduct for men and women, an appeal for an end to the objection of "indelicacy and impropriety" of women addressing public meetings, and a statement that women must secure for themselves the "sacred right of elective franchise."

When Lucretia Mott first learned of this resolution, she astonished Elizabeth Cady Stanton by saying, "Why Lizzie, thee will make us ridiculous." It seemed uncharacteristic in a woman who never trimmed her sails to public opinion. Lucretia, however, was in conflict about voting; her nonresistance, no-government principles had turned her away from the whole elective process. She was fair-minded enough to see, though, that if men were to have the right to vote, then women should also, and soon became an advocate.

Others at Seneca Falls shared her initial reaction. The oratory of Frederick Douglass, the escaped slave, however, finally swayed the assembly to accept the resolution by a narrow margin. All the other resolutions won handsomely.

At the final session Lucretia offered a resolution calling for woman's advancement in the professions: "**Resolved:** that the speedy success of our cause depends upon the zealous and untiring efforts of both men and women, for the overthrow of the monopoly of the pulpit, and the securing for women an equal participation in the various trades, professions and commerce."

Except for the resolution on suffrage, the rest of the conference had been on a rhetorical plane. It was Lucretia Mott who saw the necessity for the translation of the message into practical, and economic, terms. Her resolution adopted, she gave a final talk, urging the women to press forward with faith and courage. On this note the convention ended, and one hundred of the men and women present signed their names to the

Declaration of Sentiments. As the most prominent person there, Lucretia was the first to sign.

Pleased by the success of the meeting, the women were quite unprepared for the storm of criticism they had provoked. Almost every newspaper in the country carried an editorial attacking or ridiculing them. Many of the editors picked Lucretia as a prime target for attack. The *New York Herald* treated it as a great joke and predicted that "Miss Lucretia Mott" would soon be running for President. Later the same paper called her a modern Lucretia Borgia, full of "old maidish crochets and socialist violations of Christian dignity."

At Seneca Falls a second convention had been planned for Rochester in the first week of August. Held in the Unitarian church in Rochester, it was attended by a local Hicksite, Daniel Anthony. His daughter, Susan B., was out of town.

The Rochester meeting was smaller than the Seneca Falls Convention and created less stir. There were critics in the audience this time, however. One of them questioned Lucretia on what would happen in the family if woman was given a voice equal to that of her husband. When two heads disagree, who must decide? And did not Saint Paul strictly enjoin obedience to husbands and state that man shall be the head of the woman?

Lucretia responded that she had never seen any difficulty arising in the Society of Friends as a result of the fact that women did not promise obedience in the marriage contract of that sect. Decisions were made by appeals not to authority but to reason. And as to that famous dictum of Saint Paul's, she had a tart response: "Many of the opposers of Woman's Rights who bid us obey the bachelor Saint Paul, themselves reject his counsel. He advised them not to marry."

Was not woman mentally inferior to man? another critic asked. Lucretia was not prepared to claim full intellectual equality. Her studies of phrenology and her limited understanding of human evolution both inclined her to believe that long years of repression might have stunted the development of woman's mental powers, the very shape of her head. If so, it would take years of equal opportunity to correct the damage. But even if this were true, it was no reason to deny her rights. "Does a man have fewer rights than another because his intellect is inferior?"

she asked. "If not why should a woman?" The result of injustice should not be used as an excuse for further injustice.

There were enthusiasts as well as critics present. One black abolitionist, also present at Seneca Falls, rose to claim that in his opinion woman was intellectually and spiritually superior and man was a tyrant. Lucretia thanked him for his compliment but said she preferred that no claims be made for woman's superiority. What was needed was equality. Man was not tyrannical by nature; it was power over others that made him that way. Woman could also be made tyrannical in similar situations.

At this convention a woman presided over the sessions for the first time. There was also a female secretary. At times people had trouble hearing their voices. Lucretia insisted they speak up. Women should not plead that their voices were softer if they were going to ask for equal rights, she insisted. "I believe that with sufficient practice women can and will make themselves heard in a public assembly."

Writing to Edmund Quincy about the woman's rights meetings, Lucretia also described her visits to the Senecas, the escaped slaves, the prisoners. "All these subjects of reform are kindred in their nature and...will tend to strengthen and nerve the mind for all—so that the abolitionist will not wax weaker in his advocacy of immediate emancipation. He will not love the slave less in loving universal humanity."

Next Lucretia tried to interest her friends in holding a woman's rights convention in Philadelphia. Everyone was interested but otherwise occupied. She wrote to Elizabeth Stanton urging her and Mary Ann McClintock to come and aid her. "You are so wedded to this cause, you must expect to act as pioneers in the work."

In the same letter she expressed her delight that Elizabeth was concocting a book on woman's rights, although she cautioned that she herself must not be counted upon for a single chapter. Writing was not in her line. She urged Elizabeth not to be discouraged by the fact that so few good books had yet appeared on the subject but rather delighted with the progress the cause was now making. "Look back to the days of our grandmothers and be cheered." As to Elizabeth's own recent speech in Waterloo, Lucretia had heard good reports through Richard

Hunt. "He says some of their respectable inhabitants were well pleased. He would have preferred the headdress a little different—it looked rather Theatrical he thought—'a kind of turban and bows'—when thou comes here we can give thee an example of Quaker simplicity. I rejoice however that thou wast willing to deliver that lecture."

Elizabeth Stanton could not get away from her baby boys to come, and Lucretia was soon engrossed in preparing for the Annual Anti-Slavery Fair, as well as in her sewing rooms for poor women. In January Elizabeth Cavender's first son, Henry, was born, and in March, Thomas and Marianne had a second daughter, Emily. She now had ten grandchildren, Lucretia wrote the Webbs.

The week after Emily's birth an exciting event at the antislavery office claimed Lucretia's attention. For some time William Still, black clerk in the office, had been orchestrating the operation of the underground railroad as it passed through Philadelphia. Miller McKim and William Still were at the office when a box arrived. An escaping slave from Richmond, Virginia, had hit upon the scheme of being placed in it and shipped as goods to Philadelphia. They were delighted to find the man still alive, although he was very hungry and thirsty after his ordeal. After a breakfast and bath at the McKims he was brought to the house on North Ninth to tell his story to the Motts.

"His master is a rich man—employs an overseer, heartless as such generally are," Lucretia wrote a friend. "He was never whipped however—He was employed twisting tobacco and yielded his master $200 or more per year—He had a wife and 3 children sold from him a year ago—after their owner (not his master) had promised to let him purchase them . . . a higher offer inducing him to do so. This almost broke his heart—but from that time he resolved on obtaining his own freedom."

After telling his story the man, forever known thereafter as "Box Brown," was taken to a place of safety.

In June Lucretia made her annual trip to Auburn. Martha and David Wright by now had six children in addition to Martha's firstborn, Marianne Pelham Mott. Their second son, Mathew Tallman, did not get along with his father. Lucretia, who was rather free with advice to various members of her family, counseled David to be patient with him, but relations were growing worse. She decided, therefore, to invite Tallman to live with her and James in Philadelphia for a while.

The summer of 1849 was unusually hot and muggy, even for Philadelphia. On her return from upper New York State, Tallman in tow, Lucretia found cholera raging in the city. Her sister Eliza Yarnell's cook was ill, her cousin Mary Earle's lawyer husband had the disease; several elderly Quakers had died. Lucretia was concerned, but not particularly worried about her family. She felt sure that cholera could be prevented by paying attention to diet and sanitation, avoiding walking in the hot sun, and not giving way to "morbid fear."

On July 11 her fifty-one-year-old bachelor brother, Thomas Coffin, decided to walk from Third and Pine to the Schuylkill, although he had been ill with diarrhea. On his way back he collapsed and was taken to his rooming house. Lucretia was summoned. She immediately called a doctor and hired a nurse to help her take care of the sick man. Despite their best efforts he rapidly became dehydrated, his temperature rose, he went into shock, and within less than twenty-four hours he died.

Once more Lucretia Mott faced a deep and devastating sense of loss. Although her family was large, each member was of great importance to her. Now that Thomas was gone, she began to think of all the things she might have done to make his life happier. To assuage her grief, she decided to serve as undertaker, laying him out herself and dressing him for burial.

"Art thou sad and sorrowing my precious sister as I am?" she wrote Martha. "Such useless regrets and vain longings are my lot, that I am all the time wanting some one to dwell with me on the events of those few hours."

To avoid the cholera, Maria and Edward Davis moved to Germantown for a few weeks, leaving empty bedrooms at the North Ninth Street house. Hearing about an English mother with seven children, the Vines, who were stranded in Philadelphia, Lucretia decided to invite them to stay with the Motts for several weeks. Her daughters objected, and Sarah Pugh tried to take several of the children herself, but Lucretia would have none of it. With eight extra people to take care of, she was busy enough to blunt the pain of Thomas's death. To top it off, her servant, Matilda, became ill, and Lucretia had to nurse her.

"I ironed 4 doz. [sheets] this morng," she wrote Martha using her own inimitable shorthand, "—made soft custard, attended to stewg blackberries, potted some dutch herring of wh. Jas got a kid; besides all the dustg-sweepg the ding room etc Anne and Eliza Needles called, while thus engaged, Mary Needles sat an hour here lately & had much to say of her likg for Thomas, as well as their sadness at their loss. I was more tired when our family 13 in number gathered to dinner than since I came home.... one of the little Vines was taken with symptoms of dysentery...Dr. Griscom attended her, injections administered—all of which cause steps, a few, but glad are we to have them here."

She had been to call on Mary Earle, whose husband had died, she told Martha, but had been glad to get away. "Grief has not the effect on our cousin to make her silent." Still, she had invited Mary home for dinner and had taken her with her to call upon another bereaved family who required Lucretia's spiritual services. "Poor cousin Mary, being a widow too, took possession of the large rocking chair," Lucretia commented laconically.

By fall the epidemic was over, and the city was slowly returning to normal. Lucretia once more wrote to Elizabeth Stanton urging her to come to Philadelphia and help organize a woman's rights convention. At the same time she looked for a job in a local dry goods store for two young neighbors of Elizabeth's who, inspired by Seneca Falls, had decided to go into merchandising. Philadelphia had some successful women merchants in this period, and Lucretia was eager to extend the number.

Her concern to get women equal pay in education, born long ago at Nine Partners, was still strong. In October Horace Mann came to the City of Brotherly Love to attend a national educational convention designed to promote public schools. Lucretia was unable to attend the early sessions, since "the slave having first claim," she went to the Pennsylvania Anti-Slavery Society meeting in Norristown instead. She heard, however, that a resolution had been offered to the convention stating that no difference should be made on account of sex but that it was defeated when Bishop Alonzo Potter objected that "women were inferior by nature, and the object of the convention should go no farther than to seek to qualify her for her true position—

domestic life." As soon as she could get away from Norristown, Lucretia hurried to the conference, determined "to say a word for woman." Unfortunately Bishop Potter was too quick with the concluding prayer, and she missed her chance.

"The convention will assemble here next year," she wrote Elizabeth Stanton, "and then if life and health are spared, the latter rather failing now, see what we women will do!"

She kept up her campaign. A few years later Horace Mann wrote to his wife that the spirit of Philadelphia women was very intense and the Lucretia Mott was "too ambitious because she claimed for woman all the highest things in all departments." Yet she must have made a deep impression, for shortly after Horace Mann founded Antioch College in Yellow Springs, Ohio, he invited Lucretia Mott to be a lecturer.

Later, in the fall of 1849, Richard Henry Dana, Sr., a poet and essayist, and father of the author of *Two Years Before the Mast,* came to Philadelphia to deliver several lectures. One of these he called "An Address on Woman," and in it he launched an attack on the new woman's rights movement as being a threat to conventional society. Lucretia was appalled by the speech; she went up to Richard Dana afterward and told him she thoroughly disagreed with him. Unaccustomed to such forthrightness, Dana blushed, sputtered, and turned away. Lucretia did not pursue him, but when several prominent Philadelphians asked her if she would reply to the attack, she was happy to say yes. Her speech, "Discourse on Woman," was delivered December 17, 1849. A reporter took it down verbatim, and it was afterward published as a pamphlet.

Although she had not prepared an address and spoke as usual from inspiration, the speech was carefully reasoned. Lucretia first advanced all the scriptural arguments for the equality of men and women, beginning with the Garden of Eden, naming the prophets and leaders among women of the Old Testament, enumerating the allusions to equality in the preaching of Jesus. As for Saint Paul's injunction against women preaching in church, it could be explained by the excited conditions of that particular church at that particular time. Elsewhere, Saint Paul had set forth a list of regulations for women to follow when—*not if*—they preached and prophesied.

Moving from ancient history to modern times, Lucretia scoffed at the idea that women should avoid being active in reform movements for fear of being thought mannish. "So far from her 'ambition leading her to act the man,' she needs all the encouragement she can receive, by the removal of obstacles from her path, in order that she may become a true woman. As it is desirable a man should act a manly and generous part, and not mannish, so let woman be urged to exercise a dignified and womanly bearing, not womanish...True, nature had made a difference in her configuration, her physical strength, her voice —and we ask no change, we are satisfied with nature. But how neglect and mismanagement increased the difference!"

Quoting extensively from Catherine Beecher, the advocate of education for women, Lucretia urged the development of women's mental powers and their admission to the professions. Then men might no longer be forced to devote all their energies to business to support idle, fashionable women. With her usual optimism she informed her audience that a new generation of women were now on the scene, entering science and medicine, preferring lectures to sickly, sentimental novels, and following the examples of such reforming women as Elizabeth Fry and Dorothea Dix without sacrificing their womanly dignity. If men were to receive public praise, then why not praise equally such women as Mary Somerville, Caroline Herschel, or Maria Mitchell of her own Nantucket for their scientific achievements?

"The question is often asked, 'What does woman want more than she enjoys? What is she seeking to obtain? Of what rights is she deprived? What privileges are withheld from her?' I answer, she asks nothing as a favor, but as a right, she wants to be acknowledged a moral, responsible being. She is seeking not to be governed by laws in the making of which she has no voice."

Many women did not share these sentiments, Lucretia acknowledged. They had learned to hug their chains. Woman must therefore be placed in such a situation that through the recognition of her rights and the opportunity for growth and development she would come to appreciate the blessings of freedom. This meant the removal of roadblocks. She must be given suffrage; laws giving her husband entire control over her personal property must be repealed; she must obtain access to the education for which her tax dollars are now paid.

"Let woman then go on—not asking favors, but claiming as a right the removal of all hindrances to her elevation in the scale of being—let her receive encouragement for the proper cultivation of her powers, so that she may enter profitably into the active business of life."

The speech was well received, but with Lucretia Mott it was action that mattered more than words. When she spoke of removing obstacles from the path of women's entering the professions, she had a concrete case in mind. She had become deeply concerned about the troubles women who sought medical training were currently experiencing. Elizabeth Blackwell had finally earned a medical degree, but there were many others to whom this was denied. Among these was Ann Preston, a Chester County Quaker and a good friend. Lucretia and James were therefore delighted when William Mullen, a Quaker businessman with a wife who was interested in medicine, proposed the establishment of a Female Medical College of Pennsylvania. They helped to raise money during the winter months of 1849–50, and when the school opened its doors in October 1850, James sat on the board. In December 1851 Lucretia attended the commencement exercises. Among the graduates were Dr. Ann Preston and Dr. Hannah Longshore, also a Quaker and friend of the Motts. The happy occasion was marred by demonstrations outside so violent that the police had to be called. Male medical students objected passionately to the entry of females into the profession.

This was just the beginning of the troubles of the "lady doctors," many of them Quakers. When they attempted to attend the teaching clinics in the hospitals, they were jeered at and mobbed. The American Medical Association protested against the "lady doctors," and the graduates could find few patients. Lucretia stood by them as best she could during this stormy time. In the spring of 1852 she agreed to preside over a series of public lectures on health and hygiene, to be presented by Dr. Hannah Longshore. It was considered a dangerous step, but Lucretia's presence lent it enough respectability that a few proper Philadelphians attended. The lectures were interesting; each time there were more people in the audience. Gradually several male doctors decided to slip into the back of the room. The suspicion that the women doctors might know something after all about treating female disorders began to be entertained. A few patients, and then a few more, were actually referred by their physicians to Dr. Longshore.

A few years later Ann Preston became the dean of the Female Medical College, and the founder of Woman's Hospital in Philadelphia. She also became Lucretia's favorite personal physician.

Another enterprise in which Lucretia was interested at this time was the founding of the School of Design for Women, now Moore College of Art. Lucretia's Quaker background and education had given her a poor opinion of art per se, but her sister Martha's art studies, as well as the interest of her own Maria, had modified her prejudices. Both she and James helped to raise money for the new institution.

Lucretia believed that most women would soon cease to "hug their chains" and would join the cause. To a regional woman's rights conference meeting in Salem, Ohio, she sent a spirited message urging women not to "ask as a favor, but demand as a right, that every civil and ecclesiastical obstacle be removed." At the First National Woman's Rights Convention, held in Worcester, Massachusetts, in October 1850, Wendell Phillips predicted that women would be worse enemies to the cause than men. Lucretia corrected him sharply.

"She put, as she well knows how, the silken snapper on her whiplash, and proceeded to give me the gentlest and yet most cutting rebuke. 'Twas like her old fire when the London Quakers angered her gentleness—and beautifully done, so the victim himself could enjoy the artistic perfection of his punishment," Wendell Phillips wrote to Elizabeth Pease.

At Worcester Lucretia met a young woman who was to be her friend and colleague for many years. She was Lucy Stone, a school teacher and graduate of Oberlin College, who had been recruited for antislavery lecturing by Abby Kelley Foster. From the beginning Lucy had combined concern for the condition of women with her abolitionist position. After Worcester she devoted herself entirely to the woman's cause.

During these early years of the woman's rights movement, Lucretia Mott evidently believed that she would be able to help launch the movement, then retire to the position of senior advisor. She was, after all, in her late fifties, a generation older than Elizabeth Cady Stanton and most of the other pioneers. Moreover, she had done her share of pioneering years ago, speaking before promiscuous audiences and bearing the brunt of the wrath at the London Convention. Now she was deeply committed to the antislavery struggle as well as to a half dozen other reforms. It did not seem possible that she could give time to this new movement.

Nevertheless, because of her national stature she was by far the principal personage in the infant woman's rights struggle, and her gentle authority was badly needed to defend it from the attacks of its detractors as well as to restrain some of the excesses of its well-wishers. For the next thirty years she was to try, time and time again, to encourage younger women to take her place, only to be catapulted back onto center stage. There is no question that her role was crucial in the development of the movement, not only for the obvious leadership she gave but for the nurturing care—the encouragement, the advice, the criticism—she provided to Elizabeth Cady Stanton, Susan B. Anthony, Lucy Stone, and a host of others whose names are now part of American history.

CHAPTER
XIII

TIME
OF MANY TRIALS

In January 1851 James Mott retired from the wool business. At sixty-two, after all the years of worrying, he was finally in comfortable circumstances and hale and hearty, although white-haired. He had time to devote his leisure to his many committees and to accompany his enchanting wife.

Although Lucretia was many times a grandmother, she was determined to keep her family about her. The clan now swarmed from North Ninth Street to a larger establishment between Eleventh and Twelfth on Arch. Here Lucretia had a thirty-foot-long dining room for her immense dinner parties and a large front parlor where she could tack down bright new carpets to her heart's content. A visitor described the new house as "bright and cheery, quite gay for a Friend's, with tasteful, elegant furniture."

Into 338 Arch moved Thomas and Marianne Mott with their two little girls, and Maria and Edward Davis with Anna, Henry, and a new baby, Willie. Willie's birth in February 1850 had been followed tragically by the death of five-year-old Charlie Davis a few weeks later. Lucretia had helped to lay out the small body and to comfort Maria, but she refused to attribute the death of this beloved grandson to the ways of Providence. Rather she thought such deaths came from "ignorance of natural laws and our failure to observe them."

Two other members of the Mott household at the time were Tallman and Eliza Wright, Martha's two oldest children. The Motts had helped Tallman find a job, but his parents worried over his frittering away his salary on clothes and knickknacks. Lucretia tried to play the role of peacemaker, but Tallman was unhappy, and in March 1851 he ran away to California.

At about the same time that they moved to Arch Street, Thomas Mott and Edward Davis together bought a farm in Chelten Hills, north of the city, where the whole family might go for cool air and quiet in the summer. James Mott had always had a secret hankering to be a farmer; now during the long months at Oak Farm he could indulge his interest. Lucretia enjoyed the country and preserving country food, but worried rather perversely that people would think the family "clannish" for spending its vacations together.

National events were meanwhile transpiring that would prevent the Motts, as well as other abolitionists, from enjoying much rest and quiet for many years to come. The passage of the Fugitive Slave Act of 1850, as part of the compromise of that year, made the situation of the fleeing slaves more perilous and subjected those who aided them to a one-thousand-dollar fine or six months in prison. The abolitionists regarded the new law as evil and unjust, and many of them pledged themselves to disobey it. "Bear your testimony against this unjust and cruel edict," James Mott advised members of the Pennsylvania Anti-Slavery Society in February 1851. For many Garrisonians this pledge to civil disobedience was simply an extension of their long-term commitment to nonresistance. Other abolitionists, however, had never before broken a law, and the Fugitive Slave Act had a radicalizing effect upon their lives.

In September 1851 the Pennsylvania abolitionists were swept into the storm center by a dramatic series of events occurring in Christiana, a small town in Lancaster County. Here William Parker, an escaped slave, had organized the blacks in Sadsbury township for mutual self-defense. When Edward Gorsuch, a Maryland slave owner, came with a party of relatives and neighbors and a U.S. marshal to hunt for four escaped slaves, Parker concealed the fugitives in his house and led an armed defense against the Southerners. In the middle of the predawn struggle three white neighbors arrived on horseback in response to an appeal for help from the blacks. When ordered by the federal marshal to assist in the recapture of the slaves, they refused to do so. After they had left the scene, there was an outbreak of shooting, in which the slave owner was killed and his son seriously wounded.

This was the first case of a Southerner, in pursuit of his slaves, being shot on Northern soil. The reaction of the South was swift and angry. The federal government, fearful that the Compromise of 1850 might come apart, decided to make an example of the three nonresisters by trying them for treason against the United States, on the claim that their act had constituted making war upon the federal government. The blacks who participated in the riot were also so charged. There was some uncertainty about which of the blacks in the surrounding area these were. The authorities were not fussy; they simply wanted a good number brought to trial. For several days armed posses scoured the countryside in search of likely blacks, hunting them, as one abolitionist claimed, "like partridges upon the mountain." Finally the three white men, Castner Hanway, a miller, Elijah Lewis, a shopkeeper, and Joseph Scarlett, a farmer (the latter two Quakers), along with thirty-eight blacks, were arrested and taken to Moyamensing Prison to await trial. William Parker, the black hero of the attempted rescue, escaped to Canada.

In prison the three white prisoners were made fairly comfortable, but the blacks were crowded into ill-heated, ill-ventilated cells. September 12 and 13, when most of them had been picked up, had been warm, and the majority were dressed in scant workclothes. As the fall progressed and the cold weather came, their situation grew increasingly miserable. Hearing of their plight, Lucretia and the women of the Philadelphia Female Anti-Slavery Society took on the job of providing them with clean, warm clothing. By the time they came to trial, in late November, all were outfitted. On Saturday, December 6, when they were brought into the docket to be identified, several reporters noticed that the black prisoners wore identical costumes and appeared to have been recently bathed and shaved. Each man wore a red, white, and blue scarf around his neck. Lucretia Mott and several other Quaker women were seen in the audience, knitting furiously. They did not so much as glance at their protégés, but it was clear to the reporters that they were responsible for the appearance of the prisoners.

The charge of treason, hastily arrived at for political reasons, could not be proved, and Castner Hanway, whose case was tried first, was declared not guilty, although the presiding judge, John Kane, took the opportunity to deliver himself of the opinion that the whole unfortunate affair was the fault of the meddlesome abolitionists and "itinerant female agitators." He also refused the request of the defense that the court pay Hanway's expenses.

The trial had been expensive, and Hanway, ill and poor, had no way to meet the bill. The Pennsylvania Anti-Slavery Society and the Philadelphia Female Anti-Slavery Society contributed as much as they could afford.

Far more important than its effect on the exchequer of the Pennsylvania abolitionists, the affair at Christiana opened a debate that was to continue for another fifteen years. What should be the attitude of the abolitionists toward those blacks who took up arms in their own defense? In their original Declaration of Sentiment the members of the American Anti-Slavery Society had pledged themselves to work with moral arms alone and to influence the oppressed to do the same. If they aided those, black or white, who used violence to accomplish their same ends, were they not violating this pledge?

For pacifists like James and Lucretia Mott, the events at Christiana demanded careful thought. They must continue to fight with nonviolent weapons alone, but could they in truth make the same demand of the blacks, who had spent their life under the threat of the lash, confined to a system of slavery that was enforced in the last resort by federal bayonets? The question was to perplex Lucretia for many years. Too honest with herself to have a simple and glib solution, she puzzled time and again over the root problem, whether good could in fact ever come out of evil?

By the fall of 1852 the Pennsylvania abolitionists had had a full year to reflect on the meaning of Christiana, and lines were firmly drawn. At the annual meeting of the Pennsylvania Anti-Slavery Society, debate opened over the question of accepting the annual report, which included a glowing account of the action at Christiana. After Charles Burleigh moved that the report should be published, Lucretia Mott objected, saying it was open to criticism. Thomas Whitson also objected to the report because it said that good could come from evil. "Had the colored men not shot Edward Gorsuch it would have told more for freedom than it did tell.''

Charles Burleigh countered by reminding listeners that Harriet Beecher Stowe had been moved to write *Uncle Tom's Cabin*, recently serialized in the *National Era*, by the Fugitive Slave Act. Was this not an example of good coming out of evil? Lucretia disagreed. Good could only come from the Infinite Source of Good, she argued. To attribute good to evil was to open up a controversy without end. ''I am not willing to admit that Harriet Beecher Stowe was moved to write Uncle Tom's Cabin by that law; if she says so, I think she mistakes the influence that moved her. I believe rather that it has been the moral sentiments and truth promulgated by the *Liberator*, the *National Era*, and the public discussion of the subject upon her pure mind exciting it to feel for the oppressed.''

It was the first of many battles in which Lucretia was to advocate reliance on moral weapons, not just because she believed them to be right but also because she believed them to be the most effective in a battle for the hearts and minds of men and women.

This belief caused Lucretia Mott to take strong, sometimes even rigid, positions on the questions troubling the abolitionists of the period. She had objected when British abolitionists bought the freedom of Frederick Douglass, and she continued to be absolutely opposed to the efforts of some kind-hearted abolitionist to assure the freedom of this or that slave by buying him from the slave owner. She even went so far at times as to express the view that aiding fugitives was not the proper work of the antislavery societies, although members might do it personally, as she herself did. ''When we add all those who settle in Canada and Liberia it is not as many as are born into slavery each year,'' she told her sister Female Society members. ''Our efforts must still be to destroy the system, root and branch. To lay the axe at the foot of the corrupt tree.'' The best means to do this, she still believed, was to boycott slave products.

The usual stream of visitors were finding their way to the new house on Arch Street, among them a number of female lecturers. Lucretia was interested in them all, but her heart was with Elizabeth Cady Stanton and the new woman's rights movement. She was discouraged by the slowness of Philadelphia women to respond to the new issue. The few reform-minded women like herself were already overcommitted; the majority of Quakers still preferred "to keep in the quiet." "With the exception of a few radical Quakers—Hicksites—whose names are cast out as evil, there is too much darkness on the subject to bear such a glare as a national Convention would throw out," she wrote Elizabeth in the fall of 1851. "We must labor more in a smaller way. We want forerunners to come 'crying in the wilderness.' "

By June 1852 she and Mary Grew had managed to develop enough interest to hold a regional convention in West Chester, Pennsylvania. Lucretia gave the keynote address, an optimistic overview of the rapid progress of the women's movement and a defense of its growing militancy. To right wrongs, she said, you have to identify the oppressor. This had proved true in the antislavery struggle, and it would prove true in the women's struggle.

"Woman is told that the fault is in herself, in too willingly submitting to her inferior condition; but like the slave, she is pressed down by laws in the making of which she had no voice, and crushed by customs that have grown out of such laws. She can not rise therefore, while thus trampled in the dust. The oppressor does not see himself in the light until the oppressed cry for deliverance." She pointed out that progress had been made in the laws in New York State and in the fields of medicine and design only because woman was willing to contend earnestly for her rights.

Buoyed up by the response to the West Chester Meeting, Lucretia wrote to Lucy Stone that she was willing to go to the next national convention, to be held in Syracuse in September, but that she would certainly not preside. When the vote was called in Syracuse, however, all but one person voted for Lucretia Mott to take the chair. The exception was James Mott, who was worried about his wife's health and wanted to spare her the job. He was correct to be worried, for the session proved a stormy and taxing one. Several outspoken critics of woman's rights were present. Among them was J. B. Brigham, a New York schoolteacher, who was afraid the women were unfit for the roles they were assuming. Lucretia vacated the chair to answer him, on both religious and moral grounds. As for women's voices being too weak to be heard, did Mr. Brigham send a protest to England about Queen Victoria addressing Parliament?

Later in the meeting, when her friend and colleague Antoinette Brown, an Oberlin graduate and ordained minister, introduced a resolution on the biblical justification for woman's rights, she again vacated the chair to oppose it. In the antislavery movement much time had been wasted by both sides claiming that the Bible backed their position. It was better to let self-evident truth win its own arguments. "It is not to be supposed that all the advice given by the apostles to the women of their day is applicable to our more intelligent age; nor is there any passage in Scripture making these texts binding upon us."

During the same session the Reverend Junius Hatch, a Congregational minister from Connecticut, repeated an earlier accusation that the officers of the convention did not believe in the paramount authority of the Bible and were therefore infidel. When this argument was countered by Lucretia and others, he then turned to an attack on the women's modesty, claiming that they were trying to bring attention to themselves. To illustrate, he repeated some "coarse remarks" made by a group of men who stood by the door and watched the women come and go. Lucretia reproved him, but he continued in this vein until there were shocked murmurs from the audience. She then remarked tartly that the women present should keep their dignity, even if the speaker could not. When he still continued, she called him to order sharply and told him to terminate his remarks. The *Pennsylvania Freeman*, in its coverage of the meeting, said it had never before witnessed such firm and efficient control.

But if the *Freeman* was enthusiastic, other papers were busy attacking the convention itself. The *New York Herald*, edited by James Gordon Bennett, was the most vociferous: "The farce at Syracuse has been played out. We publish today the last act, in which it will be seen that the authority of the Bible as a perfect rule of faith and practice for human beings was voted down, and what are called the laws of nature set up instead of the Christian code.'' The offensive remarks of the Reverend Mr. Hatch were a direct result of the women inviting discussion of sexual differences in the first place, he charged.

Syracuse was the first Woman's Rights convention attended by Susan B. Anthony, a sharp-featured Hicksite school teacher. A friend of Lucy Stone, Abby Kelley Foster, and Elizabeth Cady Stanton, Susan soon won Lucretia's heart for her enthusiasm and courage in the face of public hostility. Opposition to the woman's movement was becoming stronger with each passing year. The adoption of the bloomer costume, a short skirt worn over full trousers, by some of the early feminists, and its promotion by Amelia Bloomer, editor of the *Lily*, gave critical newspaper editors an excuse for further ridicule. The fact that a great many women did not understand, and in fact feared, the demand for more rights was used by both pastors and journalists as proof that the militant women were ''unsexed.'' Since abolitionists, temperance, and woman's rights workers all tended to support each other, the three became linked in the public mind as common evils. In New York City particularly, the Democrats, under the leadership of Tammany Hall, opposed the abolitionists and their fellow travelers. Capt. Isaiah Rynders and his sporting-club mob began to show up at every meeting.

In the spring of 1853 a World's Temperance Convention was held in New York City. When its clerical leadership refused to give the women present a voice in the proceedings, Susan B. Anthony, Abby Kelley Foster, and Antoinette Brown led a group of feminist men and women in withdrawing. Subsequently they planned a Whole World's Temperance Convention—including the half of the world's population who were women—in New York, in September.

Lucretia missed the spring excitement. Early in May, Sojourner Truth came to Philadelphia to speak to the Philadelphia Female Society and to stay with the Motts. Sojourner had barely left when Yearly Meeting brought the usual flock of Quaker guests, invited and uninvited. Meanwhile Lucretia was getting ready for the marriage of her youngest daughter, Pattie, to George Lord, a bank clerk. Since George was no Quaker, the wedding was to be held at home, and Pattie was subsequently disowned by the Friends. Lucretia was becoming resigned to seeing her children slipping away one by one from the Society of Friends.

Antislavery Friends in Chester County, tired of fighting the conservatism of the Society, had organized The Progressive Friends of Longwood, which followed some Quaker procedures but was not truly a Quaker body. Lucretia was tempted to join the new group. Yet, as she wrote the Webbs, "our young people have little interest in these reorganizations and without their co-operation they must die out." So although the Motts attended the Longwood Meeting, they did not join.

There was a hint of sadness in Lucretia's letter to the Webbs. Although Ann Hopper ran the antislavery fairs, and Edward Davis supported Lucretia in most of her causes, her children and grandchildren did not feel the loyalty to the old traditions of the Society of Friends that was deep in Lucretia. Nor had she succeeded in sharing with them the sources of her spiritual strength.

After Pattie's wedding, Lucretia went to Auburn in July to visit Martha. The Wright household was happy because Tall-man, the prodigal son, had returned from California for a visit and was considering settling down and managing the farm for his father. Lucretia also visited with Elizabeth Cady Stanton, who was once more confined home with a new baby. After a string of boys she had given birth to a "noble girl" the previous November, delivering the baby herself with the help of a mid-wife and sitting up immediately afterward. Lucretia admired her young friend's spirit and wanted to see the new addition.

A busy fall of meetings and travels began the first week of September in New York. At the Whole World's Temperance Convention Lucretia spoke of the underlying unity of all reforms, and Antoinette Brown preached to five thousand. This seemed to touch off the riots, led by the Rynders mob. Lucretia had agreed to preside at the next event, the New York Woman's Rights Convention, at Broadway Tabernacle. It was at this meeting that Lucretia Mott met Captain Rynders face to face.

After this long, hot, tiring week in New York, Lucretia was no doubt delighted to set out with James on a long overland journey. Traveling was always a rest and a joy to her, perhaps some of her mariner ancestors' zest for adventure was appeased in this fashion. She loved the countryside, the people, and most of all the long days of silent companionship with James.

In Cleveland the Fourth National Woman's Rights Convention was being held. In her opening speech Lucretia referred to the opposition of women to the movement. That very day a woman in a fashionable hotel had commented to Lucretia that the bloomer costume was "an insult to decency." Yet how was this woman dressed? "Why, laced so tight she could scarcely breathe, and her clothes so long that when she went out into the dusty streets her garments formed a kind of broom to gather up the dust. This is beautiful? This is fashionable?"

Citing the mental development of her Nantucket foremothers, which she credited to their opportunity to take responsibility, Lucretia predicted that woman would continue to advance as the roadblocks were removed from her path. At the same time, she warned that exaggerated claims ought not to be made for her: "It has sometimes been said that if women were associated with men in their efforts, there would be not as much immorality as now exists in Congress, for instance, and other places. But we ought, I think, to claim no more for woman than for man; we ought to put woman on a par with man, not invest her with power, or call for her superiority over her brother. If we do, she is just as likely to become a tyrant as man is, as with Catherine the Second. It is always unsafe to invest man with power over his fellow being. 'Call no man master...' is a true doctrine. But be sure there would be a better rule than now; the elements which belong to woman as such and to man as such, would be beautifully and harmoniously blended. It is to be hoped that there would be less war, injustice, and intolerance in the world than now."

Later in the convention, a long debate arose over the biblical soundness of woman's rights. A Dr. Nevins rose repeatedly to urge women to remain under the protection of their husbands and fathers. Finally Lucretia could stand it no more.

"We ought to thank Dr. Nevins for his kindly fears," she said, "lest we women be brought out into the rough conflicts of life, and overwhelmed by infidelity. I thank him, but at the same time I must say that if we have been able this afternoon to sit uninjured by the hard conflict in which he has been engaged, if we can maintain our patience at seeing him so laboriously build a man of straw and then throw it down and destroy it, I think we may be suffered to go into the world and bear many others unharmed."

After the Cleveland meetings were over, the Motts and Martha Wright visited Folger relatives across Ohio. From Cincinnati the party went by riverboat to Maysville, Kentucky, on the Ohio River. The trip lasted from eleven in the morning until ten at night, but Lucretia found the ever-changing scenes along the shore interesting. At Maysville they were met by John Pelham, a brother of Martha's first husband, and taken by horse and carriage through the moonlit night to his large home.

In preparation for Lucretia's arrival a large public meeting had been organized for the following afternoon. Fearing that she might speak on slavery, a local official had written to her to say that she was expected to speak "especially on the peaceful doctrines of Jesus of Nazareth and George Fox." Fearing that this hint would not be enough, John Pelham spoke privately to Martha, urging her to influence her sister to avoid the controversial subject of slavery and stick to religious themes. "But slavery is a religious subject," Martha told him. She did not repeat the request to Lucretia.

Lucretia had, of course, every intention of using the occasion to speak on slavery. On the afternoon of October 16 she addressed a large crowd on "the subjects of theology, war, temperance, and slavery for an hour and a half." According to a local newspaper report, she "enchained an ordinarily restless audience." At the close of this first talk she calmly announced another meeting for that night on the subject of woman's rights. An even larger crowd came to hear her. Lucretia felt that the experiment of speaking gospel truth to the slaveholder had been such a success that she urged Lucy Stone to follow her to Maysville to speak on woman's rights.

At the Cleveland woman's rights meeting, Lucretia had been appointed to a committee to gather information on the educational and business opportunities open to American women. As soon as she got home from her long trip, and reported on it to the Pennsylvania Anti-Slavery Society's annual meeting, she developed a questionnaire on the subject. The advancement of women both in education and in the trades and professions continued to appeal to her practical mind as the best way to remove "roadblocks."

In the spring of 1854 she reported to Thomas Wentworth Higginson, a journalist and feminist, who chaired the committee, that she had employed a person to collect facts on the employment of women in Philadelphia, but the results were disappointing. "Pennsylvania is always slow to work in any progressive or new movement." She noted that many women were employed in retail dry goods stores in Philadelphia, but that they, and the teachers, received half the salary of men. "In our Model & Normal Public School in this city—the Male principal's salary was $1200—the Female's $500—the latter performing a greater task—and giving greater satisfaction—some change was lately made in the school arrangements and the salary of the Female was reduced to $300, the $200 taken from her was added to his."

In October 1854 the Fifth National Woman's Rights Convention was held in Philadelphia, with a program emphasizing equal rights in education and the professions. Lucretia continued to fear that her hometown was too backward to respond well to a national gathering, and she wrote urging all her friends to come, and to stay with the Motts. Would not Elizabeth Cady Stanton come and bring that noble girl baby? Couldn't Elizabeth Neall Gay get away from her endless domesticity for a bit? Despite her fears, there was a good attendance, and the sessions went smoothly. The chief source of annoyance was Mary Grew's aged father, Henry Grew, who came to repeat all his old arguments against women preaching. Mr. Grew did not take the Bible altogether to be his guide, Lucretia pointed out tartly. Else why, in opposition to Saint Paul's strictures against marriage, had he taken a second wife?

Present for the convention and staying with the Motts was Mary Frame Thomas, currently studying medicine in Cleveland. Chatting one day, she and Lucretia were startled to see a black man dash in off the street and crouch behind a chair in the parlor. Outside was a mob in hot pursuit. A leader of the mob came to the door and told James Mott that if he would give up the man, the crowd would disperse. Lucretia, who had joined her husband, asked, "What has the Negro done? If he has committed a crime there is a way to prove it and do him justice. Thou canst not take him out of our house without proper authority." After further discussion it was decided that James and the leader of the mob would accompany the black man to the police station. "Are you not afraid for James?" Mary Thomas asked Lucretia. "No, nothing will harm my husband," she replied. "He is doing right, and is so well known that he will be a protection to the poor man."

The next year the Motts were involved in a spectacular slave rescue. Jane Johnson, a Virginia slave, came to Philadelphia with her master, John W. Wheeler, the United States ambassador to Nicaragua. With her were her two children. According to an ancient Pennslyvania law, after having lived in the state for six months, she would be free. Passmore Williamson, a Quaker abolitionist, informed her of this fact and, working with William Still and the Vigilance Committee, helped to find a safe hiding place for her after she walked away from Wheeler's house. Unable to find her, her angry master brought charges against Williamson, Still, and five others under the Fugitive Slave Act. In the course of the ensuing trial, the defense attorney thought it would help if Jane Johnson could herself appear to testify that she had not been persuaded to run away but had made her own decision after Williamson presented all the facts. Accordingly, she was taken from her hiding place by members of the Vigilance Committee and brought to court. Lucretia Mott accompanied her and, when her testimony was completed, brought her back to the house on Arch Street.

"We didn't drive slow coming home," Lucretia wrote her sister Martha. "Miller and an officer—Jane and self—another carriage following the four officers for protection—and all with the knowledge of the State's attorney—Miller and the slave passed quickly through our house up Cuthbert Street to the same carriage—which drove around to elude pursuit. I ran to the store room and filling my arms with crackers and peaches ran after them and had only time to throw them into the carriage."

Jane and her protectors evaded pursuit, and Jane was never recaptured. Passmore Williamson and William Still, however, were found guilty of aiding in her escape. Lucretia considered the decision of the presiding judge, John Kane, an abomination. She attended an indignation meeting and worked with the Philadelphia Female Anti-Slavery Society to prepare a protest. Her youngest daughter, Pattie, was home expecting her first child, and Lucretia felt she could not be away from home for very long at a time, but she flew in and out. She decided to attend all the Quaker Monthly Meetings, both Orthodox and Hicksite, to persuade them to lodge a protest against Kane and a statement upholding Passmore. She was, as usual, doomed to disappointment. The amazing part is that she kept trying.

The causes to which she was dedicating her life—freedom for the slave and equality for women—were indivisible, Lucretia Mott was discovering. There was no use trying to concentrate on one or the other; both required total dedication. In the five years following the passage of the Fugitive Slave Law, public anger over the antislavery agitation spilled over into fury at the woman's rights movement. The radical reformers went from one crisis to the next without letup. Powered by her sense of walking in the Light, Lucretia Mott used every scrap of time and energy responding to the myriad calls upon her leadership.

XIV

THE
MOTHER
OF EQUAL RIGHTS

IN 1855 Lucretia Mott was sixty-two. She was still a striking-looking woman with dark hair, flashing eyes, and rosy cheeks, but in deep shadows around the corners of her mouth lurked the pain of stress and constant indigestion.

The pace she kept was now exacting its price. She was frequently doubled over with dyspepsia and was beginning, as well, to have problems with her back, the first symptoms, probably, of osteoporosis. Yet she never let illness interfere with her obligations. She brushed over the remonstrances of her family and set out, sick as a dog, on long, tiring journeys that a man or woman twice her size and half her years might have dreaded, with the cheerful assurance that she would be fine again shortly.

For more than twenty years her life had revolved around the antislavery movement. Now that it was no longer the concern of a few fanatics but the subject of national debate, to drop out would be unthinkable. And the new woman's rights movement would not leave her alone, nor would her own conscience permit her to refuse to participate, although she occasionally resolved to do so. Elizabeth Cady Stanton, Lucy Stone, and Susan B. Anthony continued to turn to her for counsel and advice and to beg her to chair the public meetings, where her calm authority helped to keep order and give a better image to the new movement. She had, as Elizabeth Cady Stanton once said, "a playful way of tapping a speaker in a public meeting, as a skillful driver touches his horses with the tip of his whip," using raillery, which silenced the most determined critics without offending anyone.

Lucretia had once resolved that at sixty she would give up

both preaching and public speaking and let the many younger and more able women in both the Society of Friends and the reform movements take her place. She had noticed how many elderly Quakers went on speaking in Meeting after their voices had become cracked and their messages routine, and she was resolved not to make the same mistake. She remembered, too, her mother's admonition, "Nobody wants to hear old folk talk." She sometimes disappointed herself. When she heard that Lucy Stone was discouraged by her speaking, she sympathized. "Don't I know her feelings! How often have I said let the earth open up and receive poor mortified me."

Yet now that she was past sixty, letters of invitation were pouring in from all over the east and even Ohio, and she found it difficult to refuse after all. She had a realistic view of her own abilities. She knew she was neither the most brilliant nor the most eloquent of the leaders of the woman's rights movement. "I am a much over-rated woman," she often said. But she also knew that she could stir her listeners as none of the others could. This capacity she attributed to her ability to serve as a channel for divine inspiration. It was a gift; she had no right to refuse to exercise it. She yielded, therefore, when told that only she could give leadership and encouragement to the small band of reformers. The combination of need for approval, sense of injustice, and driving Quaker conscience that had set her on her path more than fifty years ago propelled her into the lonely role of pioneer. There was no turning back.

Her interest in helping women to enter the professions led her to sponsor a budding young lawyer, Emma R. Coe, who had studied in Philadelphia in the office of a sympathetic attorney. In February 1855 Lucretia accompanied Emma to Harrisburg and stood with her while she addressed the legislature, asking to be admitted to the bar. They were given, Lucretia noted laconically, "a good hearing," and Emma was permitted to practice.

Shortly afterward she received a letter from Elizabeth Cady Stanton asking for help with the long-promised book on the history of woman's rights. Dreading to write any sort of formal epistle, Lucretia put off answering for three weeks, but she finally wrote a long letter, which included the history of some of the pioneer women of Nantucket. "In thy coming work thou must do thyself justice," she advised Elizabeth. "Remember, the first convention originated with thee."

In her letter Lucretia mentioned that she was rather busy with a family of twenty. After a brief stay in northern New Jersey Pattie and George and their baby were back under the parental roof. "Families should stay together," Lucretia said. She was probably thinking of Tallman. In late 1853 he had set off again, this time for Chile. The Wrights lost touch with him for a while, then heard he was coming home by ship. Tragically, the boom jibed in San Francisco harbor, and he was killed. Lucretia had done what she could to comfort Martha and had invited two Wright nieces to stay in Philadelphia.

But life went on. Elizabeth Cavender was expecting her third child in May, and Anna Hopper had given birth to a baby boy in January. Anna was forty-three; Lucretia wrote in the circulating family sheets that she wouldn't have been more surprised if she herself had had a baby!

In the midst of all this bustling family life, Lucretia Mott was delighted to have a family wedding to plan for. Caroline Chase Stratton, a widowed Coffin cousin, and a great favorite of Lucretia's, was marrying a widower, Charles Wood, from Auburn, New York. There were countless bridal parties to attend, linens to hem, new gowns to make. Lucretia clung to the simple Quaker style and colors, but her daughters and granddaughters were branching out, though none were so worldly as to wear the new hoop skirts.

With all the sewing to do, Lucretia decided to see if it would save time to buy one of the new-fangled sewing machines that had been exhibited at the World's Fair in New York in 1853 and were now coming into private homes. She hired a woman to come and give herself and her daughters lessons on the "masheen," but the venture was not a success. The sewing teacher arrived at noon time and was asked to have dinner with the family. As usual there was much laughter and raillery. Something was said to which the seamstress took exception, for she got up, put on her bonnet, and marched out before Lucretia could find out what the matter was. Thereafter, they figured out how to work the sewing "masheen" for themselves.

Visitors continued to arrive, as usual. Maria Mitchell, the nation's first woman astronomer and a Coffin cousin from Nantucket, came with her father. Maria, who was plagued with religious doubts centering on life after death, discussed her lack of faith with Lucretia. "She is not quite settled in her religious heresy," Lucretia wrote in a family letter after the visit.

Keeping the Coffin family letters in circulation had become an enormous chore. Lucretia insisted on including everyone and, despite the pleadings of her children, every bit of news, personal or otherwise. ("Tell us your topics, your calls, your domestic arrangements, we want to know *everything*" she wrote firmly.) She liked the whole family to gather so that each new letter could be read aloud. Since the letters came frequently, this led to almost daily family gatherings.

Lucretia's own method of letter writing was to read over the letter she was answering, comment on each item, and then give her own news in diary form. Mariner's daughter that she was, she began each letter with a description of the weather. "Cloudy, cool for May, Northwest wind blowing."

On the first of May, Lucy Stone had married Henry Blackwell, an abolitionist and the brother of Elizabeth Blackwell, the first woman physician in America. Lucretia had been in on the secret of the engagement from the start. She approved, but felt that Lucy must not follow the old custom of taking a year out of active work as a new bride. The woman's movement needed her too much. She had not heard of Lucy's decision to keep her own name and was at first surprised. "Why not add Blackwell, as the French do—Lucy Blackwell Stone?" she suggested. "Thy business." Lucy's decision ultimately caused her to reexamine her own practices. In a letter to her niece, Anna Coffin Brown, she used her name rather than addressing the envelope to her husband, Walter Brown. "Seeing there are so few to advocate woman's whole cause, it is needful for some to be ultra—so I have become quite a defender of Lucy Stone's name."

For years Lucretia Mott had objected strenuously to any wedding ceremony that involved a vow of obedience on the wife's part and on several occasions had corrected a minister when he pronounced a couple "man and wife." "Husband and wife" was the correct phrase, Lucretia insisted, since it was unfair to imply that the woman changed her role to wife without the man also changing his to husband. When people asked her for her picture or her signature, she often wrote on it a favorite motto: "In the true marriage relationship the independence of the husband and wife is equal, their dependence mutual, and their obligations reciprocal."

When the Motts congratulated a Friend who had recently inherited a house and a good deal of property, he demurred, saying that he was not really so well off, because he had to keep his mother. Did not his mother work hard for many years? Lucretia asked crisply. Should not the son rather say that he was *allowed* to live in her house?

The household at 338 Arch was beginning to thin out. Ellen Wright entered the Eagleswood School opened by Theodore and Angelina Weld and Sarah Grimké at Raritan, New Jersey, as part of a utopian community. Other Wright children were sent there as they came of age. The Wrights and Motts took an interest in the school and helped to bail Theodore Weld out when he got into financial difficulties.

A source of joy to Lucretia was her sister's chairing of the Woman's Rights Convention in Saratoga in the summer of 1855. Martha had tended to stay aloof from the reform movements in the past and to urge Lucretia to play a less active role. Now, however, she herself was becoming a leader. In part this was due to her developing friendship with Susan B. Anthony, who lived not far away. Susan was a great favorite of Lucretia's. She was less enthusiastic about another neighbor of Martha's, Emily Howland of Sherwood, who said she preferred to work quietly for the cause. "And so glad am I that there are some, besides Emily Howland, to devote time and talent to the Woman Cause. So there is another Emily. Well, let her do all the quiet work she can—but let not S. B. Anthony abate one whit from her outspoken zeal—nor E. C. Stanton one word from her vigorous writing. Lucy Stone is worth a dozen Emily Howlands or any other quiet workers—give me noise on this subject...a real Boanerges."

Having missed the Saratoga convention, Lucretia was determined to get to Cincinnati, where Martha was also going to preside. In October, after the birth of Pattie's baby, she set out alone on the four-day trip. From Cincinnati the two sisters traveled together to Cleveland, Syracuse, and Albany, where Martha chaired still another woman's rights convention.

From Albany Lucretia traveled alone to New York City, where she preached at Rose Street Meeting. Her old New York City antagonist, George F. White, was now dead, but another adversary, Richard Cromwell, took upon himself the correcting of Lucretia's theology as a personal concern. He followed her about from meeting to meeting and came to Philadelphia to see what could be done about getting her disowned.

At Rose Street, in November, Lucretia denounced "King and Priest Craft," declaring "that Protestantism was only a modification, not a thorough reform of superstition," and calling for "a religion based on faith in the perfectability of men, and patterned after Christ's example of doing good." Her sermon, reported in the *New York Times*, was regarded as eloquent and moving. Richard Cromwell, however, felt otherwise and arose to warn the listeners, "Beware lest men spoil you through philosophy and vain deceit," with a wave of his hand toward Lucretia, "or vain conceit either." The next day Cromwell was again present when Lucretia spoke at the Brookyn Meeting and again arose, this time to protest when Lucretia mentioned Elias Hicks in the same breath as William Lloyd Garrison. "Some hisses were heard in the back of the meeting and one called 'put him out' but I heard nothing of it," Lucretia reported to Martha.

This was one of the last times Lucretia Mott was to hear herself openly attacked in Quaker Meeting. Sentiment among the Hicksites was slowly swinging toward her, perhaps in part because she had gained many converts, perhaps also because she was articulating a liberal religion that fitted well with the social and economic conditions of the new age. Some of the New York Quakers, however, continued to be suspicious of her heresy. "She would make the benevolence of our natures, identical with the operation of the Divine Spirit," one minister wrote testily. "She puts no stress whatsoever upon...new birth or regeneration."

Back in Philadelphia at a planning meeting for the Annual

Anti-Slavery Fair, Lucretia heard Pliny Chase, a Quaker businessman, read some selections from *Leaves of Grass*, just published by a Brooklyn printer, Walt Whitman. Lucretia heard that Emerson liked it and thought it was "something Emersonian in style; a kind of unmeasured poetry in praise of America and telling what true poetry is." Edward Davis was so enthusiastic that he sent away for a copy for his seventeen-year-old daughter, Anna. At a time when many conventional people thought Walt Whitman was immoral, his liberal spirit appealed to Lucretia and her family.

On January 3, 1856, Lucretia celebrated her sixty-third birthday with a family party of twenty-two adults and thirteen grandchildren. Dampening the joy of the occasion was the fact that George Hopper, a beloved eight-year-old grandson, was very ill with the flu. It turned into croup, and a few days later he died. Lucretia had struggled to save him, bringing in several doctors. "Even the best of them know so little," she mourned. The flu was sweeping the city. A few weeks later she learned that Anna Coffin Brown, her niece who now lived in Germantown, had two sick babies on her hands. It was a snowy night and only a few of the street horsecars were running, but Lucretia slipped away from her vigilant family, took the cars as far as they would go, and then walked a half mile through the driving snow to reach the Browns. She told them she had been left off at the gate, but did not specify which gate, she confessed to Martha. Both children had raging fevers, and they were up all night. "Every hour something was needed, and I was glad to be there, not that I could do much, but Anna said it so relieved her of so much anxiety to have another to divide it with."

Both Brown children recovered, although the little boy was left partially deaf. Lucretia turned her attention once more to the woman's rights movement. In April Catherine Beecher came to visit the Motts and give some lectures. Lucretia had mixed feelings about Catherine, who had once objected to the Grimké sisters speaking in public on standard biblical grounds but who had become an advocate of education for women. Nevertheless, she invited her to stay with the Motts and agreed to sit on the platform with her when Catherine addressed an audience of over a thousand public school teachers, mainly women, schools having been suspended for the day to give them this opportunity.

"She addressed them well, only in too low a tone," Lucretia wrote Martha. "It takes a Quaker woman to raise her voice.... She is just publishing another work, and in true Yankee character, having an eye to the 'main chance' she called attention to that and to her letters and told where they might be procured." Lucretia reminded her that she had once prophesied that women would someday become public speakers, though she managed not to taunt her with having once been an opponent of Sarah Grimké.

The evening after the lecture Lucretia invited eight guests to join the Mott-Davis family for tea. As usual there were oysters, pickled tongue, and ice cream to make it into a real party. When the conversation turned to whether or not Shakespeare actually wrote his plays, Lucretia asked why they needed to prove that there was only one Shakespeare. Why wouldn't they be happier if it could be proved that there were ten, just as it would be more worthy of God to attribute to Him many messiahs rather than just one? Catherine Beecher, she reported, "bore the heresy better than expected. Miller stayed behind as they went to the parlor to laugh and ask me—or rather congratulate me, on delivering myself of my Messiah hobby, that's not just his language, but the quintessence, as mother used to say."

Though Miller and Sarah McKim continued to attend almost every Mott party, Miller and Lucretia quarreled continually now. Miller objected to Lucretia's pacifism, to the more extreme advocates of woman's rights, and to her heresies. Lucretia feared that his sectarian background was beginning to reveal itself once more. Yet there continued to be a deep and abiding bond between them.

Lucretia's husband and daughters were once more begging her to slow down her pace, but she would have none of it. She thought she was better this spring than she had been for some time, due to a decision she had made to give up all diets and simply eat what she felt like, following nature's promptings. She had found a book translated from French that advocated this natural system, and she sent it off to Martha, who was worried about a granddaughter with a "deranged" stomach.

Unfortunately, Lucretia's natural tastes ran to rich and spicy foods, lots of coffee, gooseberries and strawberries in cream, oysters, pickled tongue or herring, rich codfish stew, and corn pudding. She had sampled the Graham diet of bran, but thought little of it, nor did she have much use for the water cure, now much in vogue. She was sure her troubles came from too much "mental exertion," and since she had no intention of giving up that exertion, she was doomed to ups and downs.

In between the guests and the fair meetings and the housework there were always the beggars to deal with. Lucretia's reputation for philanthropy and generosity had resulted by this time in a constant stream of men and women coming to her door. Many of the callers were black, for her name as the Black Man's Goddess had spread far and wide. In a day when there were practically no social agencies to meet the needs of people who were poor or in trouble, Lucretia did whatever she could for her callers, although her family remonstrated. Intermingled with the outright beggars were men and women raising money for such causes as the School of Design for Women and the Female Medical College. Lucretia always gave generously, promising herself still stricter economy about the house to make up for the heavy drains on the family purse.

As James Mott wrote a friend during this period, "Lucretia has numerous calls almost daily from all sorts of folks, high and low, rich and poor, for respect, advice, assistance, etc., etc. I am sometimes amused to hear the object of some of the calls; it seems as though some people thought she could do anything and everything. It is true that she does a great deal; no one out of the family knows one half; and no one in the family knows the whole."

The Motts were occupied with family matters in the late spring of 1856, having decided to remodel the Showers place adjacent to Oak Farm, which James had bought, as a future home for Pattie and George Lord. The Davises were planning to move permanently to the farm next spring, and Marianne and Thomas Mott were also buying property close at hand.

But local affairs were overshadowed in the minds of the Motts by developments in Kansas. Congress had not been able to resolve a deadlock over whether to organize Kansas as a free or a slave territory. As a result it was left up to the settlers to decide. Free State proponents poured into one section of Kansas, proslavery settlers into another. Both were aided by out-of-state backers. There were many incidents, and actual civil war broke out in May. Many abolitionists who had never professed nonresistance joined to purchase rifles to send to the Free State forces. A few nonresisters dropped their scruples to do the same. In late May, John Brown with four of his sons and two other followers killed five proslavery colonists at Pottawatomie. Throughout the summer the conflict raged.

Lucretia Mott remained true to nonresistance and quarreled with Miller, who supported Brown. Even Garrison seemed to be wavering a little in his no-government stand. In the election of 1856 John Frémont was running for President on the Republican ticket, favoring the admission of Kansas as a free state. Opposed were James Buchanan on the Democratic ticket and Millard Fillmore, backed by the Know-Nothings. Garrison thought Frémont was clearly the best choice and said he would like to deliver a million votes to him if there were no moral impediment to voting. Thereafter he began to become more and more allied with the Republicans. Were none of her old colleagues prepared to remain true to the moral principles underlying the antislavery crusade?

During August the Motts put these worries behind them long enough to enjoy a special treat, a trip to Nantucket. Lucretia wanted to show her small granddaughters the island of her birth and introduce them to their roots. She found Nantucket as delightful as ever. The south shore had become a bathing place with as many as thirty hardy souls in the cold surf at any one time. "There are two dressing rooms, and such figures as come forth!" Lucretia wrote Martha.

The fall began with its usual rush of committee meetings, family gatherings, and visiting lions. Among the latter was George Curtis, the author and editor of *Harper's Monthly*. Lucretia entertained him but thought he needed educating on woman's rights. "If Harvard College and others had been closed against men as against women, I told him, we should not have the cultivated intellect in their sex which is now our glory," she reported.

She had never given up her efforts to recruit Elizabeth Neall Gay, once her traveling companion in England, into the woman's rights movement. Now she sent Elizabeth a heap of literature, including Mary Wollstonecraft's *A Vindication of the Rights of Woman*, to deliver to Curtis, who was a friend of the Gays, with the admonition that he prepare a proper speech on woman. Lizzie, she was afraid, was not getting out enough. "Men see so many humans through the day that an uninterrupted evening is pleasant, while their wives, like Lizzie Gay, long for something human," she wrote Martha.

After several postponements a woman's rights meeting was set for November in New York City, with Martha presiding. Martha came to Philadelphia so that she and Lucretia could travel to New York together, and she was with the Motts election night. Tensions between proslavery and antislavery forces had once more mounted. On the day before the election an extra was published, attacking "Abolitionists of the Lucretia Mott stamp," and E. M. Davis, her son-in-law. Martha wondered privately if the house would be attacked by a mob. But Lucretia and her family were used to this. "They felt no fear, and there was no disturbance," Martha wrote David.

Following the New York woman's rights meetings, at which Lucretia spoke, Lucy Stone was scheduled to come to Philadelphia to speak on the Kansas border problems as one of a series of lectures held at the Philadelphia Musical Fund Hall. At the last moment Lucy wrote that she was going to cancel her lecture because the hall did not permit blacks in the audience. The Motts, for all their liberalism, had evidently not given this matter much thought. They both wrote Lucy separate letters urging her not to cancel. After all, she could not change the whole series, and she had already signed a contract for her share. To break it, Lucretia pointed out, would seem "womanish and rather capricious." James added that the Motts frequently attended lectures in the hall and had ridden on city conveyances that excluded "the colored" without seeing it necessary to "exclude themselves." Lucy had given them something to think about, however. Some years later they started a campaign against discrimination in streetcars.

The year ended, as all of Lucretia's years now did, with the

Annual Anti-Slavery Fair. This yearly occasion, orchestrated by Lucretia's efficient oldest daughter, Anna Mott Hopper, now netted the antislavery cause some two thousand dollars a year. Months of preparation went into the fairs, the women gathering for sewing circles way in advance and men and women getting together for planning. These occasions were also social, and inevitably antislavery was discussed. Lucretia thought the system was excellent and objected when Miller suggested that lectures be substituted. Pragmatist that she was, she even argued that the Philadelphia Female Anti-Slavery Society, which ran the fairs, should never change its name in order to take in men. The system was working well, why tamper with it?

Through the Female Anti-Slavery Society, the Women's Medical College, and the School of Design, Lucretia had her faith renewed each year in the ability of women to advance themselves "on the scale of Being." Yet the woman's movement could not be trusted simply to evolve. It must be nudged and prodded forward. Encouraging, recruiting, defending, explaining, Lucretia functioned as a matriarchial figure in the new movement throughout the 1850s. Often she undertook to solve its conflicts by playing the role of peacemaker. "I have stacks of woman's rights letters to answer," she wrote Martha. "Is it so strange that I am bent double with dyspepsia?"

The black feminist, ex-slave Sojourner Truth *(left)* (Courtesy of Friends Historical Library, Swarthmore College)

Susan B. Anthony *(below)* (Collection of the author)

Roadside, the Motts' home in Chelten Hills, outside of Philadelphia *(top)*. From left, Mott granddaughter, Lucretia, and James (Courtesy of Friends Historical Library, Swarthmore College)

Race Street Meeting House in Philadelphia, circa 1865 *(bottom)* (Courtesy of Friends Historical Library, Swarthmore College)

CHAPTER
XV
MOVE TO THE COUNTRY

IN MID-MARCH 1857 James and Lucretia Mott moved from their home on Arch Street to a remodeled farmhouse in Chelten Hills, rolling farmland north of the city. Lucretia's health and spirits had improved, so that she did not feel the move was necessary, but James was now so happy in the prospect, she was not going to complain *"unless I feel like it,"* she wrote Martha.

There was a farewell party at old 338, at which clever Martha read some verses:

> *Weep for the glory of 338!*
> *Weep for James and Lucretia his mate*
> *Weep that the thought ever entered their pate*
> *Of selling the mansion at 338!*
>
> *Weep for the glory of 338!*
> *Weep for the lions and strangers, whose fate*
> *Never again will allow them to wait*
> *In the cheerful old parlor of 338!*
>
> *Weep for the glory of 338!*
> *Weep for the beggars who early and late*
> *Came without ceasing to knock at the gate*
> *or ring the doorbell of 338!*

A second poem by Martha, read at the same party, included twenty-two verses mentioning each member of the family as well as the many callers:

Who wearied of the world's renown
And sought a peaceful life to crown
By selling off his house in town?

James Mott

Who was it that the sale decreed
And urged him in to do the deed
And wished to close the sale with speed

Lucretia

Who first a rural homestead found
And bought the farmers homely ground
And beautified it all around?

Edward Davis

Who'll enter at the old house door
And lay their burdens on the floor
And say they'll stay a week or more?

Yearly Meeting Friends

Who'll meet them there with look aghast
And tell them that dispensation's past
And bid them turn and look their last?

Mrs. Allen [the new owner]

By the early summer of 1857 the Motts were somewhat settled in the new house, renamed Roadside. Lucretia was delighted with her old-fashioned country parlor warmed by a Franklin stove, which, she thought, added to its charm. She insisted on cutting down shrubs so that the light would pour in, and she refused to put up heavy draperies, then popular. The result was a cheerful room, lit by "Heaven's Light," and pleasantly cluttered with books and the toys of the grandchildren. She also enjoyed the daily contact with the garden, pulling weeds or picking vegetables for the dinner table. She made picking the peas, early in the morning, her special task. She loved the smell of the damp earth and the sparkle of the dew upon the grass.

Darkening her pleasure in the new house, however, was the financial panic that began in August, touched off by the failure of the Ohio Life and Trust Company. The condition of the working people disturbed her more and more as the panic grew worse. "What are thousands of men, women and children going to do thrown out of all employment?" she asked Martha rhetorically. She herself returned to the city to visit "colored" schools and distribute clothing from the House of Industry, a workshop for the poor. A Quaker doctor, she reported, was offering medical aid at a soup kitchen, where twelve hundred were fed daily, while a school and a temperance house were being used as lodgings for the homeless. "Groceries and coal sold out very cheap to the poor and yet after all, thousands are in want—in rags, in vice, in filth. Where is the radical reform?!!!"

But what exactly was the radical reform that was needed? She listened to businessmen blaming the banks for the panic and to others declaring that the lack of protective tariffs had caused the mischief and wondered if both ought not to lay more blame to "the fashionable women for sweeping up the streets with rich brocades." She felt sure that slavery was also to blame and that the panic was a result of its abuses. She would not, however, conclude, as others did, that God was punishing the nation for its sinfulness. Rather, humankind had once more failed to understand the natural laws that governed the universe: "We are all full of anxiety and pity; still this is an unavoidable result of overtrading in borrowed capital, low credits, bank discounts etc. as any natural consequence of violation of physical laws. Strange it is that sound philosophy should not be brought to bear upon mercantile proceedings as upon every other branch of natural science."

Her worry about the financial panic found its way into her sermons of the period. Preaching at Yardleyville, Pennsylvania, she said, "There is a need for preachers against the existing monopolies and banking institutions, by which the rich are made richer, and the poor, poorer. . . . It is contrary to the spirit of this Republic that any should be so rich." At Bristol, she told her Quaker audience, "It is not enough to be generous, and give alms; the enlarged soul, the true philanthropist, is compelled by Christian principle to look beyond the bestowing of a scant pittance to the mere beggar of the day, to the duty of considering the causes and sources of poverty. We must consider how much we have done toward causing it."

Despite the panic, the Motts had company during the summer

of 1857. The trip out by train and horse-drawn streetcar did not deter visitors, it soon became apparent. Even the beggars found the Motts, and Lucretia was once more busy providing food and coins. When Yearly-Meeting time rolled around again, she could rejoice that she was not still on Arch Street, but the occasional traveling Friend continued to arrive, carpetbag in hand. In January 1858 an elderly Quaker from Baltimore, a complete stranger to the Motts, came and announced that she would spend a week. She sat in the parlor most of the time reading Joseph Blanco White from cover to cover, while Lucretia, at her request, did all her laundry. Lucretia fortunately was more amused than annoyed by the old soul.

Slowly, meanwhile, the work was completed at Roadside, and Lucretia was at last able to put some of the stacks of books away onto bookshelves. "Maybe I'll have time before I die to read the 100 books I have resolved to," she wrote her sister Eliza. But she was soon back to her busy schedule and frequently away from home.

Due to the financial panic there was no national woman's rights convention held in 1857, and Lucretia was unable to attend the 1858 meeting, which was held during Yearly Meeting time. She did, however, get blow-by-blow reports from Martha Wright. Old Aunt Sarah Grimké had read a long, boring speech. ("I wish we old folks could be admonished that our day is over," Lucretia commented. "She was a good speaker a generation ago and she has no daughter to tell her she is 'a great time growing to be 60.' ") George Curtis, the editor, who had been briefed by Elizabeth Neall Gay with the help of books and pamphlets from Lucretia, had spoken exceedingly well. Stephen Pearl Andrews, an author, abolitionist, and anarchist, had advocated "free love." Eliza Farnham, a prison reformer and author, advanced the argument that woman was the natural superior of man and should rule over him, while denying him sex except for procreation.

After having resisted Lucretia's efforts to involve her in the woman's movement for years, Elizabeth Neall Gay attended this conference. She was not impressed and wrote Lucretia a "wrathful" letter condemning the women for providing a free platform for such mavericks as Andrews and Eliza Farnham.

Miller McKim joined with Elizabeth Gay in attacking the convention for allowing too many side issues to be attached to woman's rights. Lucretia had heard it all before when people argued that the antislavery cause should not be joined to side issues. She continued to believe that if everyone had a chance to express his or her opinion, the truth would be triumphant. "Let each and all expound their own creed, and then let us judge."

The Motts spent the summer at home, growing and preserving food, entertaining grandchildren, and overseeing the conversion of Thomas Mott's new house across from them. Having acquired a sharp eye for good architectural detail as a result of her background on Nantucket, Lucretia enjoyed checking on such matters as the height of ceilings and the location of corner cupboards.

Both Elizabeth Cavender and Marianne Pelham Mott had new babies, and both were drinking ale to increase their milk production. Twenty years before, Lucretia might have objected fiercely. Now she said nothing, and in fact brewed a little wine herself, though she said defensively it was just to flavor custard and to give old people a drop or so for their digestion. When her own stomach was upset, she, too, tried wine as a remedy. "I shall become quite a toper, but my health is improving."

In other matters, too, she was growing more mellow. When the Davises imported a music teacher to instruct their children, Lucretia had to admit she liked to hear the grandchildren sing. She herself could never carry a tune. Her mother had once chided her, "O Lucretia if thee were as far out of town as thee is out of tune, thee wouldn't get home tonight." But she came in her later years to enjoy music. It would be several years before she allowed dancing at Roadside, but she knew that her children danced, and rationalized that the dancing of the day was just a form of walking anyway and not as lively as the forbidden dances she and Eliza had once watched in Nantucket.

The new house was her only extravagance. She enjoyed fixing it up and eventually was willing to add a "convenience" to the bathroom and, a bit later, a bidet, which a traveling daughter-in-law brought home from Europe.

Even during the long summer months at Roadside there were many errands to run in the city, Quaker meetings and antislavery meetings to attend, shopping to do. To reach the city, one could take a horsecar down the Old York Road as far as the Penn railroad station. The horsecars stopped about a mile from their house. Sometimes James, sometimes James Corr, the farmer he employed to help him, drove Lucretia to the station and met her when she returned. On several occasions, however, there was a mix-up, and she found it necessary to walk. Once she had picked up a second-hand highchair on the way out and, finding no other good way to carry it, took off her bonnet, put the highchair on her head, and walked across the fields in this fashion.

By fall Lucretia Mott was restless. Since James felt the farm needed him, she went with Anna Hopper to Baltimore, where they stayed with cousins, the Needles. Baltimore had lost much of its former animosity to Lucretia. She reported that she and John Needles were holding a large meeting with the "colored" people. "Radical preaching seems to suit the people and good feeling prevails!"

On her return to Philadelphia she had the long-anticipated pleasure of a visit from Elizabeth Cady Stanton, whom she had been begging for years to come. Unfortunately the visit was both short and disastrous. Elizabeth's trunk was somehow lost or stolen en route. Feeling responsible, Edward Hopper asked for a list of the trunk's contents and their value in order to turn it over to the police. When the list came, Lucretia was dismayed. Imagine having a shawl that cost one hundred dollars! She had always feared Elizabeth was extravagant, but how extravagant she had never dared to guess. Nevertheless, she sent her friend one hundred dollars to help make up the loss. "To supply only the necessities, not the luxuries," she explained.

Yet her own vanity was not entirely behind her. Earlier in the year she had sat for her portrait with Willie Furness, son of the Unitarian minister and brother of the Frank Furness whose architecture was changing the face of Philadelphia. In her lap she held Joseph Blanco White's autobiography. She complained that the sittings were endless, but "the artists pronounce Willie Furness's *labored* portrait of thy sister the best painting in the Academy," she told Martha.

In November George Curtis came to Philadelphia again and

delivered the lecture "Fair Play for Women," which he had written as a result of Lucretia's promptings and with Elizabeth Gay's help. Lucretia thought it was excellent, though she wondered why he needed to refer so frequently to pantaloons and breeches.

With December, the Mott-Hopper-Davis household was once more swept up in preparations for the antislavery fair. Elizabeth Gay sent some ornamental sea pebbles, which Lucretia said she would advertise but wasn't sure of selling, considering the utilitarian attitude of many Philadelphians. The fair netted only $1,421 that year, reflecting the growing unpopularity of the abolitionists.

At the January 1859 annual meeting of the Philadelphia Female Anti-Slavery Society, where the receipts of the fair were reported, several conservative members of the organization suggested that a resolution rejoicing on the death of Judge Kane be omitted from the annual report. Lucretia had never forgiven Judge Kane for his sentencing of Passmore Williamson, and on his death she had shocked some of the women by suggesting that a resolution be prepared "expressing satisfaction that flying bondsmen had no longer cause to fear the power of this office (the judiciary)." Nice ladies did not speak ill of the dead in this fashion, but Lucretia Mott had no intention of mincing words, and her loyal following supported her.

After a quick circuit with James of the area surrounding Philadelphia, Lucretia Mott went to New York in May to preside at the Ninth National Woman's Rights Convention. She had as usual resisted the assignment and felt she did poorly. When a newspaper reporter commented that "nothing fresh was said," she entirely agreed. "To be stuck up half an hour with nothing special to inspire you at the time is an infliction and a bore on the audience. I have great faith in the Quaker creed, to speak as the spirit giveth utterance."

In the fall of 1859 the joy the Motts took in Anna Davis's marriage to Richard Hallowell was overshadowed by tragic news from Harpers Ferry, Virginia. John Brown, with a force of eighteen men, had seized the federal arsenal at Harpers Ferry and held some local citizens hostage. It was to have been the first act in a slave uprising, but the blacks did not stream to

Brown's rescue as expected. He was defeated, captured, and condemned to death. Overnight he became the hero of the abolitionists. He was eulogized in the papers, rallies were held in his honor, and several hurried to Harpers Ferry to see him before he was put to death.

Lucretia was heartsick. She could sympathize with John Brown's impatience and need to act; after all these weary years she was impatient too. But she believed as firmly as ever that the answer to slavery must be its overthrow with moral weapons. Brown's resort to bloodshed could only lead to more of the same. It was one thing for the blacks themselves to take up arms against their persecutors. When both slave owner and the state enforced slavery with bayonets, who could blame them for resisting? But the abolitionist must change hearts and minds, both North and South. Bloodshed would never work.

As the anxious days of Brown's trial passed, her heart went out to Brown's wife, who had lost two sons in the battles of Harpers Ferry. Through Miller McKim she arranged for Mary Ann Brown to stay at Roadside until the trial ended, giving her the comfort of the Mott household and what spiritual solace she could.

Brown was executed on December 2. Mary Brown arrived in Virginia a day later and was given the corpse of her husband, but not those of her two sons. Philadelphia abolitionists held a day of mourning when John Brown's body was brought through the City of Brotherly Love on the way to burial in the Adirondacks. Lucretia spoke on the great sin of slavery, predicting that it would bring bloodshed to the land. Again, at the annual meetings of the Philadelphia Female Anti-Slavery Society and of the Pennsylvania Anti-Slavery Society, Lucretia poured out some of her conflicting feelings. The abolitionists must continue to renounce carnal weapons, she believed. Nevertheless, those who elected a commander-in-chief pledged to use the army and the navy to keep the slaves in chains could not criticize the abolitionists for praising John Brown: "For it is not John Brown the soldier we praise, it is John Brown the moral hero;... Robert Purvis has said that I was 'the most belligerent Non-Resistant' he ever saw. I accept the character he gives me; and I glory in it. I have no idea because I am a Non Resister of submitting tamely to injustice inflicted either on me or on the slave. I will oppose it with all the moral power with which I am endowed. I am no advocate of passivity. Quakerism as I understand it does not mean quietism. The early Friends were agitators, disturbers of the peace, and were more obnoxious in their day to charges which are now so freely made than we are.''

The affair at Harpers Ferry brought the issue of slavery to a fever pitch in Philadelphia. On the day of Brown's execution several hundred medical students from Virginia had paraded through the streets of Philadelphia wearing red ribbons and bragging about how many "niggers" they owned. Some of their number warned that they were not going to permit the abolitionists to hold their antislavery fair, scheduled two weeks later.

Undismayed, the Philadelphia Female Anti-Slavery Society went on with their plans, and it opened as usual on the morning of December 15. The first day went smoothly enough, but on the morning of the second day the mayor ordered the women to take down the antislavery flag strung across Chestnut Street. Shortly thereafter the sheriff arrived, took possession of the building, and ordered the fair closed. The women decided to move the entire event to the Assembly Buildings, which were offered to them, and within three hours they were again in business. Lucretia Mott meanwhile told the sheriff and his lawyer that the women "did not reproach them for their part in the affair but were sorry they held offices which obliged them to do such deeds.''

That evening George W. Curtis was scheduled to give a speech at the National Hall entitled ''Present Aspects of Our Country,'' a topic that would of course touch upon slavery. The Motts attended, sitting on the platform. Present also were some 650 Philadelphia policemen, sent by the nervous mayor to keep order. Even so, there was a near riot outside, with the mob throwing rocks and bottles of vitriol, and several passersby were injured.

Some of her fellow abolitionists seemed to rejoice in the outbreak of mob violence, as they had once rejoiced in the burning of Pennsylvania Hall and the passage of the Fugitive Slave Act, predicting that good would come out of evil. Lucretia strongly objected. She took issue with her friend Ralph Waldo Emerson when he said, in "The Law of Success," that "nature utilized everything—the bad and the good. That may be in the animal economy, but in morals, I told him, wickedness works only evil and that continually."

At the same time that she was struggling to deal with the tragedy of John Brown, Lucretia was endeavoring to cope with her feelings over a painful event in the extended Coffin family. Her beloved cousin, Caroline Stratton Wood, had never said much about her life in Auburn, but it became clear that she was not happy. Charles Wood showed little interest in his step-daughters and had to be persuaded to come to the wedding when Augusta Stratton married John Needles. Finally, late in 1859 Caroline arrived home at Mount Holly tired and haggard and announced that she was not going back. Lucretia was furious. She felt that Charles Wood had driven Caroline from her home. "The meanness and littleness of some things stir up more indignation that can easily go down with the sun," she wrote. "Let us strive to keep out all desire for revenge so that, being angry, we sin not."

The phrase reveals a great deal about Lucretia's evolving character. She seemed more able, as she grew older, to admit to anger against individuals as opposed to institutions, such as slavery, sectarian bigotry, and the like. The anger had been there all along, powering her assertiveness, her ability to carry the war to the enemy. She was, as Robert Purvis had called her, a "belligerent nonresistant." Anger in the form of moral indig-nation was acceptable to her. She did not feel guilty about that, but to seek revenge, to put oneself on the same level as the enemy, was to be tarnished, in her view. In her inner economy, where every scrap of energy was put to good use, there was no room for such conflict. Generally, therefore, she had been for-giving and had tried to understand what made her opposers act as they did. She was now growing able to be outspoken about her anger, against Judge Kane, against Charles Wood, and later, about a "miscreant" son-in-law. Those of her contempo-raries who had made a living legend of her saintliness were sometimes startled by her outbursts against these few.

Lucretia had never spoken of harboring angry feelings against Samuel Gurney, the British Quaker banker who had once told her he feared her influence on his children; nor against his sister, Elizabeth Fry, who had prayed at her at a public meeting. With more pity than anger she had watched the followers of Joseph John Gurney, Samuel's brother, battling with the conservatives, called Wilburites, for the control of the Orthodox wing of the Society of Friends. Both groups were equally wrong and equally stubborn, in her view. Yet the Gurneys represented, more than any single Quaker family, the evangelical influence that Lucretia felt was reducing Quakerism to a form of sectarianism. She could not have been without strong feelings toward them.

She must, therefore, have been interested, to put it mildly, to pick up a copy of the *New York Daily Tribune* one day in 1860 and read a long, rather lurid letter by a Mary Gurney (a daughter-in-law of Joseph John Gurney), who had eloped to the Continent with her husband's groom. The letter, addressed to an unnamed friend, sought to explain those influences in the Gurney family—smugness, conformity, intermarriage—that had caused Marian, herself the daughter of a Gurney, to rebel. Her own parents, she claimed, had also reacted against the family tradition, and she had been born before they were married. The letter filled almost an entire newspaper page and was accompanied by a condemning editorial.

Lucretia wrote to Martha that she thought the letter was sickly and sentimental and ought not to have been published. Her statement that "the whole scope and measure of a woman's heart and brain and the whole purpose of her being is love" was foolish. The Woman's Rights Conventions had consistently fought the idea that love and marriage were the whole of a woman's life while only incidental to a man's.

Still, Lucretia Mott thought, when so many marriages were made for the sake of rank and money, it was not surprising that sad results followed. "We need not marvel that there are Mrs. Gurneys to step aside while the existing laws on the marriage union remain, and while the church recognizes the absolute control of the husband." The *Tribune* editorial was entirely too severe. Why attack one errant woman when so many men were known to sin against the marriage union and still be received by polite society?

Lucretia was undoubtedly thinking of Charles Wood, who

was demanding a divorce and who had been carrying on an affair with another woman. She backed Caroline in demanding as large a settlement as possible. The whole affair caused her to rethink her feelings about divorce, a subject much discussed in her circles that summer. In May Martha Wright had presided at the Tenth National Woman's Rights Convention, held in New York City. Here Elizabeth Cady Stanton had presented some resolutions on divorce that were regarded as far too radical. As a result, the entire convention was spent debating this subject, a distraction, some felt, from the main issue.

Much of the summer of 1860 Lucretia and James spent at Roadside entertaining grandchildren. In August their daughter, Maria Davis, went to Boston to be with her daughter, Anna Davis Hallowell, for the birth of her first child. It was a girl, Maria. "Tell Richard in these days girls are as important as boys so he needn't grieve that a manchild was not born to them," Lucretia wrote.

While the Motts were in Auburn in September, Bessie Lord, a one-year-old family pet, fell ill with "summer complaint," a gastro-intestinal infection, and died before her grandparents could return. Once more Lucretia served as undertaker, laying the little corpse out on ice while she tried to comfort her stricken daughter, Pattie.

Throughout the fall the national news was upsetting. The Motts knew little of the Republican nominee, Abraham Lincoln, although Miller McKim and Wendell Phillips seemed to think highly of him. Everyone was talking about the secession of the radical Southerners and the continuing turmoil in Kansas. The long antislavery struggle seemed to be degenerating into violence. One evening in October Edward Davis invited a Captain Steward to Roadside to spend the night. The Motts found his talk about the escaping slaves interesting, but not so his talk of open warfare. Although their sons and grandsons seemed to be taking an interest in the excitements of the day, "Preserve me from politics!" Lucretia exclaimed.

More interesting was a dinner party where they met Harriet Beecher Stowe and her twin daughters. Lucretia found the author of *Uncle Tom's Cabin* more handsome than she had expected and was pleased to learn that she was interested in penal reform. She and Harriet and James talked about the Auburn prison while the rest of the company talked politics.

In November the Motts made their usual trip to Baltimore for the Yearly Meeting. This time they stayed afterward for a conference on the establishment of a boarding school so that Hicksite boys need no longer go to Orthodox Haverford. Lucretia and James were among those who insisted that the new institution, Swarthmore College, chartered in 1864, be coeducational.

The telegraph brought the news that Lincoln was elected. Wendell Phillips declared that the slave had elected him, and that the nation had passed a Rubicon. Garrison was less sure, and the two quarreled in the pages of the *Liberator*. Lucretia, celebrating her sixty-eighth birthday at Roadside in January 1861, longed to return them all to the pure moral principles upon which the antislavery crusade had been founded. It was time, as never before, to speak out. When her elderly cousin, Lydia Mott, invited her to come to a woman's rights meeting in Albany, Lucretia accepted. James did not think she could bear the fatigue and refused to accompany her. "But I am better now, and this is no time to stay away," she wrote.

In Albany she went with Elizabeth Cady Stanton and Ernestine Rose to speak to the New York legislature on the subject of divorce. En route, she urged her two companions to be as moderate as possible. In front of the legislators, however, she made an impassioned speech saying that marriage was a sacred union between two people and the law had nothing to do with it at all. Let all the laws governing both marriages and divorce be swept away! It was by far the most radical statement to date on the subject. When her woman's rights colleagues teased her, she dug up an opinion in English law that backed her position.

By the time Lucretia returned from Albany, seven Southern states had seceded, elected Jefferson Davis provisional President, and seized U.S. arsenals. In his inaugural address in March 1861 Lincoln said that he did not intend to interfere with slavery but would not tolerate secession. Lucretia feared he was to prove a miserable compromiser. She was surprised when Miller McKim, Martha Wright, and even her own James took a milder view.

On April 10, in the midst of the crisis over Fort Sumter,

James and Lucretia celebrated their fiftieth wedding anniversary. All their children, grandchildren, and the one new great-grandchild were at Roadside for the party, as well as many Folger, Coffin, and Mott relatives and old friends. The wedding certificate was brought out and signed by those present, including three of the original signers. When someone noted that a corner of the parchment certificate had been cut off, unsentimental Lucretia confessed she had done so forty years ago when she had needed to mend a child's toy.

The Motts' marriage, always a good one, had been strengthened by the years at Roadside. Their children noticed how often they seemed in close communion, how frequently Lucretia ran to James with a paragraph to share from a book or newspaper. They still saw alike on the antislavery struggle. "James and I have loved each other more since we worked together for a great cause," Lucretia explained.

She was sixty-eight and frail, he was seventy-three and hearty, but having problems with his eyes. Surely now, their children thought, they would slow down their pace of involvement in the great issues of the day. But Lucretia had long ago given up fighting manifest duty, and her sense of mission now was to sweep both Motts into the center of the storm.

CHAPTER
XVI

THE
SHADOW OF CIVIL WAR

To CELEBRATE their fiftieth wedding anniversary Lucretia and James had made a trip to Nantucket in June 1861 despite the outbreak of civil war. Her cousins Phebe and Edward Gardner had waited their nice roast pig dinner for the Motts, and there was Indian pudding, pig sauce "indigenous to this Island," and stewed cranberries as well to delight the homecoming native. Ninety-three-year-old Aunt Phebe, when asked if she recognized Lucretia, drawled, "Why to be shoah." The next few days were spent in a round of visiting. Lucretia wrote home, "Your father amuses himself with long walks and rides. He seems quite as contented at home with my relatives as I am want to be with his."

On the way back the Motts stopped in Boston, where Lucretia spoke in Boston's Music Hall. "It is pleasant to see a woman called to speak in public who is characterized by that simple repose which is the best testimony to health of mind and body," an enthusiastic reporter commented. Mrs. Mott's address, he said, was like a melody by Mozart, "not an invention but an existence."

In summarizing the speech itself, the reporter said that she had spoken of the war and of her hope that "it would be prosecuted with energy and faith since it was founded on so good a cause. She thought the greatest danger would be in listening to compromise which would only result in again fighting the old battle."

Horace Greeley was one of the first to point out that Lucretia's remarks could hardly be regarded as those of a non-resistant. Upset by this, Lucretia wrote a long correction to be published in the *National Anti-Slavery Standard*. She had spoken, she said, of the fact that moral weapons had at last awakened the nation from its lethargy in regard to slavery, and moral weapons ought to be employed to fight the battle to its conclusion. The nation, feeling guilty about slavery at last, was, however, swept up by a hostile spirit, and the result was a conflict in which those who took the sword would perish by the sword. On the other hand, now that the struggle against slavery had become widespread, she hoped it would not be stopped in the name of nonexistent peace. The nation had been at war against the slaves for years and years, using the full strength of the army and the navy to back up slaveholding. No, let the struggle continue, but let the right means be employed. "So now regarding the present calamity, as the natural result of our wrong doings and our atrocious cruelties, terrible as war must ever be, let us hope it will not be stayed by any compromise which shall continue the unequal, cruel war on the rights and liberties of millions of our unoffending fellow beings, a war waged from generation to generation with all the physical force of our government and our commander-in-chief."

In midsummer her son-in-law, Edward M. Davis, received a commission as captain in the army and was posted to Gen. John Charles Frémont, who was conducting the war in the West from headquarters at Saint Louis. "Who would have thought, when Edward was exerting himself—spreading Adin Ballou's works —to make converts to peace principles, that he would be among the active officers in this war? He flatters himself that the abolition of slavery—end, justifies the means." Edward told his mother-in-law that there was a good understanding between him and his commanding officer on emancipation. Shortly thereafter the household at Roadside learned from the newspapers that Frémont was freeing slaves in the territories he won, although this was not government policy. As a result, he was relieved of his command. Lucretia was angry at the wicked machinations of the administration. Old Abe seemed to her more than ever a miserable compromiser, sacrificing young lives and then firing Frémont for "personal and partisan effect."

The Wrights, however, did not quite agree, and David confessed he backed the administration and the war effort. Lucretia admitted she could not say a word about his "fall from grace," considering "how glass our house is." She continued, however, to deplore the barbarous resort to war. The next month, when Willie Wright, now nineteen, became a soldier, she sympathized with Martha's grief over parting with him but said that it remained her conviction that a better way to solve conflicts would be found as civilization advanced.

At home there was fresh cause for grief. Lue Hopper, Anna's oldest daughter, was dying slowly and painfully of tuberculosis. Her cough was wracking in August; soon she was no longer able to leave the house. She was only twenty-three; Anna burst into tears at the sight of Lue's contemporaries. Lucretia was deeply grieved when this oldest grandchild died on the last day of the year. Why, she asked rebelliously, did old people live on and on, while the best and brightest were taken? She refused to speculate about an afterlife. It was better to concentrate on this one and assume that all would be for the best.

There remained one recipe for overcoming grief in Lucretia's book: getting busy. Early in 1862 Miller McKim was appointed general secretary of the Port Royal Relief Committee, organized to aid the slaves who were freed when Northern troops captured the islands off the coast of South Carolina late in 1861. Lucretia began a project she was to continue throughout the war: gathering clothes and raising money for the freedmen. At first she did this on her own. Later she helped to organize a Women's Association for the Aid of the Freedmen at Race Street Meeting. Lucretia thought it amusing to see some of the most conservative members of the meeting, who had long opposed her abolitionism, now sewing and packing bales of clothes and blankets for the newly freed slaves.

In June Miller McKim went to Port Royal to see the situation firsthand. With him he took his twenty-year-old daughter, Lucy, who had studied music at Theodore Weld's school, Eagleswood. Lucy was deeply moved by the black spirituals she heard, and began to collect them. On her return Lucretia invited her to sing at a party at Roadside and later encouraged her to publish them. "Roll, Jordan, Roll" and "Old Folks at Home" became her favorite songs.

Edward Davis, still in the West with the army, reported that he had seen the Frémonts and that Jessie Frémont had called Abe an ass. "Frémont says he is sold to the border states—and that we shall never succeed until universal emancipation is proclaimed." Davis himself was disowned by Cherry Street Meeting for his military position, and Maria chose to resign as well. Of the Motts' children, now only the Cavenders remained members of the Society of Friends.

With the nation wracked by war, it seemed a shame to travel. Yet Lucretia felt that Martha needed her, now that Willie was on the battlefield. In August she and James set out by horse and buggy for upper New York State. It had been several years since Lucretia had visited Martha, and she found the bushes and trees around the house overgrown. She for one would part with the trees "for a glimpse of the setting sun, or a rising thunder cloud—the other night we had to travel over these domains to have a view of the full moon's rising." Lucretia's love of light seemed to grow with each passing year. Unable to persuade Martha to prune, she herself cut down some trees as soon as she returned to Roadside.

There was bad news from the battlefront: defeats at Harpers Ferry and the second battle of Bull Run. Lucretia couldn't help but be concerned for Willie and for other young Coffin relatives who had joined up. "Nothing but defeats and retreats await us —it is some comfort I don't mean to become deeply interested in their foolish doings—such child's play from the beginning. But we must acknowledge an increase of hope for the slave."

Radical abolitionists, Lucretia among them, were not appeased by Lincoln's Emancipation Proclamation of January 1, 1863. Read closely, it freed slaves only in the rebel areas, over which the federal government had no control. It specifically exempted all areas under federal military occupation and did nothing to disturb slavery in the loyal border states. Still she felt hopeful that 1863 might become the year of Jubilee, despite her lack of faith in carnal weapons.

The continued need for fresh recruits had forced the army to accept blacks as soldiers, though they were paid less than their white counterparts. Early in January 1863 the army leased a large portion of Oak Farm from Edward Davis as a training camp for blacks, called, rather incongruously, Camp William

Penn. Soon eleven black regiments were drilling within sight of Lucretia's parlor window. Despite her strong feelings against war, she could not help but be interested. "The neighboring camp scene is the absorbing interest just now. Is not the change in feeling and conduct toward this oppressed class, beyond all that we could have anticipated?" she wrote friends working at Port Royal.

In January came word that a young Coffin cousin had been killed in battle and another wounded. Lucretia wrestled with herself to accept such losses. "Why should the young and beautiful be swept away?... Still, I wish to compare these awful sacrifices with the ten-fold, yes, manifold *in numbers*, that slavery has doomed to the most cruel deaths from generation to generation, and if, by this present means, these cruelties can be arrested and an end drawn nigh to man's claim of property in his fellow man, we need not... 'be troubled'—knowing that 'these things must needs be'...my faith however in the superior force of the 'mighty weapons' that 'are not carnal' is unshaken."

In the spring there was another death to accept. Walter Brown, the young great-nephew for whom she had once hiked through a winter snowstorm, was dying of tuberculosis. Lucretia hurried to comfort her favorite niece, Anna Coffin Brown, now living in New York, but arrived to find the crepe already hung on the door. She stayed for several weeks to be with Anna and to see old friends.

Among these were Elizabeth Cady Stanton and Susan B. Anthony, who were busy planning the initial meeting of a new organization, the Women's Loyal National League. Rather than advocate woman's rights during the war period, the two thought it best to demonstrate women's ability to help the nation achieve its highest war aims. To this end they wanted to circulate a petition calling for the complete abolition of slavery. Lucretia did not feel the need to demonstrate her loyalty, but she sympathized with the petition idea and attended the founding meeting.

The May meeting of the American Anti-Slavery Society was marred by disagreement. Swept up by his enthusiasm for Lincoln and for the Northern cause, Garrison had come to the conclusion that the abolition of the last vestiges of slavery and prejudice would now be carried forward by the momentum of the broad popular movement and that the little band of unpopular abolitionists were no longer needed to serve as goads and critics of the public conscience.

The time-battered American Anti-Slavery Society, in consequence, faced yet another schism. Wendell Phillips, long Garrison's close personal friend and associate, became the leader of a coalition of radicals—nonresistants who had stuck to their peace principles throughout the war—and blacks, such as Douglass and Purvis, who foresaw the need of white allies in the struggle ahead. Hating schism though they did, James and Lucretia Mott were inevitably drawn into the Phillips group.

After the New York meetings were over, Lucretia brought Susan B. Anthony home with her in time to attend Philadelphia Yearly Meeting. Philadelphia had now produced another woman whose lectures against slavery were drawing national attention. She was Anna Dickinson, an attractive twenty-one-year-old, who was packing halls with her pathetic accounts of the horrors of slavery. She was too warlike for Lucretia's tastes, and she refused to be drawn into the woman's movement, despite the unflagging efforts of Susan B. Anthony, who was deeply involved emotionally with the young woman. Still, Lucretia rejoiced in her success at Boston's Music Hall and later at Cooper Union and was glad to suggest her name when a speaker was needed.

The war news was ominous in the spring and early summer of 1863. Confederate general Richard S. Ewell crushed the Union garrison at Winchester, Virginia, in June, crossed the Potomac, and marched on toward York and Carlisle. Willie Wright was with General Meade near Gettysburg. The family at Roadside listened with special anxiety as news of the great battle fought there during the first days of July reached the city. Soon their worst fears were confirmed: Willie had been seriously injured. David Wright hurried to the battlefield, and Marianne Mott rushed to join him. The doctors were not sure that Willie was going to live, but his relatives found him determined to recover. "He knows his danger but means to fight it out manfully as he has all his battles, and I think he will win," Marianne wrote her mother.

In a few weeks Willie was well enough to be moved to Roadside. Once she was sure he was going to live, Lucretia accepted an invitation to preach at Camp William Penn. Whatever she thought of war, she believed these young black soldiers, too, needed her spiritual comfort. On July 12 she walked over to the camp from Roadside and was shown by the commanding officer where she could stand on some boxes (local legend has it that it was a drum) so that, small as she was, she could be seen and heard. Then some six hundred soldiers were marched in formation before her. She spoke to them stressing the theme of the one true religion and her own faith that the time would come when war would be no more.

Still more troops were needed, and the first drawing of the new draft law was put into effect. Since one could buy one's way out of service by paying three hundred dollars, the draft fell inequitably upon the poor. In New York in July there were draft riots, led by the Irish Democrats, or Copperheads. Several blacks were lynched, and the homes of abolitionists were set on fire and pillaged, among them that of James and Abby Hopper Gibbons, Edward's sister and brother-in-law.

Despite the call on her emotions from so many of her own on the battlefield, Lucretia stood behind those young pacifists, Quakers and others, who felt conscientiously impelled to refuse to fight when drafted. She spoke later that year at the Philadelphia Female Anti-Slavery Society supporting "the loftier position of those who fought only with the spiritual weapons and endured without inflicting injury." Alfred Love, a young Philadelphia conscientious objector, was drafted that fall. Lucretia supported him and went with him for his hearings. When the judge who was about to sentence him said he feared he had religious views like Lucretia Mott, "which would undermine all true religion," Love said he was proud to be associated with her. Love was eventually excused on medical grounds; he was nearsighted. Other conscientious objectors were not so lucky. A few were drafted, imprisoned, and even tortured for their refusal to fight.

In her pacifism Lucretia found herself more and more isolated. Miller McKim joined the Union League to support Northern troops. Lucretia's granddaughter, Maria Hopper, went with Abby Hopper Gibbons to be a Civil War nurse.

James Gibbons wrote a popular recruiting song, "Three Hundred Thousand Strong." Laura Stratton, Caroline Wood's daughter, married Fitz Birney, son of James Birney, once candidate for President of the Liberty party. Fitz was a Union lieutenant, and theirs was a military wedding. Lucretia, who had never before attended a church wedding, thought that "war's trappings did not make the scene more impressive." A year later Fitz was dead on the battlefield, and Laura was a grieving new mother. There was no one except James who could sympathize with Lucretia's heavy sense that all this sacrifice was a tragic waste.

There was more sadness at Roadside, too. A fourteen-year-old Cavender grandson died. The shock so upset Lucretia that she had an attack of her recurrent diarrhea and was forced to take to her bed. She recovered but worried over her daughter, Elizabeth Cavender, who slipped slowly into a deeper and deeper depression.

In October Pattie and George Lord left Roadside to move to New York City, where George was going into business with Walter Brown. Lucretia supervised the move, buying most of Pattie's new furniture and going to New York to lay the rugs. She seemed never able to conceive that this youngest child of hers was competent to manage on her own. She depended heavily on the presence of Pattie and had not taken the news of the move lightly. "Pattie belongs here. Anna D. Hallowell will claim Maria and we cannot live without chick or child." Even when the Davises decided to move into Roadside to take the Lords' place, she was not appeased.

Rarely of course was the dinner table at the Motts down to small numbers. The Motts continued to attract the visiting lions. Robert Dale Owen, son of the communitarian, came to call. James Freeman Clark and Octavius Frothingham, Unitarian ministers and transcendentalists, both were entertained at Roadside. Harriet Tubman, an escaped slave from Maryland, came and went on her way back to the Eastern shore to help more of her family and friends escape to Canada. Emily Howland stopped on her way to Washington to work among the contraband, as the escaped slaves were called. Cornelia Hancock, a Civil War nurse and a Quaker from New Jersey, visited.

Young people, especially, came to Roadside during the war years, attracted by Lucretia's special brand of warmth and encouragement, as well as by Camp William Penn. Parties at which Lucy McKim sang her black spirituals became the order of the day. In these scenes of gaiety, against the tragic background of the war, romance flourished. Ellen Wright became engaged to William Lloyd Garrison, Jr., and Lucy McKim to Wendell Garrison. It was a fitting climax to the thirty-year-old friendship between the Garrisons and the Motts.

In December of 1863, the abolitionists gathered to celebrate the thirtieth anniversary of the founding of the American Anti-Slavery Society. All the old-timers were there, including the Motts, Garrison, and Miller McKim. Lucretia reminisced about the timidity she had felt at the organization of the Philadelphia Female Anti-Slavery Society. "At that time I had no idea of the meaning of preambles and resolutions and voting. Women had never been in assemblies of the kind."

It was a nostalgic moment, but disagreements within the group continued. Garrison's optimistic notion that race prejudice was going to be swept away along with slavery was not proving the case. The Motts were soon aware of its existence in their own backyard. Many of the visitors to Roadside were black, and nearby Camp William Penn attracted the wives and sweethearts of black soldiers. The horse-drawn cars that brought visitors to Chelten Hills did not allow black passengers to ride with the whites but reserved every fifth car for them. Otherwise, they had to ride outside. Lucretia was riding home from Philadelphia one cold rainy day, when the conductor ordered an elderly black woman to ride outside in the rain. Lucretia was so indignant that she insisted on riding with her, until the other passengers protested and the conductor reluctantly permitted both women in. A few months later James caught cold because he rode outside in the rain with some black workmen he had hired to help him at Roadside.

In January 1864, when the Friends Association for the Aid and Elevation of the Freedmen was formed, the Motts suggested the creation of a committee to "investigate the exclusion of the people of color from the passenger cars." Both James and Lucretia were naturally appointed. Just as naturally, the

Philadelphia Female Anti-Slavery Society was also soon involved. Both organizations struggled without success for many months. The elimination of color prejudice was going to take many years, Lucretia sadly concluded.

The war seemed to be dragging on and on, with the new general, Ulysses S. Grant, making little progress against Lee's army. The radical abolitionists believed that a proclamation of universal emancipation and the passage of radical reconstruction measures for the South would bring more blacks flocking to the Union cause and end the war. Lincoln, however, remained cautious. lucretia thought he was a compromiser still and quarreled continually with Miller McKim about it.

Miller thought reformers ought not to criticize the government in the midst of war. Lucretia answered by quoting her favorite author, Joseph Blanco White: "'Reformers ought to be satisfied to be destructives—they are too apt to wish to be constructives.' It only lays the foundation for future trouble and fighting when, for reputation and to please men, reformers seek 'to build again the things they are called on to destroy,'" she added, citing once again the compromises made by the Hicksites after the separation.

There were other quarrels. Miller was constantly critical of the woman's rights movement, of the nonresisters, of Wendell Phillips. "He now thinks politics can't be discussed between us to much advantage," Lucretia commented rather mournfully. Miller even suggested at one point that he thought Lucretia was really becoming a heretic, losing the religious faith that had once bound them so closely together. "Thee hasn't listened to me preach if thee believes that," she told him.

Lucretia and James tried to stay out of the abolitionist controversy over Lincoln. Ellen's marriage in the fall to William Garrison, Jr., must not be marred by quarreling. Garrison was taking the whole thing too personally, Lucretia thought. It had been his movement for so long, it was hard for him to let go of control.

The Motts spent the summer at Roadside, preserving fruit and vegetables, making pies for the soldiers at Camp William Penn, sending them money for Fourth of July fireworks, entertaining grandchildren.

But Lucretia had family worries. Laura Stratton Birney was unconsolable after the death of Fritz. Maria Hopper had caught the "Saint James fever" from her Civil War nursing. Elizabeth Cavender seemed to be in a decline, and her husband Thomas was facing bankruptcy. Lucretia kept intending to spend more time with Elizabeth, but she found her home at Eddington inexpressibly sad. Fighting her own occasional battles with depression and ill health, she did not go very often.

During the summer, news came that Charles Wood was planning to marry Emma Parker, a Philadelphia Quaker with whom he had been carrying on a liaison for some time. Lucretia spoke scathingly of the "open" union of Charles and Emma and called his house in Auburn a brothel or a seraglio. Trying to guard their mother's reputation for saintliness, her daughters attempted to persuade her not to use such words, but she was angry and adamant.

Ellen Wright's wedding to William Lloyd Garrison, Jr., was set for September, and Lucretia went early to help Martha to get ready, taking Pattie Lord with her. The wedding passed pleasantly with no discussion of antislavery differences between the Motts and the Garrisons to mar the event. Lucretia, however, was tired by the journey and decided not to make her annual fall trip to Baltimore and Washington. Instead James went with a member of his Meeting, Helen Longstreth, and afterward obtained a minute from his Monthly Meeting to visit all the Meetings of the Hicksite Philadelphia Yearly Meeting in order to talk about education. It was the first and only time he ever traveled in the ministry, as his famous wife had so often done.

Lucretia was seventy-two on January 3, 1865. Her health was now deteriorating. She had almost constant diarrhea, dyspepsia, and dizziness, and complained that she shook and that her hands and feet were always cold. She lost weight and was often forced to take to her bed. Yet she continued cheerful for the most part and announced that she meant to live as long as possible. To that end she tried every cure anyone suggested to her, including the drinking of strong cider. "It is rather pleasant medicine, two or three swallow at a time."

James, now seventy-six, was sometimes ill and suffered

several bad falls, the result of his doing "improvident things," Lucretia scolded. Worse yet, his eyesight was failing. Lucretia found it touching to see him seek the strongest light and the biggest type and still lay his book aside. He had always loved to read. Maria took to reading the daily paper to him, and Lucretia read aloud from her favorite books.

Both of the Motts bore the infirmities of old age stoically. Something much more devastating absorbed their concern. It was clear now that Elizabeth Cavender was very ill. Her husband, Thomas, seemed to be doing nothing for her. Early in 1865 they moved Elizabeth to Roadside. "Some marriages break up one way, some another," Lucretia wrote Pattie. As Elizabeth grew steadily worse, relations with Thomas also deteriorated. His farm was seized by creditors and sold at auction, and he made little effort to pay back the five thousand dollars James Mott had lent him. When Lucretia decided to consult Dr. Ann Preston about Elizabeth's condition, Thomas objected to a woman doctor, and they had words. For the sake of her daughter, Lucretia avoided an open break, but she thought privately that Thomas was indeed a "miscreant."

The introduction of the Thirteenth Amendment into Congress in February 1865 lifted everyone's spirits. Perhaps slavery was actually going to be ended by the war. Lucretia grudgingly admitted that she liked Lincoln's second inaugural speech well enough. But she was disturbed by the reconstruction policies of Gen. Nathaniel Banks in Louisiana and concerned that the lands freed from the slave owners were not being broken up and given to the former slaves as farms.

Miller McKim thought all the antislavery and freedmen's aid societies ought to merge in an effort to influence reconstruction. The instrument for this influence was to be a new Union Association and a paper to be called the *Nation*, edited by Wendell Garrison and himself. He came to the Motts asking for one thousand dollars to support the effort. When Lucretia pointed out, mildly enough, that there were no women in the new association, he said that "if there seemed to be a necessity for women he thought they would be admitted." Lucretia blew up at him. "Seemed to be a necessity! For one half the nation to act with you." They had another bitter quarrel.

At least the war news was good. With Sherman's successful march to the sea the long nightmare seemed to be coming to an end. On the night of April 9 the household at Roadside heard the ringing of the church bells. They thought it must mean a fire somewhere. Elizabeth couldn't sleep and had to have a second dose of morphine. Only at breakfast did they learn what had happened: Lee had surrendered at Appomattox.

Scarcely had they absorbed the news than the church bells tolled once more, this time to announce the assassination of Abraham Lincoln. Lucretia read the news in the morning paper on April 15 and felt so stunned that she could scarcely go about her household duties. She broke the news as gradually as she could to Elizabeth, who burst into sobs. When Edward Davis arrived with a quantity of black bunting to drape across the porch, she did not object, although such display was not in line with Quaker principles.

In the face of the universal sorrow it semed to Lucretia that the sky should be clouded. Yet it was a beautiful April day, and "Heaven's Light" poured down unfeelingly. "When a great calamity has befallen the nation, we want the sun to be darkened, and the moon not give her light," Lucretia wrote Martha, "but 'how everything goes on ' as Maria said after dear little Charlie died, 'just as though such an awful event had not occurred.' "

Could good come out of all this evil? Lucretia still wasn't sure. At least the fighting was over, and the soldiers could go home. On May 2 the last regiment marched out from Camp William Penn and through the Motts' front yard. The band played, and the black soldiers shouted "Hurrah" and took off their hats to the little woman, now standing on the porch, who had been their friend for so many months. Lucretia was deeply moved. "I felt for the poor fellows—in the hope that the war is over—and over in the right way." She could not believe in her heart of hearts that carnal weapons had won a lasting victory, and she feared—correctly, it turned out—that the problems of black Americans were far from behind them.

CHAPTER

XVII

AFTER JUBILEE

THE WAR was really over at last, but Elizabeth was dying of cancer. Lucretia went to Brooklyn for three weeks to be with Pattie when a baby daughter, Anna, was born but otherwise spent the summer at Roadside, trying to keep life going as naturally as possibly while she watched her daughter fade. Dr. Ann Preston was in and out, doing all she could, and Elizabeth had some bright days. Lucretia recalled afterward how heartily she had laughed with a friend over "Catherine Beecher's Utopian plans for a housekeeping school." But there was no halting "the dread disease." On September 4, 1865, Elizabeth died.

Stoic that she was, Lucretia Mott steeled herself not to give in to morbid grief. Yet the blow was crushing. For weeks thereafter she shrank from well-intentioned visits of sympathy and avoided going to Meeting, where Friends were bound to mention her loss. She could not bear to drive past the graveyard, although she kept reminding herself that the "dear, broken, wounded spirit was at rest." Her own health remained poor, and her spirits low for more than a year afterward. "A lovely link in our circle was removed from us by death," she wrote her old friend Elizabeth Pease Nichol.

There were new calls on her heart. The war had brought an increase in Philadelphia's black population. At its end there was much unemployment and misery. Lucretia became involved in the establishment of a home for the colored aged at Front and Pine. She had relaxed her Quaker position against the celebration of Christmas for the sake of the soldiers at Camp William Penn. Now she made scrapple and baked pies for the home and gathered sugar plums and trifles "light as air" for the colored-orphan asylum at Christmastime.

She planned Christmas at Roadside for her motherless grand-children as well. Mary and Fanny Cavender were living with their Mott grandparents, while Charles, torn in his loyalties, stayed part-time with his father. Fanny was recovering not only from her mother's death but from a bad fall. Walking down Twelfth Street in Philadelphia with her uncle Edward Davis, she had been so blinded by coal dust from an open cellar door that she had tumbled down it. Fortunately she was only badly bruised.

Early in January 1866, Alfred Love, the conscientious objec-tor Lucretia had defended during the war, called a meeting of a new group, the Universal Peace Union, and invited those inter-ested to stay behind to organize a Pennsylvania Peace Society. James Mott was elected president.

Despite these activities, Lucretia remained heartsick, and the rest of the family noted that she lacked her usual enthusiasm and energy. She spoke frequently of being "old as the poles" and felt glad that there were younger, more energetic women to take her place in reform movements.

The following May 1866 a group met in New York to form the American Equal Rights Association. With the understand-ing that Elizabeth Cady Stanton, as vice-president, would do most of the work, Lucretia was named president. She was the only one who had fought equally for freedom for blacks and women. In her opening remarks Lucretia said that she rejoiced in the inauguration of a movement broad enough to cover class, color, and sex and would be happy to give her name and influ-ence if she could encourage the young and strong to carry on the good work. At the end of the meeting, when she tried to sum up the sessions with a few hopeful words, the light from a stained-glass window fell on her face, and many felt that she looked like a saint.

Quarreling between the various elements in the equal rights movement erupted a few weeks later at the Progressive Friends Meeting in Longwood. The introduction into Congress of the Fourteenth Amendment, with its use of the word *male* to define a qualified voter, had thoroughly alarmed the feminists. Susan B. Anthony, Elizabeth Cady Stanton, and Parker Pillsbury felt it was going to be necessary to start a new paper advocating woman's rights, since the *Standard* did not seem sufficiently supportive. "I weary of such everlasting complaints—then Wendell P. does not satisfy them on the woman question and so we have it—I don't think we could begin to raise money enough to conduct a paper—I'm glad sometimes that I shall not have much more to do in any of these movements," Lucretia wrote Martha.

Her uncharacteristic pessimism reflected her poor health and low spirits, which continued throughout the summer. She stayed at Roadside, occasionally accompanying James on his trips to the various local Meetings to talk about education. There was much in the immediate neighborhood to interest her. Jay Cooke, the financier of the Civil War, built a mansion nearby and came to call. Her son, Thomas Mott, now retired and wealthy, himself built a "palace" on a portion of the former Oak Farm. Where Camp William Penn had formerly stood, Edward M. Davis sold lots to black and white alike. Soon a neat row of eighteen houses could be seen from the windows at Roadside. (The community, named La Mott in honor of Lucretia, remains integrated to this day.) The usual torrent of visitors came and went. But although Lucretia Mott kept up a bright front, nothing seemed to divert her.

The family decided that a trip to Nantucket might be restorative. Since James was busy with his visits, Maria and Anna offered to go with her in late August. She was frequently sick to her stomach on the way up but recovered at Nantucket sufficiently to enjoy many of the old treats—stewed clams, corn pudding, cut tongue, mince pie. There was a heavy surf on the south shore, and Lucretia enjoyed watching the breakers, then showing her daughters the interior of the island—"the expanse of land and roads, without fences, farms—or trees." On the way home it was Anna who was exhausted. "Traveling fatigues her more than it does me—indeed few can bear more constant going from day to day than thy wife," she boasted to James. "How admirably plans can be carried out in the wonderful exactness of railroad travel. My thanksgiving are raised...that man is created with such wonderful powers."

Yet the respite was short lived. Lucretia was ill most of the fall, frequently vomiting after meals. She lost weight once more, worried about how old she looked, how bent her back was, how much she shook. She even began to try spoonfuls of whiskey as a remedy. She attempted to avoid unsettling conflict situations but was as usual unsuccessful. Visiting Pattie in November, she went to lunch at Elizabeth Stanton's house. Susan B. Anthony and Lucy Stone were also guests, and the entire time was spent discussing the next Equal Rights meeting. Just hearing them talk made Lucretia ache all over, and she was glad to get away and lie down on Pattie's sofa.

The next day she recovered her equilibrium and preached a sermon at the Friends Meeting, but on the following day Susan came with an urgent message that Lucretia go with her to meet Theodore Tilton, Horace Greeley, and Josephine Griffing to talke about forming a new paper for the equal rights movement. "I *couldn't* do it," Lucretia confessed. The following morning there was an equally pressing request that she meet with William Steadfast, editor of the New York paper, *Friend*, to see if he would be willing to add pages to give space to equal rights. Again she felt she just *couldn't* undertake it. The talk and the disagreements made her sick and dizzy.

Back in Philadelphia she enjoyed attending a wedding in the Yarnell family. Yet when Edward arrived on New Year's Day 1867 with unexpected company and a bushel of oysters, she blanched. "We were in for it until the following day...but after all it was a pleasant visit, if we *hadn't so much pleasure.*"

In the middle of January abolitionists and feminists from up and down the East Coast gathered in Philadelphia for three days of meetings, an Anti-Slavery Peace Festival, an Equal Rights Convention, and a Peace Convention. The proceeds of the Peace Festival were four hundred dollars (to be used to aid the freedmen) and might have been more if a severe snowstorm hadn't crippled Philadelphia. Lucretia thought she would have been blown away in the high winds if she hadn't had Edward's strong arm to cling to, but Edward laughed and said, "Twas mother trotted him along."

Lucretia Mott realized that she had now lived longer than her mother. "What a wonderful woman she was, to accomplish so much after 3 score." Yet she was determined to live even longer. On days that she was free of the dizziness and nausea she went in to Philadelphia as usual to make her rounds of committee meetings and to shop. One day she calculated she had covered four miles. The infirmities of her relatives and friends seemed to bother her more than her own. She worried over her sister Eliza's growing deafness and the film that was forming over James's eyes. She frequently referred to James now as "that dear old gentleman." When she heard that her old friend William Lloyd Garrison was still suffering from a sore shoulder as the result of a fall, she invited him to come to Roadside, where she was sure he would recover.

Garrison instead decided on a trip to England and France, to represent the American Freedmen's Union Commission. Before sailing he wrote Lucretia a long, sentimental letter regretting her serious indisposition: "Though you are about eleven years older than I am, if my reckoning be not at fault, I feel a strong desire that you should remain in the body until the time for my departure has come, that I may go hand in hand with you to the Spirit World."

By this time, however, Lucretia was feeling somewhat better. She went to New York in May 1867 for the annual meetings of the Anti-Slavery Society and the American Equal Rights Association, where she presided again as president. The debate over the Fourteenth Amendment had by now polarized the group. Some felt it would be necessary to pass the amendment quickly in order to provide the Southern blacks with the "shield of suffrage" to protect them against being terrorized back into peonage, as those who had gone South to aid the freedmen were now reporting. The feminists, on the other hand, felt they would have to oppose the amendment until the word *male* was struck out. Abby Kelley Foster sided with Wendell Phillips in believing that it was "the Negroes' hour," while her husband took the feminist position. Since they were both fiery orators, the sessions were lively. Elizabeth Cady Stanton advanced the questionable argument that woman's vote was needed to offset that of the freed slaves. "If all men are to vote—black and white, lettered and unlettered, washed and unwashed, then the safety of the nation, as well as the interests of woman, demand that we outweigh this incoming tide of ignorance, poverty and vice with the virtue, wealth, and education of the women of the country."

Lucretia did not care for Elizabeth's downgrading of the blacks. But she took the feminist position. She reminded her audience that in the early days of the antislavery movement it had been argued that the slave did not really want to be free, while today it was claimed that woman did not really want the vote. In either case, it was proof that the system under which they had lived had succeeded in crushing their legitimate aspirations. Many more women were now demanding the vote, and she thought that they "had the right to be a little jealous of the addition of so large a number of men to the voting class, for the colored men would naturally throw all their strength on the side of those opposed to woman's enfranchisement."

After the tumultuous sessions she returned to Roadside to rest, but a few weeks later she was on the road again, to Boston for the founding convention of a nonsectarian radical group to be called the Free Religious Association, composed of both Jews and Christians dedicated to religious reform. Of the twelve persons selected to address the opening convention, Lucretia was the only woman. She began by making it clear that she did not represent the Society of Friends or any of its branches. This was still a necessity if she wished to "keep her place" in that Society. She then went on, a bit paradoxically, to urge her listeners to follow the example of George Fox, "who was drawn away from all organizations of his time, and had to retire alone and there be instructed by a higher power than himself, by the divine word within, and had to claim that as the highest authority for action—with no Bibles, no human authorities, no ministers, no pulpits, no anything that should take the place of this divine, inward, everyday teacher, so simple in its instruction."

But although Lucretia Mott was thoroughly in sympathy with the new organization, she did not join it for several years because she objected to a phrase in the society's constitution calling for the "scientific study of theology." Rejecting as strongly as ever the concept of theology, which she defined as speculation about, as opposed to personal knowledge of, the Divine, Lucretia thought the association should devote itself to the scientific study of the religious nature of human beings. Her suggestion was eventually adopted, and the constitution was changed accordingly.

The New England Anti-Slavery Convention, which she attended the next day, was a repeat of the New York Equal Rights meeting, with the Fosters battling each other and not a single member of the Garrison family or their clique in attendance. Lucretia missed her old colleague but was angry later in the summer when she learned that Garrison had managed to arrange for the whole of a nine-thousand-dollar trust left to the Anti-Slavery Society to be given to the Freedmen's Union rather than to the *National Anti-Slavery Standard*, which was battling for its existence and for the Fourteenth Amendment. "'Tis no trifle to be thus wronged of our just dues—I have not felt any late occurrence so much, tell Ellen [Wright Garrison]," she wrote Martha crossly.

After the Boston meetings were over, Lucretia hurried home to Philadelphia to be with Eliza, whose husband, Benjamin, was mortally ill. Following his death and funeral, she settled down to a relatively quiet summer at Roadside, interrupted only by the birth of a fifth daughter, Lucretia, to Pattie and George Lord. James was still traveling from meeting to meeting, speaking on the topic of Quaker education. Lucretia assured her sister that the meetings did not tire him. " 'Plain Friends' are not apt to have a surfeit of meetings. It is so interwoven into their education," she said proudly. She did suggest at one point, however, that James take time out to look into selling his stock in a coal mine now that oil drilling was becoming practicable. "Now that oil is to be fuel, thee must hurry, so that those better able be the losers," she wrote him from Suffern.

Lucretia was still far from well and often stayed away from the dinner table because the smell of food nauseated her. But her spirits were indomitable again, and James found it impossible to persuade her to turn down invitations to speak when she felt that duty led her to accept. It was with some reluctance that he accompanied her to Brooklyn late in November so that she might give the Thanksgiving sermon at the Second Unitarian Church.

This "discourse" centered on the necessity of bringing religion into everyday life, into politics, commerce, and statecraft. Now that the slave was at last free, humankind must turn its attention to outlawing war and to achieving social justice. Let her listeners take part in the present stir about tenement houses! Let them listen to the demand for the eight-hour day! "Let this be a country, as it ought to be, the tendency in which is to equalize society, but no infringements on the rights of individuals."

The Motts returned to Roadside for Christmas, but came back to New York in January 1868 to attend the wedding of some young friends. Both caught cold on the way up, and James was soon in bed with a heavy cough and fever. Lucretia was concerned but not unduly worried—he had often had such a cold before. She allowed Pattie to send for the Lords' doctor, a homeopath, and spent her time trying to catch up with her overwhelming correspondence. Richard Mott, James's younger brother, came to see him and was from the first more worried than the rest of the household. In a few days, however, it was clear to the whole family that James was seriously ill. The doctor told Lucretia it was a form of pneumonia peculiar to old age. Lucretia began to wish Dr. Ann Preston or some other Philadelphia doctor were in attendance. "Dr. Moffatt is much sought here and I have no doubt as to his knowledge and experience and his little pills have certainly helped my cold and night sweats—at the same time you can't *command* faith," she wrote her children rather pathetically.

The household mobilized around the patient. Pattie and George carried James down in a chair to their large bedroom on the second floor. George went in person to borrow an armchair commode from some relatives. After Lucretia admitted that she had been up every hour at night tending her patient, a telegram was sent to Anna and Maria requesting that they come immediately.

James himself was quiet, patient, resigned. He asked once if James Corr, the Roadside farmer, could not come and take him home. He said to Pattie that it was pleasant to come and visit for a week or two, but "here I may be all winter." He repeated more than once, "What a pity we left home." Otherwise he said very little.

On the night of the twenty-fifth, worn out by her long ordeal of watching and worrying, Lucretia went to take a nap, leaving Maria to sit by her father. Around one A.M. Maria noticed a change in his breathing and decided to notify the rest of the family. They were all with him at two A.M. when he breathed his last.

Sad as the Mott children were over the loss of their deeply loved father, their worries centered immediately upon their frail mother. For over fifty-six years her life had been bound up with his. It seemed unlikely that she would survive long without him.

But survive she did, though sorrowing deeply. With her children around her she took James's body back to Philadelphia, where there was a funeral service at Race Street Meeting and burial at Fair Hill. The city that had once repulsed the young Motts as radicals now shared with Lucretia in her loss. There were obituaries in the papers and memorial minutes adopted by his Meeting, his many organizations, and Swarthmore College. Letters came from far and near, especially from all the old colleagues of the long antislavery struggle.

None of these were of much solace to Lucretia Mott, but she managed to pass through the first bitter months of grief with the sort of stoicism and determination to survive with which she had defeated other sorrows and ill health. A clue to her secret was her ability to voice her sense of loss, rather than bottling it up inside. On the two-month anniversary of his death, March 26, she wrote to Pattie to commemorate the date. At the time of his birthday in June she invited the family to come to Roadside as always and to join her in remembering him. Throughout that long first summer without him she spoke constantly of his absence. "Scarcely a day passes that I do not think, of course for the instant only, that I will consult him about this or that." "We were saying, as we sat in the moonlight, how we missed, in a thousand ways, the beloved occupant of the large chair there." Yet she avoided things that reminded her too poignantly of him and never again slept in the wide marriage bed they had shared for almost fifty-seven years.

As soon as he learned of his father's death, Thomas Mott returned briefly from a stay in Europe to be with his mother. Lucretia was deeply touched. Thereafter all complaints of Thomas's coolness vanished. She spoke instead of her "beloved son" and of the support he was to her in countless ways. With that instinct for self-nurturing that was one of her greatest strengths, she reached out to him and to her entire circle for the support she needed to recover from the bitter blow.

Slowly she regained interest in the world around her. There was much going on to demand it. Fanny Cavender and Bel Mott, Thomas's daughter, were to marry cousins, Thomas and Joseph Parrish. Pattie and George were moving permanently to Orange, New Jersey. Richard Webb, Lucretia's old Irish friend from 1840, now a widower, had at last fulfilled his promise to visit his friends in the United States and came to Roadside accompanied by a young cousin.

Most of all, the developing split in the woman's rights movement claimed her attention. In January 1868 Susan B. Anthony and Elizabeth Cady Stanton had begun to publish a new periodical, *Revolution*, opposing the Fourteenth and Fifteenth Amendments as written and advocating an "educated suffrage" irrespective of color and sex. The financial backer of *Revolution* was George Francis Train, a wealthy eccentric Democrat, who favored free immigration, soft currency, easier divorce, and other Copperhead notions and displayed considerable anti-black prejudice. Most of the former abolitionists were appalled by Train and angry with Susan and Elizabeth for accepting his support. "The *Revolution* is not satisfactory and I have not the littlest notion of being a subscriber.... Elizabeth Stanton's sympathy for Sambo is very questionable," Lucretia had written Martha when the news of the publication was first announced. In September 1868, when Susan and Elizabeth visited Lucretia at Roadside, Lucretia asked Susan bluntly what "thee can say in extenuation of such disloyal affiliations"?

On the other hand, she was equally dismayed when Lucy Stone and Julia Ward Howe invited her to a Woman's Rights Convention to form the New England Woman Suffrage Association and excluded Susan and Elizabeth. To go under such circumstances she felt would be too partisan. Besides, she preferred the radicals.

In the midst of these perplexities she took time out to preach a sermon at Race Street Meeting on January 3, 1869, her seventy-sixth birthday. Her topic was the religious aspect of the age, and her words were full of her faith in the progress of humanitarian concerns and the spread of enlightenment. There was a hint of her old joyousness in the talk. A few weeks later a reporter, hearing her speak, noted that her carriage was as erect and her step as light as that of a woman twenty years her junior. Somehow, in the midst of the storms, she had recovered from the worst of the pain of James's death.

A few weeks later the chaplain of the Senate opened a session of a woman's suffrage convention in Washington, D.C., with a prayer that included mention of woman being created from man's rib. According to Elizabeth Stanton's memory of the event, Lucretia Mott, who was sitting next to her, straightened up, whispering "I cannot bow my head to such absurdities." Edward M. Davis noticed his mother-in-law's reaction and slipped from the hall. When the chaplain's prayer was ended, Davis climbed back onto the platform and read from the opening chapter of Genesis. Lucretia then stepped forward and preached a short sermon, reviewing the "error" in the chaplain's prayer and insisting on "the eternal oneness and equality of man and woman." The press was amused that Lucretia should criticize a prayer in this fashion, but she thought it a good opportunity to speak truth to those in power and said she would do it again if she had the chance.

At this convention the radical wing of the suffrage movement argued forcibly against the Fourteenth Amendment. Edward Davis, who supported it, was so opposed to their position that he asked that his name be removed from the convention role. Lucretia, in the chair, permitted him, as well as many other speakers, to attack the woman's position, but several times left the chair in order to support it herself. Many in the audience were fascinated to see two members of the same family on opposite sides of the issue, apparently handling their strong disagreement without rancor.

In May the American Equal Rights Association held its annual meeting in New York, with Lucretia Mott once more in the chair. Frederick Douglass spoke, saying that suffrage for the blacks was now a matter of life and death: "When women, because they are women, are hunted down through the cities of New York and New Orleans; when they are dragged from their houses and hung from lamp posts; when their children are torn from their arms, and their brains bashed out upon the pavement, when they are objects of insult and outrage at every turn, when they are in danger of having their homes burnt down over their heads, when their children are not allowed to enter schools; then they will have an urgency to obtain the ballot equal to our own.''

It was a powerful argument, but equally powerful was that of the women who predicted—correctly of course—that if the nation settled for ''half a loaf,'' it might be many years before the opportunity came around to enfranchise everyone, women and blacks alike. And were not black women in fact equally entitled to the protection of the vote? The two positions were now so firmly held that compromise appeared impossible. Immediately after the meeting ended, Susan B. Anthony and Elizabeth Cady Stanton called a rump session of the women present and formed the National Woman Suffrage Association, devoted to fight for a federal amendment giving suffrage to women and to exclude men from leadership roles.

Lucretia chaired the Equal Rights Association sessions and tried to stem the tide of criticism against Susan and Elizabeth by pointing out that they were the real pioneers of the cause. She gave credit to Lucy Stone too, but thought privately that Julia Ward Howe had entered at the eleventh hour and was not to be compared. The tension of the irreconcilable conflict made her ''sick as a rat,'' and she hastened home to Philadelphia and took to her bed. She was slow to recover and did not travel again until the news of the death of her cousin, Nathaniel Barney, sent her to Nantucket in September to preach at his funeral.

On her way north, accompanied by Edward Hopper, Lucretia stopped in New York to talk with Susan and Elizabeth. Lucy Stone was arranging for a Woman's Rights Convention in Cleveland in November, and Lucretia wanted to urge them to attend and work for reconciliation. In Boston she saw Lucy Stone and talked with her about making peace. There was ''less asperity than in former talks,'' Lucretia reported hopefully. Still, the continued tension upset her, and she was glad to look forward to the interlude on the island of her birth.

On the boat to Nantucket she met a woman named Chadwick, from Brooklyn, revisiting the island for the first time in thirty years'':

> "Name Coffin"
> "So was mine"
> "Folger on the mother's side"
> "So was mine"
> "76 years old"
> "So am I"

> Such a coincidence, as we compared notes, made us feel acquainted and somewhat related.

Despite the sadness of the occasion, the trip gave Lucretia an opportunity to see old friends and breathe the reviving salt air. When Lucretia finally reached Philadelphia alone after a trouble-filled journey back, she was so anxious to get home that she hopped off the train while it was still moving, fell, and bruised herself rather badly. She jumped up, however, insisting that she was unhurt, and hurried off to catch the cars for Chelten Hills.

Revived by her travels, she spent much of the fall of 1869 engrossed in plans for the opening of Swarthmore College. Her daughter, Anna Hopper, had been chosen to be a member of the new board of managers, with special duties of overseeing the housekeeping. Several of Lucretia's grandchildren were considering enrolling as students. She made her first trip to Swarthmore in October to help Anna plan the laying of carpets. On inauguration day she brought her son, Thomas, and the Roadside farmer, James Corr, along with two young oak trees to plant on the Swarthmore lawn. More than one thousand people were present, according to her account, and a large number of them gathered at the tree planting, accompanied by speeches and photographs. After lunch "a good collation—*free*," the crowd assembled in the collecting room, with all the pupils present.

According to the *Friends Intelligencer*, which covered the event, Lucretia Mott said that she hoped that Swarthmore would never degenerate into a mere sectarian school and referred to the skepticism that sometimes grows out of the study of science when unaccompanied by religious faith.

On the heels of the happy day at Swarthmore came news that the Cleveland woman's rights convention had been stormy—

Lucretia was sorry to hear that Susan B. Anthony had stamped her foot—and a letter of William Lloyd Garrison attacking *Revolution* had been read, which added to the turmoil. With no reconciliation apparently possible, Lucy Stone, Henry Blackwell, Julia Ward Howe, and others of a more conservative vein had established the American Woman Suffrage Association as a parallel and rival to the national organization founded by Susan B. Anthony and Elizabeth Stanton. "It is a comfort to me that I won't be an officer to either—I'm too old anyhow," Lucretia wrote Martha.

In February 1870 Lucretia's beloved sister Eliza died of pneumonia. Except for the ten months when Lucretia taught at Nine Partners while Eliza was at Westtown, they had spent their entire lives together. To offset her bitter mourning, Lucretia undertook, that same month, to speak in all the "colored churches" of Philadelphia. "This little service among our colored people has been on my mind for a year or two passed, as a parting legacy...having long mourned with those who mourned, now to rejoice with those who do rejoice—so far in the six meetings held there has been a reciprocal all hail," she wrote Mary Grew.

The next month the pioneers of the abolition movement gathered in Philadelphia for a Jubilee celebrating the passage of the Fifteenth Amendment and the end of the long struggle for black suffrage. The other half of their mission, an end to ill treatment of blacks, was far from accomplished; the news of reconstruction from the South was disturbing. But there were too few abolitionists left with the will to keep the old societies going, and they were in consequence disbanded. In her valedictory speech to the Philadelphia Female Anti-Slavery Society, Lucretia expressed her faith in continued progress: "In our more sanguine moments we never expected to see the consummation now attained." She reminded her listeners that they had always relied on appeals to the moral force and intelligence of the people and suggested hopefully that this example might be useful "in succeeding enterprises of a similar kind."

In the midst of the Jubilee came a letter from Theodore Tilton urging her to sign an appeal to both factions of the woman's movement to resolve their differences. It meant involving herself in the controversy—as she had promised herself not to do. Yet the longing to make peace, the role that had been for years at the center of her being, was too strong to resist. She wrote back to say she would sign most willingly—"only please do not place the name first, but rather far below those who have prepared the circular."

Despite her efforts to keep her name from being prominent, Lucretia was the principal negotiator when Tilton held his attempted reconciliation meeting in April. There was no escaping the role. She was loved and respected by both branches. About a dozen were present, she reported to Martha, and several proposals made but none accepted by the Boston group. Pattie, who accompanied her, thought both Tilton and Lucretia were too partisan to be impartial. Lucretia did what she could, urging reconciliation and objecting to the "flings" in their periodicals at members of the opposite faction, but she felt that there was little thought of yielding on either side. "I went not expecting great things and I didn't get 'em—Glad to be out of it all, and I never meant to join another organization," she wrote Martha. This conflict between former comrades seemed like a defeat of everything she had stood for.

Yet she loved the old reformers, one and all, and she still believed in reform. When Miller McKim told her he had lost all faith in reform movements and could only rely on the new social sciences and the *Nation* magazine, she regarded her old protégé as "a strange talker." Her faith in progress, in people's ability to work together, remained miraculously undiminished.

The Christiana Riot of September 1851 *(top)*, in which a Maryland slave owner was killed by Lancaster Country, Pa., blacks defending four runaway slaves. From an illustration in *The Underground Railroad,* by William Still, 1872 (Photo by Ted Hetzel)

The inauguration of Swarthmore College, 1869 *(bottom).* In this photograph, although it cannot be discerned, Lucretia Mott is planting a tree on the college grounds. (Swarthmore College)

Lucretia in later years *(left) (Friends Journal)*

Sculpture by Adelaide Johnson *(below)*, showing Elizabeth Cady Stanton, Susan B. Anthony, and Lucretia Mott, and presented to the United States government in 1921 by the National Woman's Party. It is now in the crypt of the U.S. Capitol. (Library of Congress)

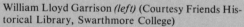

William Lloyd Garrison *(left)* (Courtesy Friends Historical Library, Swarthmore College)

CHAPTER

XVIII

AND MILES
TO GO BEFORE I SLEEP

By NOW Lucretia Mott was a famous woman. On the streets of Boston and New York, as well as Philadelphia, she was recognized, and strangers approached her to wish her well. People named their daughters after her, and clubs were established in her name, the Loyal Sons and Daughters of Lucretia Mott being one. Her daily mail contained so many requests for her autograph, her picture, her aid, that Lucretia said she wished she were in Guinea. She could not begin to keep up with the torrent. Her faithful son-in-law, Edward M. Davis, answered many of the letters. Others went long unanswered. "Skeletons in my house," Lucretia called them.

A new society for working women in Brooklyn asked for permission to name their group after her. A woman suffrage committee in San Francisco pestered her for a photograph and signature. A butcher rushed up to her in Washington market, when she was visiting New York, and told her that he had once seen her years ago in his hometown of Waterloo. A young woman in Boston stopped her on the street to present her with a copy of a new book by John Weiss.

"I'm a much over-rated woman, it's humiliating," Lucretia told her family. Thinned by ill health to a fragile eighty pounds or less, she looked angelic in her old age, and the Victorians made a legend of her saintliness. In private life, meanwhile, she was growing increasingly uninhibited. She was irritated by her great-grandchildren as she never had been by her grandchildren and began to question whether love alone was the best rule. She frequently used earthy expressions left over from her Nantucket childhood, scandalizing her proper daughters and granddaughters. "Grandmother has something beside lice in her bonnet," she said once or twice. She described physical functions—sweating or vomiting—with an explicitness that must have shocked Victorian sensibilities.

Her idiosyncrasies became the despair of her relatives. For years she had used the backs of old fliers and envelopes on which to write her letters, disdaining the fashionable French stationery her sister and daughters kept giving her. It was her way of bearing her testimony to simplicity, she said. Some of her letters were written on so many little scraps, they had to be put together almost like jigsaw puzzles. In vain Martha begged for more conventional writing paper. She even copied a whole letter from scraps in order to show Lucretia what a labor it had been to try to read the tatters.

Despite her persistent ill health, she would allow no one to dictate what she ate. She continued to enjoy coffee and to eat oysters, ice cream, codfish and onion stew, and other favorites that her family felt sure were not good for her. And although she had rather frequent colds, she would not protect herself against drafts or rain. Like her mother before her, she did not bother with an umbrella, and she even refused to use rubber sandals, declaring it was more natural to let her shoes get wet and dry out in their own good time.

Even more troubling to the family, as time went on, was her absolute insistence on traveling alone. She would not be seen to the train or helped across streets or accompanied on any of her trips, unless she happened to decide to choose a companion. Frequently on the train to and from New York she would be spotted by some Philadelphian and then would do what she could to get rid of him before she spent the entire trip in unwanted conversation. As she grew older, both family and friends worried more and more about her taking long, solitary trips to Boston, Nantucket, or Auburn, but there was no stopping her.

In May 1870 Lucretia stayed with Edward and Anna Hopper on Clinton Street in Philadelphia while she attended a round of meetings: Yearly Meeting, Quarterly Meeting, and a final meeting of the Anti-Slavery Society, the graduation exercises at the Female College, the Pennsylvania Peace Society, a Freedmen's meeting. At the latter she raised fifty dollars to send South. She then set off for Boston to take part in the anniversary meeting of the Free Religious Association. She would have gone alone, but Maria insisted on accompanying her.

At Roadside, she picked peas, entertained, and prepared for a trip to visit George and Pattie in New Jersey. (Lucretia was helping them to chop down trees from around the house.) Miller and Sarah McKim had a house at nearby Llewellyn Park, and Lucretia always managed a visit when she went to see the Lords. As usual, the visit turned into a quarrel. Miller thought Lucretia's demand for universal suffrage was too radical; only educated suffrage for blacks and women was possible, he argued. She returned home pained as usual by the bitterness of the battle.

Quarreling continued between the two factions of the woman's rights movement. Lucretia found it upsetting after her abortive efforts to make peace. She decided to stay out of it and did not attend the Washington Woman's Rights Convention of 1871. Edward Davis, who went to Washington to attend a "colored convention" at the same time, gave his mother-in-law a report of how well Susan B. Anthony, and Victoria Woodhull, a newcomer, had spoken before the Judiciary Committee, claiming that the Fourteenth Amendment had in fact already given the right of suffrage to women.

On their way home from Washington Paulina Davis and Sarah Pugh came to see Lucretia Mott full of their plans to get signers for a petition backing up this interpretation of the Fourteenth Amendment. Would Lucretia get Ann Preston and the whole faculty of the Female Medical College to sign? Would Martha Wright and Anna Hopper help? Their determined plans so upset Lucretia that she spent the whole night throwing up. The next year, when Elizabeth Stanton suggested that Lucretia organize a Philadelphia chapter of her group, she said she would have to remain a "cipher."

"Such a new set as are now interested in the suffrage question, able young minds ought to inspire new life, and would if my days were not so nearly over." Thereafter for several years she tried to stay out of the limelight and the controversies. "It is so provoking that we are needlessly two," she wrote Martha.

Yet when Pattie said something sarcastic about the quarrels, Lucretia answered heatedly that she need not go to another woman's meeting but she must not say a word against the "brave pioneers."

Brave pioneers of other struggles were dying fast. In February 1871 Lucretia and Edward Davis drove to Wilmington to attend the funeral of their old friend Thomas Garrett, one of the foremost conductors of the underground railroad. "Such a concourse of all sects and colors as we never saw—thousands—the street lined for half a mile and nearly as many outside as in," Lucretia wrote describing it.

More cheering was a visit from her sister Martha. Together the two went to hear Victoria Woodhull make her first Philadelphia lecture. With Edward Davis they visited Westtown, the Orthodox boarding school, and the new institution, Swarthmore, which was serving at the time as both boarding school and college. Swarthmore was said to be as much better than Westtown as it was more expensive, Lucretia had heard. After leaving Westtown, Edward said, "Blessed be simplicity." After leaving Swarthmore his comment was, "Blessed be culture."

Times were certainly changing. At Yearly Meeting that spring a suggestion was made that men and women serve on Representative Meeting, an interim decision-making body, on an equal basis. Lucretia could scarcely believe her ears. This was a reform she had fought for in the old days, when she was discounted as a radical and a heretic. Now it was actually considered. The next year she was put on a committee to discuss the change. (It became official five years later.) It was about time, Lucretia thought. In all human institutions there had to be equality. Otherwise there would always be despots. "'Tis not in the nature of things for man to be empowered over his fellow being and preserve his original mercy and purity of right."

Another great change was in the attitude of New York Yearly Meeting. For years they had hated Lucretia as a heretic. Now she was urged to come and was warmly accepted. How few were left, though, of the old friends and enemies she had once known! "But glad am I to see some of the young coming out wiser than their teachers," she wrote Martha.

From New York she went on by boat to Boston for the spring

Meetings, and in August made her annual visit to Auburn. During the brief intervals between trips, Lucretia was busy with her usual assortment of good causes. She continued to be interested and active in the Northern Association for Poor Women, taking to the workshop wagonloads of produce from the farm. Packing boxes and raising money for the freedmen was a constant task. She sent clothes to Harriet Tubman, who had established a home for poor blacks in Auburn, New York; to the freedmen settling in Iowa and later Kansas; to Josephine Griffing, who was working for the freedmen still in Washington, D.C. She continued to raise money to support the schools for freedmen in the South run by a number of women who had visited Roadside during or after the Civil War.

Increasingly, however, as she grew older, she became absorbed in local concerns. She was present at the cornerstone laying of the Aged Colored Home, now renamed the Stephen Smith Memorial Home. She helped to put on a fair for the "colored" children's orphanage. At Christmastime she never forgot to take food and gifts to both these institutions. As snow changed to sleet, on Christmas Eve 1871, James Corr drove her on her rounds while she delivered seven turkeys, thirty mince pies, fifty aprons, fifty "head handkerchiefs" for the "colored aged," and picture handkerchiefs and boxes of candy for the orphans.

Overriding all these other interests, however, was the cause into which she poured the fire of her remaining years, the cause of peace. Her long, painful struggle with her principles during the Civil War had awakened within her a strong desire to devote the rest of her life to trying to make sure that war and its barbarities never came again.

She had been for years vice president of the Universal Peace Union, and in 1870 she was elected president of the Pennsylvania Peace Society, a post she held until her death. She brought to the cause of peace all the freshness and optimism she had poured years before into the antislavery movement. Alfred Love, her colleague, reported that she "seemed like a child, full of enthusiasm."

A goal of the Peace Society under Lucretia Mott's leadership was to get military training out of the public schools. She believed that the love of peace was implanted at birth in each child but that parents sometimes failed to nourish it by giving the children guns to play with, teaching them to stick up for their rights with physical force, and using corporal punishment as a form of discipline. If, in addition, children learned to be little soldiers at school, what hope could there be for raising a nation geared to peace? she asked.

Her pacifism was thoroughgoing. She objected to capital punishment and insisted that society hold to "the absolute sacredness of human life." She saw a relationship between economic exploitation and war. Peace did not mean the absence of war. It meant the arbitration of disputes and justice for all—the Indians, the working classes, the blacks, women. "There can be no true peace without justice," she often said. At an early peace meeting she had startled her audience by talking about justice for American Indians: "We have never considered the wrongs of the Indians as our own. We have aided in driving them farther and farther west, until as the poor Indians say 'you will drive us away, until we go beyond the setting sun.' " If the Indian took revenge on white settlers, it was because the white man had taught him to take the sword, she argued.

At the Annual Meeting of the Pennsylvania Peace Society, held in December 1871, a delegation of forty from the International Workingmen's Association, probably a branch of the First International organized by Karl Marx, was present. Some of the more conservative members thought they ought not to be there, but Lucretia defended them and said she thought it would be possible to work with them. "While we aim to be thorough and maintain the highest peace principles, at the same time we can labor with those who do not go as far as we do. The working men. . . resolved that they would no longer submit quietly to being used in war, and some of them went so far as to resolve to put an end to war even if they had to fight for it."

After the meetings she wrote to her old friend Richard Webb to ask if it were indeed true that the Workingmen's Union of England had come out with a protest against war? "Even the woman question, as far as voting goes, does not take hold of my every feeling as does war."

The Franco-Prussian War had ended with a settlement against France that many thought too harsh. Richard Webb was raising money for French war sufferers. Lucretia told him that the Quakers in Philadelphia, both Orthodox and Hicksite, were raising money for the relief of war sufferers on both sides of the conflict. (It was during this war that the red and black star, now the symbol of Quaker service all over the world, was first used.)

Preaching against war became as habitual with Lucretia as preaching against slavery had once been. In May 1872, making good her welcome at New York Yearly Meeting, she preached a sermon about the U.S. claims against Great Britain in regard to the warship *Alabama*, which were then being adjudicated by an international tribunal. She said she thought all international conflicts should hereafter be settled by such peaceful means, as the Society of Friends had long advocated. The admiring reporter from the *New York Herald* thought her words had both grace and strength. Lucretia was nevertheless annoyed by the account. The reporter had said she removed her bonnet and handed it to a sister, "a thing I never do—nor was a handkerchief unfolded and laid over the railing."

Lucretia could not stay over to attend a meeting of the New York Peace Association where Julia Ward Howe intended to launch the first "Mother's Day," an annual event when women could demonstrate against war (it was celebrated thus for several years). She hurried off to Boston for meetings and to hear an excellent lecture on the Darwin theory: "no hard words—only 'anthromorphism' (if that's it) once." The new acceptance of scientific thought, for which Lucretia's liberal preaching had helped to pave the way, had come at last.

At home there was continuing anxiety over Marianne Pelham Mott. She had been ill for several years, following menopause, and Thomas had taken her to Switzerland to see if a change of air might cure her. The news grew worse, and in late June Martha Wright set off for Europe to be with her. Early in July word came that she had died.

There had been so many deaths. In April a beloved great-grandson had died after an accident in the Roadside barn. The same month Ann Preston, Philadelphia's pioneer woman doctor and one of Lucretia's best friends, had died at fifty-eight. Now Marianne. Who next? In self-protection, Lucretia tried to look at the bright side. The family circle was still large, she reminded her grieving sister. "How many we have to love and to feel for."

The fall brought fresh excitement to help distract Martha's grief. Susan B. Anthony had decided to go ahead and vote in the presidential election in Rochester, New York, as a way of claiming once more that the Fourteenth Amendment gave suffrage to women. She was arrested, indicted, and held for trial. Here a hostile judge fined her without permitting the jury to render a decision. Although Susan refused to pay the fine, the case was never carried to the higher courts, as she had hoped.

At election time also came word that Victoria Woodhull was in jail! She had been imprisoned for libel, after publishing an account of a liaison between Henry Ward Beecher and Elizabeth Tilton. Earlier Lucretia had stoutly defended Victoria when the more conservative women had feared her "free love" reputation might tarnish their cause. Now she once more rushed to Victoria's defense. Perhaps she had suffered some sort of mental lapse, causing her temporarily to depart from the truth? At any rate "it was wrong for her to be punished when so many greedy monopolizers can come off scot free." The cause would never be harmed by radicals like Woodhull but rather by the conservative Boston clique, who were so proper that their meetings caused no stir.

In early 1872 Anna Davis Hallowell traveled in Europe to write and paint. Her mother, Maria Davis, took charge of the Hallowell children at Roadside. Lucretia found them demanding, a result, she thought, of the modern use of nursemaids. Maria seemed to her to be a slave to the children. As often as possible Lucretia hurried off to Orange to be with Pattie and pick up her running battle with Miller McKim. "Tell Miller I have quite forgotten the last talk and am longing to see him again, but Sarah must keep us in order," she instructed Pattie.

In May 1873 she took the night boat from New York to Boston. Thinking this would be her last such visit, she spoke at the Free Religious Association from her heart, urging her listeners to pay attention to the Light within:

> Therefore I say, preach your truth; let it go forth, and you will find, without any notable miracle, as of old, that every man will speak in his own tongue in which he was born. And I

will say, that if these pure principles have their place in us, and
are brought forth by faithfulness, by obedience, into practice,
the difficulties and doubts that we may have to surmount will
be easily conquered. There will be a power higher than these.
Let it be called The Great Spirit of the Indian, the Quaker's
"Inward Light" of George Fox, the "Blessed Mary, Mother
of Jesus" of the Catholics, or Brahma, the Hindoo's God—
they will all be one, and there will come to be such faith and
such liberty as shall redeem the world.

After the meeting she was urged to attend an evening reception where "no poor old lady was ever so heartily welcomed."
The young people brought her flowers, plum cake, and ice
cream and urged her to speak a few words. "So the old goose
did that too and begged the dear young people to simplify their
costume etc." Garrison was present to see his old comrade
honored. It seemed like the end of an era. Lucretia, however,
surprised them all by returning to the meetings in 1875.

When Lucretia Mott spoke of the Great Spirit of the Indians,
she may have been thinking of the Modocs who, under a brave
leader, Captain Jack, had been resisting forced resettlement in
California. Early in June word came that six of them had been
captured and condemned to death. Both the Universal Peace
Union and the Pennsylvania Peace Society decided to intervene.
A committee of the former waited on President Ulysses S.
Grant and urged him to pardon the Modocs. Not sure that this
would bring results, Lucretia decided to call upon the President
when he was in the neighborhood of Roadside visiting the financier Jay Cooke. Several versions of the story were told afterward:

"But mother, thee has no invitation," Edward Davis said.

"My spirit says 'go' and it will not wait for etiquette, my business is urgent, I am going," Lucretia replied. At Cooke's she
was shown immediately into Grant's presence, and the President listened thoughtfully to her earnest pleas. When she turned
to leave, he stooped down to whisper in her ear. "Madam, they
will not all be executed." The following month the six condemned Indians were led to scaffold, but only four were hanged.

The Pennsylvania Peace Society made a great deal of this partial victory, but Lucretia regretted that she had been unable to
save all the Modocs, including their leader, Captain Jack. "He
told me that they would not all be hanged, but I must know the

feeling both North and South. Of course we knew that a plea for mercy for Captain Jack would be in vain,'' she wrote Martha after the Grant interview.

A few weeks later came the tremendous financial crash of 1873 and the ruin of Jay Cooke. There was talk of his selling all his earthly possessions and of his palace being bought by a Catholic order. Lucretia's heart went, however, to the poor workingmen who were suffering from the ensuing depression. She determined once more to study finance and usury. Surely there were laws of nature that man could follow in the management of such things? In 1874 she eagerly went to hear Victoria Woodhull lecture on political economy, banking, land monopolies, and the rights of workingmen and the people.

Members of her own family were growing prosperous, especially her son, Thomas, who had bought a place at Newport, Rhode Island. Lucretia worried that all their wealth was at the expense of the working people and tried to preach simplicity. Yet she never overcame her old fear of failure, based on her father's troubles. When her nephew, Willie Wright, had considered a delay in accepting a business offer in Florida until his new wife, Flora, had had her first baby, Lucretia thought it might hurt his reputation as a rising young businessman. "What would Nantucket say, for husband not to sail when ship was ready but wait 4 or 5 months for a baby?"

She was eighty-one. Every letter now brought news of the death of some contemporary. She continued to try to bear it bravely, but 1874 was a heartbreaking year. In March word came that Miller McKim was ill. Lucretia sent him butter from Roadside and wrote anxiously for news. Despite all the bitter quarrels, the bonds between the two remained tender. Lucretia grieved for him, after his death in June, as she might have for one of her own family.

One of her very own, in fact, was ill. In the spring Anna Hopper was diagnosed as having a tumor of the throat. "It is all inexpressibly sad," Lucretia wrote. It was Elizabeth all over again. Anna had her good days and her bad days, but the decline continued, and in August she died. It was as Lucretia wrote Lydia Love, "a longed-for termination of a fatal malady. ...Still the tender ties of nature and affection are not severed without many pangs.'' To add to the pain, Anna's nineteen-year-old son, Isaac Hopper, died the next month, leaving Edward and one unmarried daughter, Maria, alone in the house on Spruce Street.

Lucretia had barely caught her breath from this double blow when news came from Boston that her beloved sister Martha Wright had taken ill with pneumonia visiting the Garrisons and in a few days had died. She had been sixty-nine.

Lucretia Mott believed that one should never court death but peacefully await its coming. However, for a little while after Martha's death she evidently thought that the end had come for her. She began to gather up and destroy as many of her old letters as she could find "before I depart this state of being." She quoted Ecclesiastes: "The grasshopper shall be a burden." She looked for ways of getting rid of the piles and piles of peace circulars that Alfred Love regularly inundated her with. She even abandoned letter writing for several months. But her love of life and her ties to the living soon reasserted themselves. She began to worry about David Wright's future and to correspond with her niece Eliza Wright Osborne. Maria Davis, constantly at her side, reminded her more and more of James. "Precious Pattie's" visits were cherished, and, sure of her daughter's love, Lucretia felt perfectly free to demand that she come more often.

On April 14, 1875, the old Pennsylvania Abolition Society observed its centennial and invited Lucretia to be an honored guest. Since this society had never admitted women to membership and had opposed the antislavery societies as too radical, Lucretia may have been surprised at the invitation. Yet James had once been a member and had served as secretary in 1822 and 1823. Other women, including even the controversial Abby Kelley Foster, had been invited to be present. Lucretia decided to attend and was met with warmth and delight. She was introduced by the Vice-president of the United States, Henry Wilson, who said, "I propose now to present to you one of the most venerable and noble of the American women, whose voice for forty years has been heard and tenderly touched many noble hearts. Age has dimmed her eye and weakened her voice, but her heart, like the heart of a wise man and wise woman, is yet young." After a storm of applause, Lucretia stepped forward and recited in a firm, clear voice a stanza from a poem by Wordsworth:

> *I've heard of hearts unkind, kind words*
> *With coldness still returning*
> *Alas, the gratitude of man*
> *Hath oftener left me mourning.*

She then went on to say that she had come to the meeting without the slightest intention of speaking to a society where women were not expected to take part. She would, however, say a few words to remind her listeners that much remained to be done for the education of the black people and to stop the outrages being perpetuated against them in the South. It was the moral influence of the antislavery cause that had won them emancipation, and that influence must be brought to bear once more in reconstruction.

In May she spoke at the Mother's Day celebration of the Women's Peace Festival. She still did not think that women differed widely from men, she said; at least the facts did not substantiate it. She could not therefore believe that if women got their just rights, all evils in society would cease. Very few women had been active in the peace movement until recently. The fact that women were now active was one of the encouraging signs of the times.

"Within thirty or forty years there has been more remarkable success than before in all reforms. The people are learning that the weapons of our warfare are not carnal, to the pulling down of strongholds."

The following year, when she again spoke on Mother's Day, she startled her audience by saying that while she was in favor of peace, she was also in favor of war: "I mean the firmness and combativeness that marked the antislavery warfare.... I want that there should be a belief, a faith in the possibility of removing mountains to the side of right. If we believe that war is wrong, as everyone must, then we ought to believe that by proper efforts on our part it may be done away with."

It was 1876, the year the Centennial of the Declaration of Independence was celebrated in the United States. With their usual flare for showmanship, Elizabeth Cady Stanton and Susan B. Anthony decided to hold a convention of the National

Woman Suffrage Association in Philadelphia on the Fourth of July. A headquarters was opened on Chestnut Street, and preparations for the event were begun. Somehow Elizabeth managed to persuade Lucretia to serve as vice-president of the association, and to preside at the convention, which was to be held at the First Unitarian Church.

As a tribute to their veteran leader, as well as an acknowledgment of the role of women in American life, the officers of the association decided to ask the Centennial Commission to permit Lucretia Mott, accompanied by Elizabeth Stanton, to present a women's Declaration of Independence, rewritten and updated for the occasion, to the Vice-president during the July Fourth ceremonies at Independence Hall. When the request was denied, the women were angry, and one of their number went to the offices of the commission to make a formal protest.

By the afternoon, word had been received at the National's headquarters that they were not to be allowed to present their declaration. As a sort of sop, however, they were offered five seats among the honored guests in the hall. Lucretia Mott and Elizabeth Cady Stanton decided to decline the offer, but to go directly to the First Unitarian Church. Susan B. Anthony, Matilda Joslyn Gage, Sara Andrews Spencer, Lillie Devereux Blake, and Phoebe Couzins, however, took the tickets. On the morning of the fourth they attended the ceremonies. Just as Richard Henry Lee, of Virginia, a descendant of one of the signers, finished reading the original declaration and the band was preparing to strike up the Brazilian national anthem in honor of the emperor of Brazil, who was present, Susan B. Anthony rose and presented the women's document in silence to the flustered master of ceremonies. The five women then walked down the aisle, distributing printed copies of their declaration to the right and to the left. Men stood on their chairs to grab copies while the officials shouted for order. Outside, the women climbed onto a bandstand erected for later entertainment, and while Phoebe Couzins held a parasol over her head, Susan B. Anthony read the women's declaration to the crowd.

The convention at the First Unitarian Church was due to begin at twelve noon. After the reading of the declaration the five women, followed by some curious strangers, walked to the church in time to see Lucretia Mott open the sessions. Several people in the back of the church complained that they could not see her and suggested that she use the pulpit. She complied, saying, "I am somewhat like Zaccheus of old, who climbed the sycamore tree, his Lord to see. I climb the pulpit, not because I am of lofty mind, but because I am short of stature that you may see me." At this, the Hutchinson family singers struck up the song "Nearer My God to Thee." Many in the audience wept.

"Weep not for me," Lucretia said, according to press reports. "Rather let your tears flow for the sorrows of the multitude. My work is done. Like a ripe fruit I await the gathering. Death has no terrors, for it is a wise law of nature. I am ready whenever the summons may come."

The convention lasted all afternoon. Elizabeth Cady Stanton read the Declaration of Rights for Women; Belva Lockwood, the second woman to run for the presidency, discussed abuses of the judiciary. Matilda Gage spoke on marriage laws, Sara Andrews Spencer on the evils of a double standard in the moral code for men and women, Susan B. Anthony on taxation without representation.

Lucretia Mott stood on her feet throughout the four-hour session, speaking at times to review the history of the movement and to add words of enthusiasm and encouragement.

To celebrate the Centennial, an International Exposition was held in Philadelphia from May 10 to November 10. On the west bank of the Schuylkill, the exposition covered 236 acres and consisted of 167 buildings. Lucretia made several visits to the Centennial grounds. Many trophies of war were exhibited there, she acknowledged, but "this we must expect in the present state of mankind." She was glad that so many representatives of the so-called heathen nations were present, and she thought it interesting that one of these commented on his surprise in finding so many warlike preparations in a Christian country.

The one issue, however, that did excite her was the agitation to close the exposition on Sunday, mounted by many Protestants and opposed only by the Catholics, Unitarians, and a few Hicksites. Lucretia felt that a Sabbath closing would not only be giving way to religious formalism but would prevent working-class people from enjoying the exposition on their only day off. She spoke at the Women's Peace Festival in June of her disapproval: "The attempt of the Commission to keep the gates closed, it seems to me, is a lamentable sign of the times; a war-like sign and there are rumors that some of the people will demand their rights by force. I hope that as lovers of Peace, for there is no true Peace that is not founded on justice and right, we shall show our love for the whole people without distinction, by using all proper means to have this opened and by a free and open recognition of the rights of all."

When the Commission finally voted in September to close the exposition on Sundays, Lucretia decided that she would protest by no longer going into the city on First-days to attend Meeting for Worship or for any other reason. She continued this boycott until the end of her life, although she went regularly to Fourth-day Meeting at the Race Street Meeting House to watch the children file in and settle into silence.

More and more, as she grew older, she placed her faith in the spark of the Divine that she saw in children. "Children love peace. The little child knows when it says, mother, I love everybody. There is a Divine Instinct in them which prompts this feeling." Amid all the discouragements of the 1870s, the decline in reform, the corruption of the "Gilded Age," the failure of reconstruction in the South, the persecution of the native Americans, along with the sorrows of her advancing years, she clung to her faith in this principle.

CHAPTER

XIX

A GENTLE PARTING

SHE LIVED from the days of George Washington to those of Rutherford B. Hayes, from the times of Thomas Paine and Thomas Jefferson to those of Karl Marx and Charles Darwin. She had seen the invention of the locomotive and the steamboat, the telegraph and the telephone, the oil well and the typewriter. She had watched the nation grow from thirteen colonies clustered along the Eastern Seaboard to thirty-eight states spread across the entire continent. She had seen Philadelphia grow from 50,000 to over 800,000 while losing its preeminence as American's largest city. She watched a population of craftsmen and tradesmen replaced by barons of industry and a growing working class.

She had fought all these years for equality and she had seen some victories. The slave was freed, although recent news from the South revealed that he was reduced again almost to the status of a serf. The woman's rights movement was a going concern, captained by her old comrades. She had played a role in bringing Swarthmore College into being. Now one of its graduates had become the first American woman to earn a Ph.D. The Female Medical College was thriving and had over two hundred graduates. An affiliated hospital was on strong footing, thanks to the money left it by Ann Preston. Men and women were playing an equal role in decision making in the Society of Friends, although they still met separately for business. Even the campaign for integrated streetcars to Chelten Hills had finally succeeded.

There had been many defeats too. The treatment of American Indians was increasingly disturbing. Corruption in government,

even in William Penn's City of Brotherly Love, was the order of
the day. The peace societies had had no success keeping military
training out of the schools, and the increasing tendency of
American presidents to want to involve themselves in the affairs
of Latin America promised poorly for the cause of peace.

She was old now, so old and frail that she was ethereal, more
spirit than body, almost luminous with the light she loved. Simple woman though she was, she had been obedient, a child of
Light. Now it was time to wait patiently and cheerfully for the
end.

The family she had loved so faithfully was widely scattered.
Her grandson, Henry Davis, lived abroad with his ailing wife;
Fanny Cavender Parrish and her husband were in Colorado
Springs; Thomas Mott spent a good deal of his time in Newport, Rhode Island; the Davises went to Bar Harbor every summer. The last remaining Folger relative on Nantucket had died,
but there were still many directions for the family letters to be
sent, and Lucretia kept them circulating as faithfully as ever.

Only Maria and Edward Davis, themselves aging, remained
with her at Roadside. She often spoke rather unsentimentally of
selling the place, now that the family was so small, but she
stayed on year after year. She loved the farm's largess in summer and brought eggs, cream, fruit, and vegetables on every trip
to the city. Once she arrived in town carrying under her huge
cloak "eggs by the dozen, chickens, and a little *sweet* piece of
pickled pork, mince pies, vegetables of the season....We do
not know for she concealed how much of the way she had
walked from the station or how broad a trail of dropped eggs
she left behind her, but as she at last reached Anna Hopper's
and tugged at the stiff bell cord, the big bottle of cream slipped
from her tired hands and smashed upon the top shelf, a libation
at the threshold, but so much better in coffee. Wasn't that
hard?"

She continued to like to pick peas in the early morning
although Lucretia confessed that it made Maria "rave" to see
her out in the garden with the sun beating down on her head.
The smell of the earth refreshed her, and she was determined to
continue to do her share of the work of the household. She often ate only peas for her dinner, unless one of her grandchildren
brought a special treat of ice cream.

So she stayed and continued to try to make Roadside more like Nantucket by cutting down the remaining trees and shrubs around the house. Heaven's light, clear, brilliant, stark, uncompromising, a light that matched the Light within, mattered to her more and more with each passing year.

In 1876 after the Centennial celebration, she paid a final visit to the island of her birth, where her granddaughter, Anna Davis Hallowell, had rented a house for the summer. She took Anna and her children to see the sights of her childhood: the old well, the house on Fair Street, the windmill to which she had once taken corn, the spot where she had seen a woman whipped. Anna was touched to see Lucretia stop every aged person to ask about matters that went back seventy years or more. At eighty-three, Lucretia was one of the oldest survivors, and few could answer her questions. She left promising to be back the next year. As she had written her cousin Mary Earle, she still believed that happy times were more lasting and social relations more enduring on Nantucket.

She never managed the return trip, but in 1878, at the age of eighty-five went to Rochester, New York, to attend the thirtieth anniversary of Seneca Falls. Sarah Pugh, only seven years younger than she, was her companion. The family at Roadside saw the two off with mixed feelings, but the trip was an entire success. Lucretia appeared rejuvenated and spoke to the convention at length, calling for not only equal civil, religious, educational, and industrial rights but "an equality of political exertion. Give woman the privilege of cooperating in making the laws and there will be harmony without severity, justice without oppression," she promised. At the end of the session the whole convention rose to its feet in her honor, and the veteran abolitionist Frederick Douglass, on behalf of all of them, said, "Good-bye, Lucretia Mott."

But her long career in reform was still not over. If she did not make as many trips to conventions during her last five years, she was just as diligent as ever in attending meetings in Philadelphia. Right up until the end she chaired most meetings of the Pennsylvania Peace Society. Elizabeth Buffum Chace, of Rhode Island, thought she was in her dotage and manipulated by Alfred Love, but William Eyre, a closer associate, thought her "intellectual powers wonderfully preserved": "She is very weak physically. Comes in seven miles from her country home. Non approval is shown in her facial change, and the brilliance of her eyes. Nearly 4 score 10. Did she ever have her equal in mental ability and broadness and liberality of view and divine inborn charity for all?"

When Lucretia came in to the peace committee meetings, Alfred Love confided to his diary, she often spent the entire day, eating soda crackers and resting between sessions, rather than go home to her family, who might not permit her to return. In 1879 Edward M. Davis spoke at the annual meeting about his mother-in-law's diligence: "I want to say a word about my mother-in-law, Lucretia Mott, who will be eighty-six the third of next month. The tears came into my eyes when I saw this good woman here yesterday, who ought to have been home receiving the blessings there. But she came here almost fainting, for the purpose of standing before this community, and bearing her testimony in favor of Peace. Is it not enough to inspire you, my friends, to this cause?"

At home at Roadside her new enthusiasm was Dean Arthur Stanley's valedictory address at Saint Andrews, which she digested for the *Voice of Peace*: a publication of the Universal Peace Union. "We often hear of reconciliation of theology and science. It is not reconciliation that is needed, but the recognition that they are one and indivisible. . . . Whatever enlarges our ideas of nature, enlarges our ideas of God."

While Edward Davis shared her enthusiasm for suffrage and the peace movement—now that the Civil War was over—and Thomas Mott gave money to some of her causes, none of her children remained active in the field of reform, nor were any of her daughters or granddaughters active advocates of woman's rights. Only Anna Davis Hallowell had any interest in an independent career, as a writer. Lucretia supported her in this but was content for the rest to devote themselves to the more traditional role of wife and mother. When Ellen Lord left Swarthmore early, she even wrote to Pattie that the girl did not need more educaton, beyond the training in domestic arts Pattie could give her at home. It was freedom of choice for all women that she had advocated all along.

None of her children were members of the Society of Friends any longer, and few of her grandchildren were more than nominal Quakers. This, too, Lucretia seemed to accept. She had felt ambivalent toward the Society of Friends for so many years —loving it but hating its reluctance to change—that she could understand the impatience of the young with the bonds of "sect." Her own faith was stronger than ever, but it was a faith so inextricably bound up into her everyday life—in a worshipful attitude toward the good in men and women and in the laws of nature—in unhesitating action in response to Divine impulse—that it was hard to separate out and transmit. It was her whole life that spoke of her faith and profoundly affected men and women. "She little knows 'what arguments she to her neighbors' creed hath lent,'' William Ellery Channing once said. Her sermons seemed truly inspired, but it was the spirit, as much as the words themselves, that moved people.

Robert Collyer, a Unitarian minister, once wrote that he felt Lucretia Mott was too radical in religion, "steering by the head—a little too steadily, and giving faith a poor show against reason.'' Yet it was she, he acknowledged, who helped him understand the appropriateness of the Catholic faith for many people. Lucretia did believe in reason, but to her it was God's gift, to enable men and women to understand God's world. Hers was a faith that could be caught better than it could be taught. The result was that many of her listeners, as well as those in her inner circle, turned to Unitarianism, which she continued to feel was too cold, rather than join her in trying to awaken the sleeping fires of Quakerism. Only today is her full influence on the Society of Friends coming to fruition.

Whether the realization that she had failed to convert the ones she loved to the causes to which she had devoted her life was a source of pain to Lucretia, we can only guess, for she never spoke of it. Once, addressing the Peace Society, she said that nothing gave her greater joy than seeing her children walking in the Truth and, "as Sojourner Truth said, 'you are all my children.' '' Like Elizabeth Cady Stanton, she may have made up her mind that her descendants in reform would be the men and women she had inspired rather than those to whom she had given birth.

Many of those protégés came to see her during her last years. Susan B. Anthony visited Roadside in July 1876, after the Centennial celebration, and came away with ten dollars that Lucretia insisted she take. "It is too hard for our widely extended National Society to suffer thee to labor so unceasingly without a consideration." Laura Towne called, and Martha Schofield wrote from Aiken, South Carolina, to thank her not only for recent gifts for the freedmen but for her lifelong inspiration. Belva Lockwood, newly admitted to practice before the Supreme Court, came to tea and talked about the settlement of international disputes by arbitration. William Lloyd Garrison made two trips to Roadside, one only a few months before his death in May 1879.

Children, grandchildren, nieces, and nephews continued to visit. In April 1879 Lucretia commented that there had been only eighteen for lunch and it was enough. Increasingly she kept to her room during mealtime and saw the great-grandchildren only when they came up to her room to get a mint drop. One spotted Lucretia's false teeth in a dish beside her and cried, "What's that!" in great astonishment. She was becoming self-conscious about her bent back and thought, with just a trace of her old vanity, that she ought not to be seen walking the streets.

Nevertheless, she continued to commute to Philadelphia when duty called. On her eighty-sixth birthday the officers and employees of the North Penn railroad wrote her a letter expressing their appreciation of the "happy intercourse" that had existed between her family and the North Penn Line for so many years. Throughout 1879 she traveled regularly to the city for Fourth-day Meeting, and in November she was present at Quarterly Meeting and made a stirring appeal for the freedmen now pouring into Kansas and being aided by a Quakerly acquaintance, Elizabeth Comstock.

"Maria Hopper *would* keep with me quite to the 51st street cars," Lucretia reported crossly.

In November she attended the anniversary meeting of the Pennsylvania Peace Society but was too weak to stay to the end. She could not manage the reception for President Grant in December, where a picture of herself was presented to him, and he spoke of his memories of her. She was well enough in the spring, however, to attend Yearly Meeting at Race Street. Maria, who went with her, reported to Pattie that "it was an ovation every day, in the multitude which came just to take her by the hand," and "the only way to escape this, for it was very exhausting, was to leave before the closing minute was read."

Lucretia spoke once when the meeting seemed to be slow in taking action on a temperance petition. She was tired of the phrase "way has not opened," she said. So often in the past it had been used to serve as an excuse for inaction. Maria overheard one Quaker whisper to another, "Lucretia has outlived her persecutors."

Rejuvenated by this meeting, Lucretia thought she might go up to Boston and Medford for a visit. She seemed, however, to grow weaker from this time on and rarely left Roadside. By early fall it was apparent that she was failing each day, gradually and without complaint. She stayed in bed most of the time, where she liked to hear the family read the news of the day or a favorite great-grandson sing "John Brown's Body" or "Old Folks at Home." She knew she was going to die and said several times that she was quite ready. Her only concern was that her burial be simple. "Remember, mine has been a simple life, let simplicity mark the last done for me. I charge thee, do not forget this." Word spread among friends and family that it was finally time to say good-bye. Pattie arrived to help Maria with whatever care Lucretia required and to stay until the end.

On November 1, 1880, Lucy Stone wrote from Boston to report that at the thirtieth anniversary of the First National Woman's Rights Convention, held in Worcester in 1850, a resolution had been unanimously passed: "Resolved, that this convention presents its greetings to its venerable early leader and friend, Lucretia Mott, whose life in its rounded perfection as wife, mother, preacher and reformer is the prophesy of the future of woman. The large liberty which the Society of Friends has always given to women has been justified in her example; have we not a right to believe that the larger measure of freedom to church and state we are here to claim will be alike blessed to all American women?"

"We think of you, dear Mrs. Mott, with loving tenderness," Lucy wrote, "and sympathy in your feeble health, but we remember the other days of strength, and the help given so freely to our inexperience, in the sure belief that the good cause we have sought to establish will surely be carried at no distant day.''

A few days after this letter reached Roadside, Lucretia's mind, which had remained so bright, began to wander. She seemed to think she was directing her own funeral and kept stressing that it must be ''decorous, orderly, and simple.'' On November 11, 1880, with all her remaining children and grandchildren about her, she peacefully breathed her last.

In keeping with her last wishes, the funeral was simple. Relatives and close friends gathered at Roadside for a memorial service at which several old friends spoke. Then the small coffin was taken to the Fair Hill burial grounds, where several thousand gathered silently. At the graveside only one Peace Society colleague, Henry Child, said a few words. The silence became profound. ''Will no one speak?'' a low voice asked. ''Who can speak?'' another said. ''The preacher is dead.''

News of Lucretia Mott's death spread quickly throughout the nation. There were obituaries in New York, Boston, Rochester, and Philadelphia papers as well as in the *Nation, Harper's,* the *Christian Ledger,* the *Baptist Weekly,* and the *Voice of Peace.* Walking up Broadway a few days after her death, Robert Collyer reported he saw her picture in a store window, set there evidently that all could once more see ''the beautiful face.''

A memorial service was held at Mother Bethel Church in Philadelphia, at which Robert Purvis spoke. William Furness preached a sermon on the message of her life at the First Unitarian Church in Philadelphia and Robert Collyer at the Church of the Messiah in New York; others in Brooklyn, and Germantown. Race Street Meeting wrote a long memorial minute. The National Woman Suffrage Association held an elaborate memorial service in Washington in January—Frederick Douglass thought Lucretia would have hated all the music and flowers—and the Peace Society remembered her on her birthday, January 3, 1881.

Letters of sympathy poured in to Roadside from all over the country. Susan B. Anthony wrote to say how sorry she was that she had missed the funeral and to urge Maria and Pattie to start immediately on a life of their mother. "No one else can do it, as you two loving daughters—and I do hope you will set about it, what a loving occupation it will be for you."

To Ella Sargent, who was preparing material for the National Woman Suffrage Association's memorial service, Susan wrote, "Mrs. Mott fought a triple battle—1st in the Religious Society—Quaker—of which she was a member, she being Hicksite—Unitarian she was persecuted and ostracized by many of her old and best friends.... Then 2nd—Anti-Slavery—for her work for that she was almost turned out of the Society—the Hicksites—then for her woman's rights—she again lost the favor of many of her oldest and best friends, but through it all she was ever sweet tempered and self poised."

In his diary Alfred Love wrote, "Lucretia Mott is dead.... I did love that woman. She was more closely connected with Deity than anyone I ever met. Now there is the higher work she always craved. She used to say she never wanted to be so at rest that she would have nothing to do."

She lies, as she would have wished, close to James. Around her are grouped her children and her grandchildren. A young birch has been planted nearby, but its shadow does not touch her grave, which is open to "heaven's light." The long grass stirs in a light breeze this clear summer day.

The little graveyard is a still-green oasis in one of the worst sections of north Philadelphia. All around are houses that look as though they have been bombed, doors and windows gaping open or temporarily boarded up with sheets of metal. Abandoned cars sit on their axles at the curbs. Garbage, trash, and graffiti are everywhere. In the midst of the desolation a few black and Puerto Rican children play. A pregnant teen-ager stands at the corner, drinking a soda, watching the intruder with dull eyes.

O Lucretia, what would you say to this? Whatever became of that bright vision of radical reform, just down the road a bit, which kept you going all those years? Where is that progress that seemed to you so natural, so inevitable, when men and women turned to the Inward Guide?

The grass stirs, the children shout. Otherwise there is nothing, only that clear light that she loved pouring down upon me. Only the memory, out of the silence, of the many, many times she said it: The Light is as available today as it was yesterday as it has been everywhere, for all eternity. Only after a bit, a gentle nudging. "What is thee doing about it?" Lucretia wants to know.

NOTES

Abbreviations Used in the Notes

Boston Public Library — Department of Rare Books and Mss., Boston Public Library

Foster Papers — Abigail Kelley Foster Papers, American Antiquarian Society, Worcester, Mass.

Garrison Papers — Garrison Papers, Sophia Smith Collection, Smith College

Hallowell — Anna Davis Hallowell, ed., *Life and Letters of James and Lucretia Mott* (Boston: Houghton, Mifflin and Co., 1884)

History of Woman Suffrage — Elizabeth Cady Stanton, Susan B. Anthony, and Matilda Joslyn Gage, comps., *History of Woman Suffrage,* 3 vols. (New York: Fowler and Wells, 1881)

Mott MS — Mott Manuscript Collection, Friends Historical Library, Swarthmore College

Willis Papers — Phebe Post Willis Papers, Department of Rare Books, Manuscripts and Archives, University of Rochester Library

CHAPTER I

P.2 l.26 "The uproar and confusion..." *History of Woman Suffrage,* Vol. I, pp. 557-558.

P.2 l.37 "I think it was really a beautiful..." ibid.

P.4 l.29 "That man over there..." ibid., p. 116.

P.4 l.35 "I know it feels kind of hissin..." ibid., p. 567.

233

P.6 1.6   "Well, she seemed like a good, sensible woman." *Hallowell,* p. 131. This story, which is told by Lucretia's contemporary biographers, is hard to pin down. One version is an obituary appearing in *The New York Times,* November 14, 1880, quoting from the black minister, the Reverend Henry Garnet Highland, who may have been her escort. I have placed it at this 1853 convention since it is the only meeting in New York City attended by Lucretia Mott which was totally disrupted by mob violence. In several versions, Lucretia appealed to "the leader of the gang," who must have been Rynders.

CHAPTER II

P.10 1.23   Additional Coffin children as registered in the Monthly Meeting records of Nantucket and Lynn, Massachusetts:

Elizabeth	12-22-1794*
Mary	11-20-1796, died 9-29-1797
Thomas Mayhew	6-19-1798
Mary	3-20-1800
Lydia	3-14-1804
Martha	12-25-1806

*Quaker usage is to write dates as numerals only.

P.12 1.5   "What I had done left no impression. . ." Lucretia Mott to Martha Wright, 8-28-1840. *Mott MS.* This letter was misdated by LCM, since she was in England at the time.

P.12 1.13   In an undated letter to her sister, Martha Coffin Wright, Lucretia describes the visit that Marianne Pelham Mott had paid a medium. The medium had told Marianne she had a message for the family "Queer on earth; queerer in the spheres." Marianne had concluded it could only be Aunt Sarah. *Garrison Papers.*

P.17 1.22   "How odd it would seem. . ." LCM to "My precious home circle," 6-9-1861. *Garrison Papers.*

CHAPTER III

P.20 1.21   "It gave me. . ." Lucretia Mott's memoir to Sarah Jane Hale, in rough draft form. *Mott MS.*

P.22 1.29   "Friends, we have. . ." *Hallowell,* p. 37.

P.26 1.15   "The injustice of this distinction. . ." Lucretia Mott's memoir. *Mott MS.*

CHAPTER IV

P.30 1.12   Births and Marriages, Philadelphia Yearly Meeting Records. On microfilm at Friends Historical Society, Swarthmore College.

P.32 1.10   "Classified. . ." Lucretia Mott to Elizabeth Cady Stanton, 11-27-1852. *Stanton Papers* (typescript), Library of Congress.

P.33 · 1.26 "Ever taught..." Lucretia Mott to Martha Wright, 2-4-1871. *Garrison Papers.*

P.34 1.37 "I shall rest satisfied..." *Hallowell,* p. 53.

P.36 1.18 "Far safer..." Lucretia Mott to George Julian, 11-14-1848. *Mott MS.*

P.36 1.34 "As all our efforts..." Prayer as remembered and transcribed by LCM, 5-10-1879. *Mott MS.*

P.38 1.33 "My husband and self..." Lucretia Mott to Richard and Hannah Webb, 2-25-1842. Boston Public Library.

CHAPTER V

P.44 1.4 "To the Christ..." As quoted by Lucretia Mott in sermon delivered at Bristol, Pa., 6-6-1860.

P.45 1.27 "to find that she must part..." Robert Collyer Discourse, *New York Daily Tribune,* November 22, 1880.

P.47 1.39 "the history of the birth, life, acts,..." Epistle to London Yearly Meeting from Philadelphia Yearly Meeting (Hicksite), 1830. Friends Historical Library, Swarthmore College. Rough draft bears suggested changes in Lucretia's own handwriting.

P.48 1.23 *Hallowell,* p. 107.

P.49 1.19 "to learn to bear evil report..." Lucretia Mott to Phebe Post Willis, 3-16-1831. *Willis Papers.*

P.50 1.3 "You may meet Lucretia Mott..." Mary Biddle to Clement Biddle, 6-13-1830. *Biddle MS,* Friends Historical Library, Swarthmore College.

P.51 1.12 "Saul had said..." Lucretia Mott to Phebe Post Willis, 10-22-1833. *Willis Papers.*

CHAPTER VI

P.54 1.17 "William, if thee expects..." New York *Daily Graphic,* November 18, 1880.

P.57 1.8 "If our principles are right,..." *Proceedings of the 3rd Decade Meeting of the American Anti-Slavery Society.* New York: Arno Press, 1969.

P.59 1.19 "We deem it our duty..." Minutes of the Philadelphia Female Anti-Slavery Society, 1833-1870, part of the collection of The Pennsylvania Abolition Society, housed at the Historical Society of Pennsylvania, Philadelphia, Pa.

P.60 1.22 "Her principles and long cherished..." Anna Coffin and Lucretia Mott to Martha Wright, 6-2-1838. *Mott MS.*

P.63 l.24 "I can never willingly submit..." Lucretia Mott to Phebe Post Willis, 9-13-1834. *Willis Papers.*

P.64 l.4 "He never liked to hear preachers..." Lucretia Mott to Phebe Post Willis, 1-28-1835, *Willis Papers.*

P.64 l.39 "a deathlike silence reigns..." Lucretia Mott to Phebe Post Willis, 4-20-1835. *Willis Papers.*

P.65 l.14 "Our foolish women..." Lucretia Mott to Phebe Post Willis, 3-26-1836. *Willis Papers.*

CHAPTER VII

P.66 l.23 "Such inspection..." Lucretia Mott to Miller McKim, 7-19-1839. *James Miller McKim Papers,* Cornell University.

P.67 l.3 "Look at the heads of these women..." *Proceedings of the Woman's Rights Convention, Cleveland, Ohio, 1853.* Cleveland: Gray, Beardsley, Spear and Co., 1854.

P.67 l.10 Combe's findings were published in the *American Phrenological Journal* of April 9, 1839, with an interpretation by Orson Squire Fowler.

P.67 l.37 "When people are so over particular..." Lucretia Mott to Martha Wright, 6-4-1855. *Mott MS.*

P.68 l.24 "She is proof..." *Dublin Weekly Herald* as quoted in *Hallowell,* p. 190.

P.68 l.31 "remarkably bearing..." Lucretia Mott to Martha Wright, 2-27-1853. *Mott MS.*

P.70 l.13 "I want thee to have done..." Lucretia Mott to Miller McKim, 3-13-1838. *Mott MS.*

P.71 l.12 "Without a pause..." I had this story directly from Mrs. Alan Valentine, great-granddaughter of Sarah Miller.

CHAPTER VIII

P.73 l.19 "when our brothers and sisters..." Minutes, Philadelphia Female Anti-Slavery Society, January 2, 1837.

P.74 l.24 Chapman poem. *History of Woman Suffrage,* Vol. I, pp. 82-83.

P.75 l.5 "the Low Estimate..." Lucretia Mott to Miller McKim, 3-13-1838. *Mott MS.*

P.76 l.24 "perched by the parlor window..." Maria Davis to Edward Davis, 5-15-1838. *Mott MS.*

P.77 l.12 "Let us hope..." *The History of Pennsylvania Hall Which Was Burned by a Mob on the 17th of May.* Philadelphia: Merrihew and Gunn, 1838.

P.77 1.26 "by a little appearance of danger." ibid.

P.79 1.5   "The color prejudice lurking within me..." James Mott to Anna Weston, 6-7-1838. Boston Public Library.

P.79 1.39 "have the cause of human rights...our right and duty." Lucretia Mott to Abby Kelley, 3-18-1839. *Foster Papers.*

P.81 1.3   "unnecessary walking with colored people..." *Proceedings of the Third Annual Anti-Slavery Convention of American Women. Hall of the Philadelphia Riding School, 5-1-1839.* Philadelphia: Merrihew and Thompson.

P.82 1.19 "record them more sparingly in his paper." Lucretia Mott to Maria Chapman, 12-19-1839. Boston Public Library.

P.83 1.17 "That while we are applying..." to P. 83 1. 32 "punishment." *Proceedings of the First Annual Meeting of the New England Non Resistance Society, September 25, 26, 27* as carried in the *Non Resistant,* Nos. 19, 20, 21 and 22. Library Company of Philadelphia.

P.84 1.9   "imperious women." Charles Burleigh to Miller McKim, 10-26-1839. *Mott MS.*

P.84 1.30 "I pled hard..." Lucretia Mott to Maria Chapman, 5-13-1840. Boston Public Library.

CHAPTER IX

P.86 1.13 "most companionable," This, and many other quotations in this chapter, are taken from Lucretia Mott's diary. *Mott MS.*

P.86 1.27 "So if any do come..." Letter of Joseph Sturge of Birmingham, published in the *Emancipator* and reprinted in the *Liberator,* 5-8-1840.

P.89 1.1   The information about Stephen Grellet is from a letter to be found at the University of Rochester Library, Department of Rare Books, Manuscripts and Archives, addressed to "Dear Children" by Lucretia Mott and dated 6-14-1840. This letter bears the inscription "3rd letter" on the first page. Lucretia speaks of her past letter as having brought them as far as London. She urges her children to save the letters since "they are all the memorandum we take." The letter is ten finely written pages. It agrees with the diary, but gives more detail, and is more explicit about the attitude of the London Friends. Lucretia asks that the letter be shown to Isaac Hopper, since she mentions some of his acquaintances. Since Charles Palmer was Isaac's grandson, it would appear that he copied the letter for the Hopper family, and this copy survived, whereas the original was destroyed.

P.91 1.22 "one of the most interesting..." Proceedings of the Convention, as annotated in *Slavery and the Woman Question,* by Frederick Tolles. Friends Historical Association, Haverford, Pa., 1952.

P.92   l.3   "Seeing how the thing..." LCM to "Dear Children," as above. *Willis Papers.*

P.92   l.10   To read more about Anne Knight, see Marian Ramelson, *The Petticoat Rebellion,* London: Lawrence and Wiseheart, 1967. It has also been claimed that hearing Lucretia Mott made such an impression on a Julia Smith that she influenced her cousin, Florence Nightingale, into nursing during the Crimean War. *Revolution,* 9-21-1868.

P.93   l.19   "sacrificed principle at the altar of peace." Lucretia Mott to Maria Chapman, 7-27-1840. Boston Public Library.

P.95   l.26   The correspondence between Elizabeth Cady Stanton, Mary Grew, Wendell Phillips, and Edward M. Davis about this snubbing is in the *Mott MS.* Stanton's letter is dated 12-5-1881. The other two are not dated.

P.96   l.10   "Yes but immortal beings..." *History of Woman Suffrage,* Vol I, p. 421.

P.97   l.4   "brush away the silken fetters..." *London Christian Pioneer,* September 1840, as in *Hallowell,* p. 172.

P.96   l.37   "During his visit to us, his manifestations..." George Combe to Lucretia Mott, 2-8-1841. *Mott MS.*

P.99   l.1   "I found in this new friend..." *History of Woman Suffrage,* Vol. I, p. 422.

CHAPTER X

P.100   l.7   "A patient and respectful..." Lucretia Mott to Elizabeth Pease, 2-18-1841. Boston Public Library.

P.101   l.2   "They might have had Colver..." Lucretia Mott to Webbs, 8-9-1841. Boston Public Library.

P.101   l.30   "I long for the time..." *Liberator,* October 15, 1841.

P.101   l.38   "I am very sorry..." *Hallowell,* p. 246.

P.103   l.15   "Let them go on and rend..." Lucretia Mott to Phebe Willis, 4-28-1842. *Willis Papers.*

P.104   l.18   "One of the richest..." J. E. Snodgrass, 11-26-1842. Vassar College Library Autograph Collection.

P.104   l.27   "I am as much opposed to slavery as anyone..." *Hallowell,* p. 236.

P.105   l.13   "it was like the rumble of an earthquake..." *The Letters of Ralph Waldo Emerson,* edited by Ralph Rusk. New York: Columbia University Press, 1939.

P.106   l.3   "the best person in Philadelphia...suspect her faith." ibid.

P.106 l.12 "My friends, a body with two heads; what an anomaly!" Hannah Truman to Joseph Turner, 5-16-1843. *Turner MS,* Friends Historical Library, Swarthmore College.

P.106 l.22 "I did not spare her, stranger though she was...." *Hallowell,* p. 248.

P.106 l.28 "join not these associations..." Sermon by George White delivered at Cherry Street Monthly Meeting 10-8-1843. Published as a pamphlet at the office of the *Independent.*

P.106 l.21 "When one compromise of principle is made for peace sake..." Lucretia Mott to Sarah Dugdale, 10-7-1845. *Mott MS.*

P.107 l.16 "seek Truth for authority, not authority for Truth." Lucretia Mott to Mary P. Allen, 6-5-1877. *Mott MS.*

P.107 l.28 Edward Hicks, *Memoirs of the Life and Religious Labors of Edward Hicks, late of Newton, Bucks County, Pa., Written by Himself,* Philadelphia, 1851, p. 211.

P.109 l.32 "How little Marianne knew us..." Martha Coffin Wright to "My Dear Husband," 4-17-1844. *Garrison Papers.*

P.110 l.37 "But Jas Mott didn't incline to go with me..." Lucretia Mott to Elizabeth Pease, 4-28-1846. *Mott MS.*

P.111 l.6 "If she thinks thee wrong..." *New York Times,* January 4, 1881.

CHAPTER XI

P.113 l.36 "which it is intended..." Draft of Address from the Women of Philadelphia, U.S.A. in answer to the Friendly Address of the Women of Exeter, England, on the Subject of Peace, 1846, Friends Historical Library, Swarthmore College.

P.114 l.30 "Considerable uneasiness..." *Friends Intelligencer,* 1-30-1847.

P.115 l.3 "It appeared to me..." Edward Hicks, *Memoirs,* cited before, p. 211.

P.115 l.19 "As to theology..." Lucretia Mott to Richard Webb, 4-22-1841. Boston Public Library.

P.115 l.35 "I sympathized especially with Blanco White's..." Lucretia Mott to Richard Webb, 2-25-1842. Boston Public Library.

P.117 l.26 "from laying aside the whip stick..." Abby K. Foster to Stephen S. Foster, 8-24, 25-1847. *FosterPapers.*

P.118 l.7 "Lucretia, I am so deeply afflicted..." *Hallowell,* p. 294.

P.119 l.19 "it is regarded a greater crime..." Extracts from the Address of Lucretia Mott to the Anti-Sabbath Convention held in Boston, March 23, 24, 1848 as reprinted in *Hallowell,* p. 482.

P.120   l.7   "But a reformer now, the Jesus of the present age,..." *The National Anti-Slavery Standard,* 5-18-1848.

P.120   l.27   "I confess to you, my friends,..." *A Sermon to the Medical Students, preached at Cherry Street Meeting House First day, Second month, 1849, Philadelphia.* Philadelphia: Merrihew and Thompson, 1849.

P.121   l.39   "Those who go forth ministering to the wants and necessities of..." Sermon, 3-17-1850. *Mott MS.*

CHAPTER XII

P.124   l.3   "Commenting on the incidents of the day..." *Eighty Years & More, 1814-1897,* Elizabeth Cady Stanton, Schocken Books, pp. 82, 83.

P.125   l.16   "It was far from me to say..." Lucretia Mott to Edmund Quincy, 8-24-1848, published in the *Liberator,* 10-6-1848.

P.125   l.30   "long be necessary..." ibid.

P.127   l.17   "But it will be a beginning..." Lucretia Mott to Elizabeth Cady Stanton, 7-16-1848. *Stanton Papers,* Library of Congress.

P.128   l.15   "Why Lizzie..." From *Elizabeth Cady Stanton as Revealed in Letters, Diary and Reminiscences,* edited by Theodore Stanton and Harriot Stanton Blatch. New York: Harper, 1922.

P.129   l.28   "Many of the opposers of Woman's Rights..." *History of Woman Suffrage,* Vol. I, p. 79.

P.129   l.38   "Does a man have fewer rights than another..." ibid.

P.130   l.15   "I believe that with sufficient practice..." ibid.

P.130   l.20   "All these subjects of reform..." Lucretia Mott to Edmund Quincy, published in the *Liberator,* 10-6-1848.

P.130   l.29   "You are so wedded to this cause,..." Lucretia Mott to Elizabeth Cady Stanton, 10-30-1848. *Stanton Papers,* Library of Congress.

P.131   l.25   "His master is a rich man..." Lucretia Mott to Sarah Dugdale, 3-28-1849. *Mott MS.*

P.132   l.27   "Art thou sad and sorrowing my precious sister..." Lucretia Mott to Martha Wright, 7-25-1849. *Mott MS.*

P.133   l.1   "I ironed 4 doz. [sheets] this morning..." Lucretia Mott to Martha Wright, 7-28-1849. *Mott MS.*

P.133   l.38   "women were inferior by nature,..." Lucretia Mott to Elizabeth Cady Stanton, 10-25-1849. *Garrison Papers.*

P.135 l.3 "So far from her 'ambition leading her to act the man'...." *Discourse on Woman,* Lucretia Mott. Philadelphia: Merrihew and Thompson, 1849.

P.137 l.21 "ask as a favor, but demand as a right...." Address to the Women of Salem, 4-13-1850, *National Anti-Slavery Standard.*

P.137 l.27 "She put, as she well knows how...." Wendell Phillips to Elizabeth Pease Nichol, 3-9-1851. Boston Public Library.

CHAPTER XIII

P.140 l.18 "Bear your testimony against this unjust and cruel edict." *Pennsylvania Freeman,* 2-13-1851.

P.143 l.9 "I am not willing ...." *National Anti-Slavery Standard,* 11-18-1852.

P.143 l.30 "When we add all those who settle in Canada ...." Philadelphia Female Anti-Slavery minutes, 4-10-1856.

P.144 l.4 "With the exception of a few radical Quakers ...." Lucretia Mott to Elizabeth Cady Stanton, 9-11-1851. *Stanton Papers,* Library of Congress.

P.144 l.19 "Woman is told that the fault is in herself, ..." *History of Woman Suffrage,* Vol. I, p. 159.

P.145 l.12 "It is not to be supposed ...." *Proceedings of the Woman's Rights Convention, Syracuse, 1852.* Syracuse: J. E. Masters. 1852, p. 62.

P.145 l.35 "The farce at Syracuse has been played out. ...." *New York Herald,* as reprinted in the *Liberator,* 10-15-1852.

P.147 l.7 "our young people have little interest in these reorganizations ...." Lucretia Mott to Richard and Hannah Webb, 4-5-1852. Boston Public Library.

P.148 l.8 "Why laced so tight she could scarcely breathe, ..." *Proceedings of the Woman's Rights Convention, Cleveland, 1853.* Cleveland: Gray, Beardsley, Spear and Co., 1854.

P.150 l.8 "Pennsylvania is always slow to work ...." Lucretia Mott to Thomas Wentworth Higginson, 4-6-1854. Vassar College Autograph Collection.

P.151 l.1 "What has the Negro done? ...." *Woman's Journal,* February 14, 1881.

P.151 l.29 "We didn't drive slow coming home ...." Lucretia Mott to Martha Wright, 9-4-1855. *Mott MS.*

CHAPTER XIV

P.154 1.23 "a playful way of tapping ..." *History of Woman Suffrage*, Vol. I, p. 383.

P.152 1.10 "Don't I know her feelings ..." Lucretia Mott to Martha Wright, 1-30-1854. *Mott MS.*

P.155 1.1 "In thy coming work thou must do thyself justice ..." Lucretia Mott to Elizabeth Stanton, 3-16-1855. *Stanton Papers,* Library of Congress.

P.156 1.27 "Why not add Blackwell, as the French do ..." Lucretia Mott to Lucy Stone, 10-31-1856. *Blackwell Family Papers,* Library of Congress.

P.156 1.32 "Seeing there are so few ..." Lucretia Mott to Anna C. Brown, n. d. *Mott MS.*

P.157 1.5 "In the true marriage relationship ..." signed autograph. *Mott MS.*

P.157 1.30 "And so glad am I that there are some ..." Lucretia Mott to Martha Wright, 10-14-1858. *Mott MS.*

P.158 1.24 "Some hisses were heard in the back of the meeting ..." Lucretia Mott to Martha Wright, 11-16-1855. *Mott MS.*

P.158 1.35 "She would make the benevolence of our natures ..." Samuel Haines to Rebecca and Rowland Haines, 7-29-1859. Haines Collection, Friends Historical Library, Swarthmore College.

P.159 1.4 "something Emersonian in style ..." Lucretia Mott to Martha Wright, 11-26-1855. *Mott MS.*

P.159 1.27 "Every hour something was needed, ..." Lucretia Mott to Martha Wright, 1-18-1856. *Garrison Papers.*

P.160 1.3 "She addressed them well, ..." Lucretia Mott to Martha Wright, 4-3-1856. *Garrison Papers.*

P.160 1.20 "bore the heresy better than expected. ..." ibid.

P.161 1.23 "Lucretia has numerous calls almost daily ..." *Hallowell,* p. 329.

P.162 1.30 "There are two dressing rooms ..." Lucretia Mott to Martha Wright, 8-7-1856. *Garrison Papers.*

P.162 1.36 "If Harvard College ..." Lucretia Mott to Martha Wright, 2-19-1857. *Mott MS.*

P.163 1.8 "Men see so many humans through the day ..." Lucretia Mott to Martha Wright, 1-26-1856. *Garrison Papers.*

P.163 l.20 "They felt no fear ..." Martha Wright to David Wright, 11-6-1856. *Garrison Papers.*

CHAPTER XV

P.165 l.9 "Weep for the glory..." to P. 166 l. 20 "Mrs. Allen." These verses appear in *Hallowell,* and in their most complete form in *Flight to the Suburbs (Anno 1857),* by H. Justice Williams, in *Quaker History,* Vol. 64, August, 1975, No. 2. In a letter to Martha in the *Garrison Papers,* 3-17-1857, Lucretia says that Sarah Pugh and Abby Kimber added some stanzas.

P.167 l.1 "What are thousands of men,..." Lucretia Mott to Martha Wright, 10-12-1857. *Garrison Papers.*

P.167 l.8 "Groceries and coal..." undated fragment, circa 1857. *Mott MS.*

P.167 l.21 "We are all full of anxiety and..." Lucretia Mott to Martha Wright, 10-12-1857. *Garrison Papers.*

P.168 l.24 "I wish we old folks could be admonished..." Lucretia Mott to Martha Wright, 5-27-1858. *Garrison Papers.*

P.170 l.17 "Radical preaching seems to suit the people..." Lucretia Mott to "all at Home," 10-27-1858. *Mott MS.*

P.171 l.20 "expressing satisfaction that flying bondsmen..." Minutes of the Philadelphia Female Anti-Slavery Society, 4-8-1858.

P.171 l.30 "To be stuck up half an hour..." Lucretia Mott to Martha Wright, undated fragment, circa 1859. *Mott MS.*

P.172 l.35 "For it is not John Brown the soldier..." Report of the Pennsylvania Anti-Slavery Society in the *National Anti-Slavery Standard,* 11-3-1860.

P.173 l.24 "did not reproach them for their part..." *Hallowell,* p.392.

P.174 l.1 "nature utilized everything..." Lucretia Mott to Martha Wright, 12-27-1858. *Mott MS.*

P.174 l.16 "The meanness and littleness of some things..." undated fragment, circa November, 1859. *Mott MS.*

P.175 l.25 "the whole scope and measure of a woman's heart..." Lucretia Mott to Martha Wright, 8-12-1860. *Mott MS.*

P.175 l.32 "We need not marvel that there are Mrs. Gurneys..." ibid.

P.176 l.15 "Tell Richard in these days girls are as important..." Lucretia Mott to Maria Davis, 8-23-1860. *Mott MS.*

P.177 l.19 "But I am better now, and this is no time..." Lucretia Mott to "My dear cousin, Lydia Mott," 1-22-1861. *Mott MS.*

CHAPTER XVI

P.179 l.14 "It is pleasant to see a woman..." Boston *Atlas and Bee* as printed in the *National Anti-Slavery Standard,* 6-29-1861.

P.180 l.13 "So now regarding the present calamity,..." *National Anti-slavery Standard,* 7-13-1861.

P.180 l.24 "Who would have thought,..." Lucretia Mott to Martha Wright et al., 8-18-1861. *Mott MS.*

P.182 l.2 "Frémont says he is sold to the border states..." Lucretia Mott to Martha Wright, 8-1-1862. *Osborne Family Papers,* George Anson Library, Syracuse University.

P.182 l.14 "for a glimpse of the setting sun,..." Lucretia Mott to Martha Lord et al., 7-15-1862. *Mott MS.*

P.182 l.23 "Nothing but defeats and retreats..." Lucretia Mott to Martha Wright et al., 12-27-1862. *Mott MS.*

P.183 l.3 "The neighboring camp scene is the absorbing..." Lucretia Mott to the Heacock sisters, 1-7-1863. *Mott MS.*

P.183 l.10 "Why should the young and beautiful be swept away?..." Lucretia Mott to Martha Wright, 9-12-1863. *Mott MS.*

P.184 l.38 "He knows his danger..." Marianne Pelham Mott to Martha Wright, 7-12-1863. *Garrison Papers* (typescript).

P.185 l.25 "the loftier position of those..." Minutes, Philadelphia Female Anti-Slavery Society, 11-6-1863.

P.185 l.31 "which would undermine..." This account is from the diary of Alfred Love, 7-12-1863. Friends Historical Library, Swarthmore College.

P.186 l.25 "Pattie belongs here..." Lucretia Mott to Martha Wright, 6-2-1863. *Mott MS.*

P.188 l.16 "Reformers ought to be satisfied to be destructives..." Lucretia Mott to Martha Wright, 12-5-1861. *Mott MS.*

P.188 l.24 "He now thinks politics can't be discussed..." Lucretia Mott to Martha Lord et al., 7-3-1864. *Mott MS.*

P.191 l.19 "When a great calamity has befallen the nation,..." Lucretia Mott to Martha Wright, 4-17-1865. *Mott MS.*

P.191 l.31 "I felt for the poor fellows..." Lucretia Mott to Martha Wright, 5-2-1865. *Mott MS.*

CHAPTER XVII

P.194 l.2 "I weary of such everlasting complaints..." Lucretia Mott to Martha Wright, 6-11-1866. *Mott MS.*

P.194 l.30 "the expanse of land and roads,..." to P. 194 l. 37 "wonderful powers." Lucretia Mott to James Mott, n. d. *Mott MS.*

P.195 l.24 "We were in for it until the following day..." Lucretia Mott to "My dear Sister," 1-1-1867. *Mott MS.*

P.196 l.14 "Though you are about eleven years older than I am,..." William Lloyd Garrison to Lucretia Mott, 4-8-1867. *Mott MS.*

P.196 l.35 "If all men are to vote—black and white, lettered and unlettered..." *History of Woman Suffrage,* Vol. II, p. 215.

P.197 l.9 "had the right to be a little jealous..." ibid., p. 199.

P.197 l.23 "who was drawn..." *Remarks by Lucretia Mott at the founding meeting of the Free Religious Association, May 30, 1867.* Boston: Adams and Company, 1869.

P.198 l.9 "'Tis no trifle to be thus wronged of our just dues..." Lucretia Mott to Martha Wright, 8-26-1867. *Mott MS.*

P.199 l.2 "Let this be a country, as it ought to be,..." *The Friend,* New York, Vol. III, November, 1867.

P.199 l.18 "Dr. Moffatt is much sought here..." Lucretia Mott to "Dear Children," 1-24-1868. *Mott MS.*

P.202 l.36 "When women, because they are women, are hunted..." *History of Woman Suffrage,* Vol. II, p. 382.

P.204 l.3 "Name Coffin..." Lucretia Mott to Pattie Lord, 9-12-1869. *Mott MS.*

P.204 l.31 "a good collation,—." Lucretia Mott to "My dear One & All," 11-13-1869. *Garrison Papers.*

P.205 l.16 "This little service among..." Lucretia Mott to Mary Grew, 2-24-1870. (This letter is catalogued 1872, but appears to me to be correctly 1870.) Vassar College Library Autograph Collection.

P.205 l.31 "In our more sanguine moments..." Minutes, Philadelphia Female Anti-Slavery Society, 3-24-1870.

P.206 l.4 "only please do not place the name first,..." Lucretia Mott to Theodore Tilton, 3-18-1870. Rare Book Room, James Fraser Gluck Collection, Buffalo and Erie Library.

P.206 l.17 "I went not expecting great things..." Lucretia Mott to Martha Wright, 4-7-1870. *Mott MS.*

CHAPTER XVIII

P.210 l.8   "Such a concourse of all sects..." Lucretia Mott to Martha Wright, 2-4-1871. *Garrison Papers.*

P.210 l.30   "Tis not in the nature of things for man..." Lucretia Mott to Martha Wright, 5-13-1872. *Mott MS.*

P.212 l.15   "We have never considered the wrongs of the Indians..." *The Bond of Peace* (publication of Universal Peace Union), later it became the *Voice of Peace,* October, 1869, p. 89.

P.212 l.27   "While we aim to be thorough and maintain the highest..." *Voice of Peace,* January 1, 1876, p. 147.

P.212 l.35   "Even the woman question, as far as voting goes,..." Lucretia Mott to Richard Webb, 1-22-1872. Boston Public Library.

P.213 l.13   *New York Herald,* May 26, 1872.

P.213 l.17   "a thing I never do—nor was a handkerchief..." Lucretia Mott to Martha Wright, 5-27-1872. *Mott MS.*

P.213 l.24   "no hard words—only 'anthromorphism'..." ibid.

P.214 l.30   "Tell Miller I have quite forgotten the last..." Lucretia Mott to Pattie Lord, 3-2-1873. *Garrison Papers.*

P.214 l.37   "Therefore I say, preach your truth;..." Discourse, Free Religious Association, May 30, 1873, as reported in *Hallowell,* p. 555.

P.215 l.11   "no poor old lady was every so heartily welcomed." Lucretia Mott to Martha Wright, 6-1-1873. *Garrison Papers.*

P.215 l.30   "But mother, thee has no invitation." *Voice of Peace,* November and December, 1873, p. 9.

P.215 l.40   "He told me that they would not all be hanged,..." Lucretia Mott to Martha Wright (scraps recopied by Martha), 10-5-1873. *Garrison Papers.*

P.216 l.22   "What would Nantucket say, for husband..." Lucretia Mott to Martha Wright, 7-16-1870. *Mott MS.*

P.217 l.34   "I propose now to present to you one of the..." *Proceedings of the Centennial Anniversary of the Pennsylvania Society of the Abolition of Slavery.* Grant, Faires & Roberts, Printers, 1875. Also *Hallowell,* p. 451.

P.218 l.24   "Within thirty or forty years there has been..." Report of the Third Woman's Peace Festival, June 2, 1875, in *Voice of Peace,* July, 1875.

P.218 1.30 "I mean the firmness of combativeness that marked..." Report of the Fourth Annual Woman's Peace Festival, June 2, 1876, as reported in *Voice of Peace,* July, 1876, p. 54.

P.220 1.5 "I am somewhat like Zaccheus of old,..." *Philadelphia Times,* November 23, 1880.

P.221 1.4 "The attempt of the Commission to keep the gates..." *Voice of Peace,* July, 1876, p. 52.

CHAPTER XIX

P.223 1.25 "eggs by the dozen,..." Marianne Mott? to ?, undated fragment. *Garrison Papers.*

P.224 1.26 "an equality of political exertion...." Report of Third Decade Woman's Rights Meeting, in *Woman's Journal,* July 27, 1878.

P.225 1.1 "She is very weak physically...." Diary of William Eyre. Eyre Collection, Friends Historical Library, Swarthmore College.

P.225 1.12 "I want to say a word about my mother-in-law,..." *Voice of Peace,* January, 1879, p. 151.

P.225 1.23 "We often hear of reconciliation of theology and science." *Voice of Peace,* December, 1878, p. 135.

P.226 1.35 "as Sojourner Truth said, 'you are all...'" Minutes of the Pennsylvania Peace Society, 7-8-1876, as reported in *Voice of Peace,* August, 1876.

P.227 1.4 "It is too hard for our widely extended National Society..." Lucretia Mott to "Dear Susan," 7-21-1876. *Garrison Papers.*

P.228 1.2 "It was an ovation every day..." *Hallowell,* p. 466.

P.228 1.21 "Remember, mine had been a simple life, let simplicity..." *Hallowell,* p. 463.

P.228 1.29 "Resolved, that this convention presents its greetings..." Lucy Stone to Lucretia Mott, 11-1-1880. *Mott MS.*

P.230 1.6 "Mrs. Mott fought a triple battle..." Susan B. Anthony to Ella Sargent, 12-3-1880. *Susan Brownell Anthony Papers,* Department of Rare Books, University of Rochester.

P.230 1.14 "Lucretia Mott is dead..." Diary of Alfred Love, 11-12-1880. Friends Historical Library, Swarthmore College.

PRINCIPAL MEMBERS OF LUCRETIA MOTT'S EXTENDED FAMILY

COFFIN FAMILY

Anna Folger Coffin **Mother**

Thomas Coffin, Jr. **Father**

Sarah Coffin, unmarried **Sister**

Elizabeth (Eliza) Coffin, married Benjamin Yarnell **Sister**

Thomas Mayhew Coffin, unmarried **Brother**

Mary Coffin, married Solomon Temple **Sister**
their child: Anna Coffin Temple, **Niece**
married Walter Brown

Martha Coffin, married first Peter Pelham **Sister**
their child: Marianne Pelham **Niece**

married next David Wright
their children: Eliza, Tallman,
Ellen (married William
Lloyd Garrison, Jr.),
William, Frank, and Charles

Rebecca Bunker, married Daniel Neall **First cousin**
once removed

Ruth Bunker Chase **First cousin**
once removed
her daughter: Caroline Chase Stratton, **Second Cousin**
married Charles Wood

Mary Hussey, married Thomas Earle **First cousin**

MOTT FAMILY

James Mott **Husband**

Anna Mott, married Edward Hopper **Daughter**
their children: Lucretia, Maria,
George, Isaac

Thomas Mott, born 1814, died 1817 **Son**

Maria Mott, married Edward M. Davis **Daughter**
their children: Anna Davis (married Richard
Hallowell), Henry, Charles,
and William

Thomas Coffin Mott, married Marianne Pelham **Son**
his first cousin
their children: Isabel,
Emily, Maria

Elizabeth Mott, married Thomas Cavender **Daughter**
their children: Fanny, Henry, Charles, Mary

Martha (Pattie) Mott, married George Lord **Daughter**
their children: Ellen, Bessie, Mary,
Anna, Lucretia

B

PRINCIPAL SERMONS
AND SPEECHES
OF LUCRETIA MOTT
(listing prepared in collaboration with Dana Greene)

Remarks delivered at the First Anniversary Meeting of the New England Non-Resistance Society, Boston, September 26, 1839. *Non-Resistant,* November 16, 1839.

Sermon delivered at Marlboro Chapel, Boston, September 23, 1841. *Liberator*, October 15, 1841.

Sermon delivered in the Unitarian Church in the City of Washington, January 15, 1843. B. B. Davis, stenographer (Salem, Ohio: Davis and Pound Printers, 1843).

Remarks delivered at the Twelfth Annual Meeting of the Pennsylvania Anti-Slavery Society, Norristown, Pa., October 15, 1844. In the Records of the Pennsylvania Abolition Society, housed at the Historical Society of Pennsylvania.

Speech delivered at the Semi-Annual Unitarian Convention, Philadelphia, October 20, 1846. *Christian Register*, October 31, 1846.

Remarks delivered at the Anti-Sabbath Convention, Boston, March 23-24, 1848. *Proceedings of the Anti-Sabbath Convention* (Port Washington, N.Y.; Kennikat Press, 1971).

Speech, "The Law of Progress," delivered at the Fourteenth Annual Meeting of the American Anti-Slavery Society, New York, May 9, 1848. *National Anti-Slavery Standard*, May 18, 1848.

Sermon to the Medical Students, delivered at Cherry Street Meeting, Philadelphia, February 11, 1849. (Philadelphia: Merrihew and Thompson, 1849).

Sermons delivered at Cherry Street Meeting House, Philadelphia: September 2, 1849; September 16, 1849; September 30, 1849; October 14, 1849; November 4, 1849; December 23, 1849; March 17, 1850; March 31, 1850. Mott Manuscript Collection, Sermons, Friends Historical Library, Swarthmore College (hereafter cited as *Mott MS, Sermons*).

"Discourse on Woman," delivered in Philadelphia, December 17, 1849, in the hall of the Assemblies Building (Philadelphia: T. B. Peterson, 1850).

Remarks delivered at Woman's Rights Meeting, West Chester, Pa., June 2, 1852. Reprinted in *History of Woman Suffrage*, comp. Stanton, Anthony, and Gage, vol. 1, pp. 359-60 (New York: Fowlers and Wells, 1881).

Remarks delivered at the Woman's Rights Conventions, Syracuse, N.Y., September 8-9, 1852. *Proceedings of the Woman's Rights Convention* (Syracuse, N.Y.: J. E. Masters, 1852).

Remarks delivered at the Fifteenth Annual Meeting of the Pennsylvania Anti-Slavery Society, West Chester, Pa., October 25-26, 1852. *National Anti-Slavery Standard*, November 18, 1852.

Address delivered at the Whole World's Temperance Convention, Metropolitan Hall, New York, September 1-2, 1853. *Proceedings of the Convention* (New York: Fowlers and Wells, 1853).

Remarks delivered at the Woman's Rights Convention, New York, September 6-7, 1853. *Proceedings of the Woman's Rights Convention* (New York: Fowlers and Wells, 1853).

Remarks delivered at the National Woman's Rights Convention, Cleveland, October 5-7, 1853. *Proceedings of the National Woman's Rights Convention* (Cleveland: Gray, Beardsley, Spear and Co., 1854).

Remarks delivered at the Woman's Rights Convention, Philadelphia, October 18, 1854. Reprinted in *History of Woman Suffrage*, comp. Stanton, Anthony, and Gage, vol. 1, pp. 382-83 (New York: Fowlers and Wells, 1881).

Sermon delivered at Rose Street Meeting House, New York, November 11, 1855. *New York Times*, November 21, 1855.

Remarks delivered at the Seventh National Woman's Rights Convention, New York, November 25-26, 1856. *Proceedings of the Woman's Rights Convention* (New York: Edward O. Jenkins, 1856).

Sermon delivered at Yardleyville, Bucks Co., Pa., September 26, 1858. *Liberator*, October 29, 1858.

Sermon delivered at Bristol, Pa., June 6, 1860. Reprinted in *Life and Letters of James and Lucretia Mott*, ed. Anna Davis Hallowell (Boston: Houghton, Mifflin and Co., 1884).

Remarks delivered at the Twenty-Fourth Annual Meeting of the Pennsylvania Anti-Slavery Society, West Chester, Pa., October 25-26, 1860. *National Anti-Slavery Standard*, November 3, 1860.

Speech delivered at the American Anti-Slavery Society at its Third-Decade Meeting, Philadelphia, December 3-4, 1863. *Proceedings of the American Anti-Slavery Society at Its Third Decade* (New York: Arno Press, 1969).

Remarks delivered at the Eleventh National Woman's Rights Convention, New York, May 10, 1866. *Proceedings of the Woman's Rights Convention* (New York: Robert J. Johnston, 1866).

Discourse delivered at Friends' Meeting, Fifteenth Street, New York, November 11, 1866. *The Friend*, December 1866.

Remarks delivered at the Pennsylvania Anti-Slavery Society, Philadelphia, November 22, 1866. *National Anti-Slavery Standard*, December 1, 1866.

Address delivered at the American Equal Rights Association, Church of the Puritans, New York, May 9-10, 1867. *Proceedings of the First Anniversary of the American Equal Rights Association* (New York: Robert J. Johnston, 1867).

Remarks delivered at a meeting held in Boston, May 30, 1867. *Free Religion: Report of Addresses at a Meeting Held in Boston*, May 30, 1867 (Boston: Adams and Co., 1867).

Discourse delivered at the Second Unitarian Church, Brooklyn, N.Y., November 24, 1867. *The Friend*, January 1868.

Remarks delivered at the Pennsylvania Peace Society at Its Second Anniversary, Philadelphia, November 19-20, 1868. *Bonds of Peace*, February 1869.

Sermon delivered at Race Street Friends' Meeting, Philadelphia, January 3, 1869. Mott MS, Sermons.

Address delivered at Friends' Meeting, Race Street, Philadelphia, March 14, 1869. Mott MS, Sermons.

Remarks delivered at the Abington Peace Meeting, Abington Meeting, Pa., September 19, 1869. *Voice of Peace*, October 1869.

Address delivered at Friends' Meeting, Race Street, Philadelphia, January 23, 1870. Mott MS, Sermons.

Remarks delivered at the Thirty-Sixth Annual Meeting of the Philadelphia Female Anti-Slavery Society, Philadelphia, March 24, 1870. Records of the Pennsylvania Abolition Society, Historical Society of Pennsylvania.

Extracts from Reports of Addresses delivered at the Annual Meetings of the Free Religious Association, Boston, 1870, 1871, 1872, 1873, 1875. Reprinted in *Life and Letters of James and Lucretia Mott*, ed. Anna Davis Hallowell (Boston: Houghton, Mifflin and Co., 1884).

Sermon delivered at Hester Street Meeting, New York, May 26, 1872. *New York Herald Tribune*, May 26, 1872.

Remarks delivered at the funeral of Mary Ann W. Johnson, New York, 1872. Boston Public Library.

Remarks delivered at the Meetings of the Pennsylvania Peace Society, Philadelphia. *Voice of Peace,* February 1873, January 1875, November 1875, June 1877, August 1877, January 1878.

Remarks delivered at the Centennial Anniversary of the Pennsylvania Society for Promoting the Abolition of Slavery. *Proceedings of the Pennsylvania Society for Promoting the Abolition of Slavery* (Philadelphia: Grant, Faires and Roberts Printers, 1875).

Remarks delivered at the Women's Peace Festivals. *Voice of Peace*, July 1875, July 1876.

Remarks delivered at a Special Meeting of the Universal Peace Union, Camden, N.J., September 16, 1877. *Voice of Peace*, November 1877.

Remarks delivered at the Thirtieth Anniversary of the Seneca Falls Convention, July 1878. *Woman's Journal*, July 27, 1878.

BIBLIOGRAPHY

MANUSCRIPT COLLECTIONS—CORRESPONDENCE

The principal source of Lucretia Mott's letters is the Mott Manuscript Collection, Friends Historical Library, Swarthmore College. Another large group is among the Garrison papers, Sophia Smith Collection, Smith College. Others include: Department of Rare Books and Mss, Boston Public Library; Elizabeth Cady Stanton Papers, Blackwell Family Papers, and the National American Suffrage Association Papers, Library of Congress; James Miller McKim Papers, Cornell University; Sydney Gay Papers, Columbia University; James Miller McKim Papers, New York Public Library; Susan B. Anthony Papers, and Phebe Post Willis Papers, University of Rochester; Thomas Mott Osborne Papers, George Arnets Research Library, Syracuse University; Woman's Rights Collection, Schlesinger Library, Radcliffe College; James Fraser Gluck Collection, Buffalo and Erie County Public Library; Autograph Collection, Vassar College; Abigail Kelley Foster Papers, American Antiquarian Society, Worcester, Mass.; Foster Papers, Worcester Historical Society, Worcester, Mass; Society Collection, Gratz Collection, Logan-Fisher-Fox Collection, Clark W. Unger Collection, Drear Collection, Historical Society of Pennsylvania; Papers, Pennsylvania Abolition Society, housed at the Historical Society of Pennsylvania.

MANUSCRIPT COLLECTIONS—DIARIES

There are two diaries of Lucretia Mott: an autobiographical fragment prepared for publication by Sarah Hale, and her diary of her trip to the London Anti-Slavery Convention, both in the Mott Manuscript Collection, Friends Historical Library, Swarthmore College. Other diaries consulted were the following: Alfred Love, in the Universal Peace Union Collection, Friends Historical Library, Swarthmore College; William Eyre, in the Eyre Collection, Friends Historical Library, Swarthmore College; Deborah Fisher Wharton, in the Wharton Collection, Friends Historical Library, Swarthmore College.

MINUTES AND PROCEEDINGS—MANUSCRIPT

SOCIETY OF FRIENDS: Nantucket Monthly Meeting Minutes; Salem Monthly Meeting Minutes; Nine Partners School Committee; New York Yearly Meeting, Committee on Education; Ledger, Westtown School; Philadelphia Yearly Meeting, Record of Marriages, 1811; Philadelphia Monthly Meeting for Western District Minutes 1821–24; Women's Minutes 1821–24; Philadelphia Yearly Meeting (Hicksite) Minutes, 1828–81, including Women's Minutes, Indian Committee, Education

255

Committee; Philadelphia Monthly Meeting (Hicksite) Minutes 1828–81; Women's Minutes, 1828–81. (Also Minutes of Yearly Meeting of Progressive Friends of Longwood, not strictly within the Society of Friends.)

ANTISLAVERY: From the Papers of the Pennsylvania Abolition Society, housed at the Historical Society of Pennsylvania: Philadelphia Female Anti-Slavery Society Minutes, 1833–70; Board of Managers, Minute Books, 1833–41; Correspondence, 1833–70; Anti-Slavery Society for Eastern Pennsylvania, New Jersey and Delaware, Executive Committee Minutes, 1837–70; Pennsylvania Abolition Society General Minutes, 1820–30; American Free Produce Society Minutes, 1838–40.

Minutes of the Friends Association for the Aid and Elevation of the Freedmen, 1864–65 (Friends Historical Library, Swarthmore College).

OTHER: Minutes of the Northern Association of the City and County of Philadelphia for the Relief & Employment of Poor Women, Annual Reports, 1845–1918 (Friends Historical Society, Swarthmore College); Minutes of the Pennsylvania Peace Association, 1851 and 1867–80 (Friends Historical Library, Swarthmore College).

PERIODICALS CONSULTED

Pennsylvania Freeman, Liberator, National Anti-Slavery Standard, Liberty Bell, Friends Intelligencer, The Friend N.Y., Non-Resistant, Godey's Ladies Book, New York Herald, New York Times, New York Daily Tribune, Woman's Journal, Revolution.

ARTICLES by Lucretia Mott: "Diversities," *Liberty Bell*, 1844; "What Is Anti-Slavery?" *Liberty Bell*, 1846.

INDEX